Parkland

ALSO BY DAVE CULLEN

Columbine

Parkland

Birth of a Movement

Dave Cullen

HARPER LUXE

An Imprint of HarperCollins*Publishers*

HarperCollins books may be purchased for educational, business, or sales promotional use. For information please e-mail the Special Markets Department at SPsales@harpercollins.com.

FIRST HARPERLUXE EDITION

ISBN: 978-0-06-288797-9

HarperLuxe™ is a trademark of HarperCollins Publishers.

Library of Congress Cataloging-in-Publication Data is available upon request.

19 20 21 22 23   ID/LSC   10 9 8 7 6 5 4 3 2 1

FOR THE SEVENTEEN PEOPLE MURDERED AT
MARJORY STONEMAN DOUGLAS HIGH SCHOOL:

Alyssa Alhadeff, Scott Beigel, Martin Duque,
Nicholas Dworet, Aaron Feis, Jaime Guttenberg,
Chris Hixon, Luke Hoyer, Cara Loughran,
Gina Montalto, Joaquin Oliver, Alaina Petty,
Meadow Pollack, Helena Ramsay,
Alex Schachter, Carmen Schentrup, and Peter Wang

And for all of the March for Our Lives kids, and all you
young activists inspired by them to get off your
butts to make something change

Contents

Part III: The Long Road

Parkland

Prologue

1

Gun country. Half the country. Fighting them, provoking them, alarming them, was doomed to failure, more failure, decades of failure—they had to try something new. They had to engage them. So Jackie Corin had come to North Carolina six weeks after escaping her high school, but she was scared. It was just one guy. One guy was all it took. "It was nerve-racking, because there was a guy staring me down and . . ." He was an older white guy with gray hair under an NRA cap. "An average-looking grandpa," she said. "He just had a blank stare on his face the whole time, like I couldn't tell if he was there to hear us out or he was coming to make some chaos."

Jaclyn Corin, more comfortable as Jackie, is a petite blond teenager with fair skin, flowing hair, and a soprano voice that doesn't carry in crowds. But she has a presence. After she spoke, Jackie left the podium but remained seated onstage, out in the open. Just like the kids at her high school who were no longer at her high school, because they had been in the open. "The people that went to the bathroom in the freshman building, they were easy targets," she said. Jackie had just left the freshman hallway when that jerk started shooting. "It was all about timing. I literally walked out the doors that he walked into; it was like a span of fifteen minutes . . ." She didn't complete the thought, but couldn't stop picturing it.

Jackie's new friend Sarah Chadwick spoke after her at the rally, and then local college kids energized by their visit took the stage. The scary guy's eyes barely skimmed them, they just kept burrowing into her. "I felt like he was going to pop out a gun the whole time," she said. Alert security? Say what to security? And there was hardly any security.

Just four days earlier, Jackie had spoken to hundreds of thousands filling Pennsylvania Avenue, plus huge banks of TV cameras, but the contrast only heightened her fear. "Obviously, the march on Washington was very well protected," she said. "There was so much security, I was like, 'OK, if something happens to me onstage, the whole world's going to see it.' But at this event, there weren't really a lot of people there to react."

The march on Washington had been covered as the culmination of their movement, but the kids had engineered it as a launchpad. Where they were headed was still hazy—they were making it up as they went along. But they had an instinct. Jackie had come to North Carolina as part of an intentional sharp right turn. She had arrived with two objectives: to rally the waves of young new supporters eager to join the movement, but also to engage Second Amendment warriors. Preaching to the converted was easy. The real slog, if they wanted to get serious, was to convince hunters, collectors, and enthusiasts that no one was coming for their guns. They would not convince them today, or this year. But eventually. It didn't feel safe, though, and Jackie couldn't wait to get out.

Jackie's fear has since faded, but it lurks and swells unpredictably, in waves of silent terror that can knock her back at any moment. Fear was a constant stealth companion in the first strike she engineered in Tallahassee, the five-week sprint to the March for Our Lives (MFOL) in Washington, DC, and the grueling Road to Change bus tour, consolidating their network all summer along ten thousand miles of American highway. Fear was with her all the way to the midterms, which were their primary objective from that first weekend, when they concluded they would never break the logjam on gun legislation without changing some legislators. And putting the rest on notice.

It's a particular sort of fear Jackie shares with survivors of Columbine and the Pulse nightclub shooting. Most mass shootings end within fifteen minutes, but Jackie and her friend Cameron Kasky were crouched in lockdown on the day of the shooting for three and a half hours. Throughout it, they got updates on the carnage by text and Twitter, as seventeen students and staff were murdered around them—long enough to ride the waves of panic, fear, and helplessness to settle on simmering rage. By the time Jackie and Cameron hit their beds that night, this movement was in motion.

It was speed that launched this movement, and a breadth of talent that packed its punch. That first night, Cameron, Jackie, and David Hogg started simultaneously on separate tracks to completely different movements, which they fused forty-eight hours later to form a juggernaut. Cameron's first and best move was assembling talent. By Saturday, when Emma González went viral, two dozen creatives were conjuring up a new movement in Cam's living room.

I spent ten months shadowing these kids, and they were relentless, frequently racing around the country in opposite directions. That was their secret weapon: waging this battle on so many fronts with a host of different voices, perspectives, and talents—healing each other as they fought.

2

I swore I would never go back. I spent ten years researching and writing *Columbine*, and discovered that post-traumatic stress disorder can strike even those who have not witnessed a trauma directly. First responders, therapists, victim advocates, and journalists are among the vulnerable professions, but I had never heard of secondary traumatic stress, or vicarious traumatization (VT), until it took me down, twice, seven years apart. I learned that it comes in many forms, that PTSD is very specific, and less common than depression, which struck me. I was sobbing all day, mostly in bed, then slumped in a chair, unable to work effectively, or to do much of anything. That's when I agreed to some of my shrink's terms: read no victim stories the first week after a tragedy; watch no TV tributes or interviews with survivors unless I promised to hit the mute button if I started to feel the warning signs. I could study the killers at will, because they didn't burrow inside me—it was the survivor grief that did me in.

Even years after Columbine, I had no idea it had drawn me in for life. Since that day, I have tracked every major tragedy in some capacity as a journalist—but always at a distance of either time or space. In the immediate aftermath, I engage with a cadre of mental health and criminology experts, and with countless informal survivor networks, especially the many Columbine survivors I now count as friends. Months, or preferably years, later, I have gone back to the scene of some of the worst crimes. I work with John Jay College's Academy of Critical Incident Analysis (ACIA), which brings a small team of experts and survivors together for a three-day study of one critical event each year. I studied the Virginia Tech and Las Vegas tragedies on-site, and Norway's 2011 Worker's Youth League attack from New York City. But I could never plunge back into the scene of the crime while the wounds were still raw. Nor could I bear the prospect of documenting horror another time.

Parkland changed everything—for the survivors, for the nation, and definitely for me. I flew down the first weekend, but not to depict the carnage or the grief. What drew me was the group of extraordinary kids.

I wanted to cover their response. There are strains of sadness woven into this story, but this is not an account of grief. These kids chose a story of hope.

The Parkland uprising seemed to erupt out of nowhere, but it had been two decades in the making. The school-shooter era began at 11:17 a.m. MDT, on April 20, 1999, at Columbine High School, in Jefferson County, Colorado. There is a photograph that became iconic, which I described in *Columbine*: a blond girl, head thrown back in anguish, caught by her own hands, palms against her temples, fingers burrowing into her scalp. Her mouth is open, eyes squeezed shut. She mirrored what I witnessed when I arrived that first afternoon: girl, boy, parent, teacher—everyone clenching something: their hands, her knees, his head, each other. But nothing prepared me for the same kids the next morning. Their eyes were dry, their faces slack. Their expressions had gone vacant. That's why I'm still on the story two decades later: I never wanted to see that look again. But what we see today is worse: unsurprised survivors who *expected* a shooter.

The media coverage of Columbine was unprecedented. CNN logged its highest ratings ever, and the *New York Times* covered the story on its front page for nine straight days. It was an exceptional moment, demanding exceptional action. Law enforcement and the education system responded with significant changes, including the Active Shooter Protocol, and then . . . we came to accept it.

There were no vacant stares from the Parkland survivors. This generation had grown up on lockdown drills—and this time, they were ready.

3

Sadly, I've become a talking head: the mass-murder guy whom reporters and producers call to interview after every big shooting. Minutes after I learn of a new horror, I know whether the media will play it as a megastory or a minor one—because our media runs in only two gears. My phone is soon exploding, or it's silent. It melted down on Valentine's Day 2018.

Fifty-four minutes after the shooting started, I learned about it by a text from an *Anderson Cooper 360°* producer. "Another fucking school shooting," she wrote. That was fast, and not because of the carnage. It was something entirely different; something the producer was sensing, but couldn't put her finger on. "This one feels like Columbine," she said. Producers kept repeating versions of that all afternoon: The images look strangely familiar. Why?

I felt it too, and was equally puzzled at first. Parkland wounded America again, even before we met David, Emma, or Jackie, because it took us back to Columbine in a way that none of the intervening horrors had. We can all picture that ghastly footage of Columbine kids running for cover with their hands on their heads, men in black with SWAT stamped on their jackets motioning them with assault rifles to line up for pat-downs. Victims as suspects. Yet we had gone nearly two decades without seeing this horrifying sight again, because after Columbine, law enforcement threw out the old rulebook and developed the Active Shooter Protocol. Now police charge in immediately, and these spectacle murders end abruptly. Of the horrors post-Columbine, only one lasted more than fifteen minutes. Most perpetrators die in the act, often by their own hand, as authorities close in. The Pulse nightclub attack was the exception, raging for nearly four hours, but it unfolded while most of the nation slept. Orlando police tweeted that the killer was dead before dawn.

Most of these tragedies are reported in the past tense. By the time news hits the national networks, it's over. Columbine was different, and now Parkland was too. In both cases, the killing actually ended quickly— but the fear dragged on for hours. Columbine began at 11:17 a.m. Denver time, and played out on national television as a murderous hostage standoff until a SWAT team reached the library, and police announced at a 4:00 p.m. news conference that the killers' bodies had been found. The Parkland shooting began at 2:21 p.m. EST, but the perpetrator fled the campus and escaped. That is exceptionally rare. He was picked up around 3:40 and then arrested, but there was doubt for some time about whether he was the right man, and the only man. It was three and a half hours before the SWAT team cleared the last classrooms and gave the all clear.

Americans respond to most mass shootings with shock and grief. Columbine and Parkland provoked fear. *Hours* of fear. Human responses to those emotions are dramatically different. Fear floods the brain with norepinephrine, a hormonal cousin of adrenaline, which appears to be a primary culprit in the genesis of PTSD. "The outpouring from the adrenal gland and the related chemicals already in pathways in the brain appear to be implicated in the creation of trauma memory," said Dr. Frank Ochberg, a trauma expert.

A confession. Just three months before Parkland, one of the worst shootings ever—(can we stop awarding them titles?)—tore apart the town of Sutherland Springs, Texas, and I turned away. Twenty-six people were killed in a church, which made it worse, but when a friend relayed the info from the back seat of a car, I asked how bad it was, said "That's horrible," and changed the subject. Much of the country had begun to do the same.

Journalists were sensing the malaise or feeling it themselves, and had been scaling back coverage. *The Trace*, a nonpartisan, nonprofit newsroom that reports on gun violence in America, analyzed news coverage of Parkland against the seven deadliest shootings in the prior five years. The Pulse shooting in 2016 seems to have been the point when millions of Americans decided they couldn't bear it anymore. Nothing ever changed, except the body count, which kept rising. *The Onion* famously reruns the same headline after every time: "'No Way To Prevent This,' Says Only Nation Where This Regularly Happens."

Hope for gun reform swelled after Columbine, but even the Colorado legislature failed. Guns laws actually grew much looser when the federal assault weapons ban expired five years later. Virginia Tech brought another push, which didn't quite get there—but momentum seemed to be building. Finally, Newtown was such a horror that gun safety advocates were sure something substantial would pass. No. That defeat felt like the death knell of hope. Polls indicated huge majorities favoring several gun reforms, but most of us went silent about them. Even raising the possibility of closing the gun show loophole or fixing the background-check system drew eye rolls and jabs about political naivete. A new assault weapons ban, or limiting large-capacity magazines, ideas heavily supported by the public, drew jeers. The NRA kept introducing new bills to weaken gun laws, and they were passing in legislatures around the country. The opposition folded. If dead six-year-olds couldn't change this downhill course, it was hopeless.

So when the Las Vegas massacre obliterated all records in October 2017, it drew intense coverage, but for only a few days. Sutherland Springs came just a month later. Two months after that, two students were killed and sixteen wounded at Marshall County High in Kentucky, and the media barely bothered. I'm their go-to mass-murder guy, and I didn't even hear about it until the next day.

Paradoxically, the fog of defeatism wouldn't smother the Parkland uprising but fuel its lift-off. And it felt so amazing once the fog suddenly lifted. An axiom of addiction is that you have to hit rock bottom before you are ready to take on the harsh reality of recovery. America had hit rock bottom.

4

A brief note on names: I use first names for the Parkland kids, and other youth activists, because that's who they are: they're kids. One name will not appear in this book: that of the killer, who quickly grew irrelevant. Although he inadvertently set off an uprising, he is of little significance himself. We must examine the perpetrators as a class, both to spot threats and address underlying causes. And it's fruitful to study influential cases—influential to subsequent killers—particularly the false narrative of the Columbine killers as heroes fighting for the bullied and outcasts everywhere. Most of the perpetrators buy into that myth, which is why it's imperative that the media avoid creating new ones by jumping to conclusions too soon. Sadly, Columbine ignited the school-shooter era, which we're still dealing with, and it's getting much worse. While keeping top-ten lists of these massacres is part of the problem, it's notable that Columbine no longer even makes that list. For the first fifteen years or so of that era, the first question I got, and the most consistent and insistent, was always "Why?" Why did the Columbine killers do it, or what drove these killers collectively? What were the patterns, what were the causes? That changed rather abruptly, in the mid-2010s. It wasn't immediately after Newtown, but further in its wake, after the defeatism had set in, and the horrors grew worse and worse: Pulse, Las Vegas, Sutherland Springs. The question I get now is always some variation of "How do we make this stop?"

After two decades of research based on the voices of victims and victim advocates, and responses from the best minds in academia, psychology, criminology, and journalism, plausible roads out seem clear: major reforms to the easy access to deadly weapons and ammunition; a targeted approach to mental health in the form of screening for teen depression, every semester, in every high school in the country; and a major change in the media's coverage of these killers, which lionizes them in the eyes of unraveling future perps. It may take a combination of these strategies, and of course the smart money is on doing all three. Yet in twenty years, America alone has lost 683 lives in 81 mass shootings, and we've done virtually nothing. Concealed-carry and a host of other laws have made quick access to guns easier and easier. The "mental health" component has always been addressed with that absurdly broad label, so of course we have failed to move an inch. Only the media angle has begun to show some progress, or at least the early rumblings, in which journalists are beginning to accept our role in the star-making cycle.

The Parkland kids seem to have accidentally solved the problem of celebrity shooters simply by becoming bigger celebrities themselves. It took David Hogg twenty-four hours to become the first survivor to surpass his attacker in fame. Emma González went viral shortly thereafter. Meanwhile, the killer's name has already been forgotten, and few people could pick him out of a lineup.

He is irrelevant, but his mental health issues are not. The Parkland kids talk passionately about mental health when asked, but it is not their cause. They made two crucial decisions immediately: speak with one voice, and hammer one topic. They recognized that several different strategies for solving this problem are worth fighting for, all of them are daunting, and adversaries have stalled progress on each one by deflecting to the others. But one of these initiatives called out to them as the overwhelming priority. They chose guns.

PART I

Uprising

Nonviolence holds that suffering can educate
and transform.

—MARTIN LUTHER KING JR.'S
FOURTH PRINCIPLE OF NONVIOLENCE

1

Valentine's Day

1

Speed. That was the first answer to the question on everyone's lips when this movement erupted, suddenly and unexpectedly, just one day after the attack: *Why this time?*

They didn't wait a moment. David Hogg was the first to reach the public. On Valentine's Day, Laura Farber was gearing up for the film festival circuit. She had finished postproduction on her documentary feature, *We Are Columbine*, about her freshman class surviving that tragedy. It had taken nineteen years.

David Hogg filmed his Parkland ordeal as he lived it. He laid down his commentary track in real time huddled in lockdown, and conducted his first on-camera interviews with the kids trapped alongside him. David was the news director at the school's TV station, WMSD, and he had recently landed a gig as stringer for the Fort Lauderdale *Sun-Sentinel.* Media was in his blood.

After the SWAT team burst in, David fled the school and found his dad, a retired FBI agent. But they couldn't find his sister, Lauren. His dad sent him home, finally—it was too dangerous—and when David got in his car he started screaming. He pounded on the dashboard and screamed "fuck" over and over. He screamed the whole way home. He was angrier than he'd ever imagined, but intent on finishing his documentary. "Action is therapeutic," he thought.

David's dad got home with Lauren, and the teens' mother, Rebecca Boldrick, met them there. Lauren was unscathed physically, but deeply wounded. "I was screaming and wailing like a possessed person," she wrote. Their mother, who has a wicked sense of humor and refreshing candor, later described the sound as "subhuman." Lauren had lost two close friends. "They said they were missing, but I knew they weren't missing, they were dead." (The next day, their deaths would be confirmed, along with those of two other friends: Jaime Guttenberg, Alaina Petty, Alyssa Alhadeff, and Gina Montalto.)

David announced he was going back. He needed B-roll footage, exterior shots. He had the intimate horror on film, but splicing in cops and paramedics in chaos would seriously goose the intensity. David understood the media. He had done this before. And he needed to address the news vans he could already picture rolling in. He had to vent this anger. And he had to escape Lauren's subhuman wail.

No way, his mom said. His dad got more aggressive and blocked the door.

"Dad, I need to do this," David said. "If they don't get any stories, this will just fade away."

David can be a force of nature, and one way or another, he was getting back to that school. "Well, we're not taking you," his dad finally said.

David hopped on his bike, and pedaled furiously back.

Twenty years. The pace has changed. So has kids' connection to media. In the Columbine age, teachers sought to make their students wiser media consumers. The members of David's generation spent much of their waking lives on Snapchat, Instagram, and YouTube—they were already amateur media creators. David was semipro.

David got his B-roll and approached the news vans. At 10:05 p.m., he was live with Laura Ingraham on her prime-time Fox News show, with Ash Wednesday ashes on her forehead. For seven minutes, David dutifully answered her questions, highly composed, but looking a bit nervous, head nodding rhythmically through some extended questions. Ingraham mostly asked about his experience that afternoon, and what he knew about the killer, which was secondhand. But when she started to wrap with "Our emotions are with you—" he interrupted.

"Can I say one more thing, to the audience?"

"Yes."

David took a long pause and then a deep inhale, began to speak twice, and took another moment to get it right. "I don't want this to be another mass shooting. I don't want this just to be something that people forget." He said it affects every one of us "and if you think it doesn't, believe me, it will. Especially if we don't take action to step up and stop things like that. For example going to your congressmen and asking them for help and doing things like that. For example—"

"All right."

She cut him off, but he finished the thought: "Going to your congressmen."

First call to action on national television: February 14, 2018, 10:12 p.m. EST. Less than eight hours after the shooting began.

2

David Hogg startled America. Day one victims didn't talk that way. They were still in shock and mourning, sometimes lashing out in anger. Stepping back to assess the wider malady, and leaping straight from diagnosis to prescription—that was days or weeks away. David was different, and by noon I would discover he was only the tip of the spear.

David kept talking, all evening, to one news van after another. He pedaled home after midnight. He tried to sleep for a few hours, and then a car pulled up at his curb. ABC had booked a predawn interview on *Good Morning America*, and then CNN had him on its morning show, *New Day*. Alisyn Camerota, the program's anchor, met him in front of the school shortly after the sun rose.

That's when David Hogg hit my radar. I was at the Time Warner Center, CNN's headquarters in New York, watching a live feed on an elevator monitor. I had done an interview on the same show and watched David as I rode down to the lobby. I didn't get off.

There was little foot traffic, so no one disturbed me, and I watched it straight to the end.

David is a thin, wiry senior, a dead ringer for a young David Byrne, though slightly better looking. Same angular face, but higher cheekbones, cleft chin, and exceptionally thin snub nose. They even share the big mop of dark brown hair, piled high on top, shorter on the sides. David normally slicked his back, but didn't mess with product that morning, or change his black V-neck T-shirt. David stood beside Kelsey Friend, a freshman, on camera, as she described her experience rushing back inside to take cover in her classroom:

"My geography teacher unlocked the door and I ran in thinking he was behind me, but he was not."

"What happened to your teacher?"

"He unfortunately passed away in the doorway of our classroom."

David's mouth dropped open, just a little, and his eyes widened. Then they closed and he grimaced as Kelsey continued: "I heard the gunshots and I heard the shooter walk down the hallway shooting more kids. I heard a young man, crying for his mother, dying. It was just hard because you don't imagine this happening to you. . . . I thought at the beginning that this was just—it was a drill, just a drill, until I saw my teacher dead on the floor."

Kelsey believes her teacher, Scott Beigel, saved them by blocking the door, giving the kids time to huddle around his big desk, so the room looked empty.

"And how long did you stay like that?"

"If I'm going to be honest, it felt like five years. More than that. I was so scared. I wanted to go home."

After five more minutes of that, David's mouth was clenched. But he told his story calmly, with none of the anger that would come to define him. It flickered on his face, when he paused midsentence to label the experience—"This atrocity"—and when the gunman entered his story as "this sick person" who pulled the fire alarm. (That detail was widely believed but was ultimately proved false. Smoke from all the gunfire set off the alarm.) Douglas High is a large, decentralized campus, with 3,200 students in fourteen buildings. David was in environmental science class, about two hundred feet from the freshman building. Kids heard gunshots, so his teacher closed the door, but then the alarm rang. "We started walking out without even thinking about it twice. . . . When we were walking out towards our designated fire zone, there was a flood of people running in the opposite direction, telling us to go the other way. So I started running with the herd."

The herd was wrong. They were headed straight for the freshman building. "Thank God for a janitor that stopped us," he said. "They funneled us all into the culinary cooking classroom, about like forty students I'd say, if not more, and because of those heroic actions and the actions that she took, just a split-second decision, in thirty seconds, she saved my life and she saved easily forty others there." David hadn't yet learned her name, but thanked her again. "I'm pretty sure that's why I'm alive today."

David thought it was a drill. Everyone thought it was a drill—"An extremely realistic one," he said. They soon discovered it was not. "This was life or death."

"And how did you find this out? From—"

"Our phones. We're looking it up."

Their phones told them the worst of it, possibly all of it, but at the time no one knew what was happening in the freshman building nearby. "We need to realize there is something seriously wrong here, and policy makers need to look in the mirror and take some action," David said. "Because ideas are great but without action ideas stay ideas, and children die."

In the next six minutes, David demanded action twelve times. "Any action at this point, instead of just complete stagnancy and blaming the other side. . . . We're children. You guys are the adults. You need to take some action."

That was the moment. February 15, 2018, 8:22 a.m. EST. David Hogg called out Adult America for letting our kids die. The uprising had begun.

3

I got home and flipped through channels on the TV. David Hogg was popping up around the dial. Conservatives were already chiding the Left for "politicizing" the mourning period, before an "appropriate" time had passed. A steady parade of Parkland students called out "thoughts and prayers" for the stall tactic it was. Politicians were going to think and pray and legislate to keep the deadly system precisely the same. What had begun with good intentions after horrors like Columbine rang hollow nineteen years and 81 mass shootings later. The Parkland kids welcomed thoughts and prayers *in addition to* solutions, not instead.

Sunday, the journalist in me got ahold of David Hogg's number, and began texting. We spoke that afternoon, he put me on speaker, with the entire Never Again group. I wondered where they were, exactly, and learned later that it was the extended sleepover in Cameron's living room. David was funny, self-deprecating, and incredibly cheerful. He said he was still in shock, and felt the pain worst through Lauren, who was devastated. But they had found a purpose; it was right there in their name, and he seemed electrified by it. They all did.

David told me it was too late to get a seat on the buses to their first rally in Tallahassee, but I could caravan up with them. Tallahassee? Wasn't the march going to be on Washington? That was weeks away, he said—their first big insurrection would be underway in forty-eight hours.

"I'm taking the lead on that," a girl said. She introduced herself as Jaclyn Corin.

She was conducting an organizational meeting the following day, and David promised to follow up with the location. But remind him, repeatedly, he advised. They were getting buried in press calls. I kept trying, and landed on Monday to a single cryptic text from Cameron: "Pavilion by the amphitheater at Pine Trails Park." Huh. I figured his friends would understand that, but . . . My first taste of the months to come.

Google Maps matched a Pine Trails Park, 1.9 miles from the school, so I raced to it, and asked my way to an outdoor amphitheater, but there were dozens of tents and gazebos that could qualify as a pavilion. As I dashed about, asking kids, and focused on my objective, I noticed crosses and Stars of David in every direction, each one piled with memorabilia, and realized I was standing inside the sprawling memorial. A wave of sadness knocked me to my knees, and all I could feel was Columbine. This one had promised to be different, but these spontaneous memorials are horribly familiar. All the memorials include flowers, candles, and teddy bears, but each tragedy has its own iconography: thirty-two Hokie Stones at Virginia Tech, painted bedsheets and small cardboard angels at Newtown, and the line of enormous crosses towering over Columbine atop Rebel Hill. As I took in the lush park on the cusp of the Everglades for the first time, I saw them under the huge awning of the outdoor amphitheater: seventeen life-size angels, in flowing white gowns, with gold wings and halos, brilliantly lit from within.

The sun was setting and a storm threatened: rolling thunderheads streaked in amethyst by the sun's dying rays. Hundreds of mourners roamed the area. Most were silent or whispering in hushed tones, but a group of young women sang out loudly to their savior, lilting sopranos riding the gentle notes of an acoustic guitar: "Yours is the kingdom / Yours is the glory / Yours is the Name above all names / Now and forever God you reign." They were beautifully backlit by a bank of stadium lights in the distance; their shadows stretched across the field as they raised their arms to the heavens, which were opening just then to sprinkle us with a gentle shower. No umbrellas; no one seemed to notice or care.

The voices were heavenly, as beautiful as their refusal to surrender, for that moment at least, to the pain devouring much of the crowd. A girl staggered by, trembling, other kids sobbing, a few giggling. A Chihuahua pranced by and snapped at a Jack Russell terrier, their owners exchanging smiles, tightening the leashes and hurrying on. A group settled down with hearty plates of stew served up fresh from the Red Cross tent nearby. Every stage of grief.

2
Lightning Strike

1

J ackie was annoyed when the fire alarm sounded. Again? They had already drilled that day. And she had a lot on her plate. Jackie was junior class president, and Valentine's Day was a fund-raising opportunity. She personally delivered the carnations to freshman classes, and what a joy that was. Some kids were expecting them, but others were overwhelmed. She had hurried back from the freshman building, with just twenty-one minutes left of study hall, which she needed because she had gotten a B plus sophomore year—"My one B plus my entire life"—and she wasn't going to let that happen again. Valedictorian was out, but she could still graduate in the top 1 percent, and she was going to. She had loaded down her schedule with five AP courses, but she loved a challenge, and learning, and it mattered. She had even given up dancing. God, that had been hard. "Dance was my life and my love," she told me. She had started at the age of three, with her best friend, Jensen, and they were inseparable: camping, preschool, and dance, dance, dance. "I did everything: musical theater, ballet, lyrical, jazz, tap, hip-hop—it was like my whole world." They performed *Don Quixote* and *The Nutcracker*, and her passion was pointe. But student government forced a reckoning. Jackie ran for class vice president as a freshman, won, and then served as class president every year after. Dance had been her first love, but when she hit sixteen, she had to cut it loose.

The alarm sounded at 2:19, twenty-one minutes before the final bell. Jackie was seventeen. "We ran out to the bus loop and then—We were really far out," she said. "We were near the gates, towards the far end." It was two weeks later when Jackie first described this to me, and to that point, she was her typical, deliberate self. Then it all spilled out in a jumble: "Then I turned around and my friend said she heard like— Everyone was screaming and running back inside and I was really confused, and then my friend said she heard a gunshot, and I was like, 'No, no you didn't,' because I didn't hear it and I usually have good hearing, so I was in denial, and I was in denial for like the first fifteen minutes while we were hiding when we got back into the room, because I had no idea it was real, and my mom is an elementary school teacher down the road. And she wasn't on lockdown for fifteen minutes! Because they weren't aware. So I was texting her and she was like, 'Relax, Jackie, this is not real, we're not on lockdown, we would have been on lockdown by now.' And then she texted me after like fifteen minutes, 'This is real. Active shooter. Just listen to your teacher.' I was kind of gaining all my information through Twitter. We weren't supposed to be talking or on our phones, but I couldn't just sit there in the darkness for two hours, so I didn't listen, which is really bad. So I was just on my phone on Twitter and I was just getting updates, like from the helicopter view, and I was just watching like kids run out and we were stuck in there until almost five p.m. We were one of the last people the SWAT team broke out. We were sitting in the dark for quite a long time, which was really scary."

A distressing factor in so many Parkland survivors' stories is the fact that they ran back inside, toward the danger. For several years now, the Department of Homeland Security has championed the simple "Run. Hide. Fight." concept, with the key proviso to attempt them *in that order.* Hide only if all escape routes are blocked; fight only as a last resort. Otherwise, *run, run, run!* So why did they go back inside?

"Because we didn't know if there were other shooters around the campus and we needed to take cover—we couldn't just run away. I know a lot of kids just ran away to the local Walmart, but like—we had to run back inside. There were gates surrounding the bus loop and the gates were really high and we could not jump them. Who knows, there could be another shooting like— When I was running inside it was so scary because I didn't know who was behind me. It could have been a whole team of shooters. You never know. It was really scary."

Many kids fleeing Columbine also encountered a chain-link fence, but it was only about chest high and they went right over. Teachers and other students helped kids who were having trouble. The tall fence around Douglas was considerably higher. It was erected for security—but it trapped many students inside.

Cameron Kasky was one of the kids running with Jackie. They were good friends, but in different classes, on opposite sides of campus, thrown together by a series of coincidences. Broward County schools use a block scheduling system, meaning that students meet for periods one through four on silver days, alternating with five through eight on burgundy days. Wednesday was a silver day, which ends with drama class for Cameron—and drama fun for his younger brother, Holden, who has autism. The special-needs kids get out thirty minutes early, to get to the bus loop. On silver days, Cameron excuses himself to pick up Holden and bring him back to drama class, where he has a wonderful time. But Cameron was working on a song that day and lost track of time. Around 2:25, he realized his mistake and ran out of rehearsal to retrieve Holden. That put them across campus when the fire alarm rang. Fire drills were already stressful, because there were several kids with autism, and some of them have trouble dealing with situations like that. Then all hell broke loose: the screaming, running, and frantic calls to take cover in the school. Cameron and Holden sprinted. Cameron thought he could get them back to drama class, but a teacher, Ms. Driscoll, said, "Go into that room!"

"We can make it to drama," Cameron said.

"No, go into that room right now!"

Ms. Driscoll ushered in several of the kids with autism, and Jackie as well. Then she locked the door, shut out the lights, and they all crouched in the dark. Cameron looked for a weapon, chose a chair, moved to grab it, but the teacher said, *No! Try not to make a sound.*

"Look Holden, we're going to be here for a while," Cameron told him.

"I didn't let go of that kid for an hour and a half. Everybody was spreading rumors," Cameron would post on Facebook when he got home. "I heard at least three names dropped as to who the shooter was. We were all so distracted looking at our phones that we forgot somebody was shooting up our school." Then kids started posting video. "People being shot. People bleeding. Dead bodies. All over Snapchat." Kids were crying, texting their parents. "You could smell the anxiety. . . . We just wanted to hear that the shooter was gone. We didn't want to be shot. We had no idea what that even entailed. We're young. We don't know real pain."

That went on interminably, then someone smashed the glass out of the door. "All the glass shattered," Jackie said. Five hulking men burst in barking orders and pointing assault weapons. "They all screamed, 'It's the police! Put your hands up!'" It was terrifying, Jackie said. But she was most afraid for the kids with autism. "They were making noises, and some of them didn't know to put their hands up when they were told to. My teacher had to tell the SWAT team and the police that there were kids with autism in the room, and they might not be able to follow orders, which is scary because if they had made the wrong move, who knows what could have happened."

2

Marjory Stoneman Douglas High School is an unwieldy name. The kids call it Douglas or MSD. The campus is supersized too, and not much to look at. Its 3,200 students are dispersed among fourteen buildings, nestled among scrub oaks and acres of sports facilities. Most of the structures are homey-looking—two stories, cream colored, with arched roofs covered in brown Spanish tiles. They were constructed together when the school opened in 1990, and connected by breezeways, so they appear crammed together like an assortment of La Quinta Inns. The flagship building, at the corner of Holmberg Road and Coral Springs Drive, features a large rectangular edifice rising over the treetops bearing the school name and a diamond-shaped mural of a rainbow over the Everglades. Off to the side, two stand-alone buildings were added in 2009. One of them is an anomaly: a three-story structure that could pass for a parking garage—still cream colored, but with a flat, gray roof. That's building 12, also known as the freshman building, where all the shooting took place.

Emma González liked to write. The best profiles written about her were written by her. "I'm 18 years old, Cuban and bisexual," she wrote in an early one. "I'm so indecisive that I can't pick a favorite color, and I'm allergic to 12 things. I draw, paint, crochet, sew, embroider—anything productive I can do with my hands while watching Netflix." When someone suggested she run for president, she joked that she'd already accomplished that. She had been president of Douglas's Gay-Straight Alliance for three years. The alliance came up with a fun activity for Valentine's Day: it created "Proclamation of Love" certificates, with a space to write in your name beside your recipient's. Emma worked a lunch table encouraging kids to take part.

The killer began his day very differently, but the horror he would unleash began long before. Tune in to the coverage of any mass shooting, and you will hear the word "snap" bandied about. Journalists can't seem to resist the term: *When did he snap? Why did he snap? What made him snap?* I'm frequently asked to advise journalists on covering these tragedies, and my number one recommendation is to yank that word from the discussion. It's not a terminology problem we're quibbling over; it's our basic conception of the shooters. These are not impulsive acts or bursts of rage; there is rarely a moment when the perpetrator flips from good to bad. It's a long, slow simmer, a gradual evolution, or more often, a devolution.

The planning phase typically lasts weeks or months. In the case of the deeply depressed, it typically comes at the tail end of a far longer downward spiral into depression. The definitive study on school shooters reported that nearly 95 percent of perpetrators planned the attack in advance, just over half spent a month or more doing so, and some planned for an entire year. The Secret Service conducted that investigation in 2004, and studied every targeted school shooting in the United States until that point: thirty-seven incidents from 1974 to 2000. The FBI did a companion study with similar findings and has recently done more exhaustive work on the broader cohort of mass shooters. In all cases, same result.

The Secret Service report made a startling statement, backed by all the others: "There is no accurate or useful 'profile' of students who engaged in targeted school violence." Shooters encompass all racial, ethnic, and socioeconomic factors, parenting styles, and so forth. However, most of the major studies have indicated that mental health disorders play a big factor. The FBI's June 2018 study examined "concerning behaviors" in major mass shooters, and only one of those broke 50 percent: mental health issues afflicted 62 percent of all shooters studied. Depression, anxiety, and paranoia were the issues most frequently cited.

"Mental health" covers a huge range of conditions, but for these shooters, it's useful to examine two broad categories: those suffering from depression, and those with a profound mental illness, sometimes causing them to break with reality. The Virginia Tech and Newtown killers are prominent examples of the latter. The Secret Service study found much greater prevalence of depression: 61 percent of the school shooters had "a documented history of feeling extremely depressed or desperate," and a staggering 78 percent "exhibited a history of suicide attempts or suicidal thoughts" prior to their attack. From the perpetrator's point of view, many of these attacks are best understood as vengeful suicides: a profound hunger for suicide, coupled with the overwhelming desire to lash out, to demonstrate pain and power in a final act.

3

The Parkland killer was a nineteen-year-old former student. He had been expelled from Douglas High for bad grades one year and six days earlier, on February 8, 2017. Three days later, he legally bought from a local gun store the Smith & Wesson M&P15 .223 he would use in the shooting.

The shooter had a shockingly well-documented history of depression and mental health issues, dating back to an early age. He had been devolving for months, and acting out so aggressively that both state and local officials had been warned. After the attack, Broward County sheriff Scott Israel said his office had received about twenty calls concerning the perpetrator over the prior few years. In September 2017, the FBI had been notified of a YouTube comment bearing the shooter's name, saying, "I'm going to be a professional school shooter." In January, someone close to the gunman alerted the bureau that he owned a gun and had talked of committing a school shooting. It did not investigate.

The shooter's adoptive mother died in November 2017, which seemed to leave him distraught. He moved in with the family of a friend who was a junior at Douglas.

Around the start of February, he was ready to act. A few weeks before Valentine's Day, he drafted a simple plan: go shoot people at a local park. He never got as far as choosing which one, he would later tell the FBI. Why didn't he do it? they asked. He gave no explanation. "I didn't want to do it."

By February 8, the one-year anniversary of his expulsion, he had chosen a new course. He recorded a video on his phone that day describing the attack, another three days later, and a third on Valentine's Day. "All the kids in the school will run in fear and hide," he said. "From the wrath of my power they will know who I am." He also expressed undying love for a girl mentioned by her first name: "I hope to see you in the afterlife."

"I'm going to be the next school shooter of 2018," he said in another segment. "My goal is at least twenty people with an AR-15. . . . Location is Stoneman Douglas in Parkland, Florida. . . . Here's the plan: I'm going to take an Uber in the afternoon before 2:40 p.m. From there, I'll go into the school campus, walk up the stairs, load my bags and get my AR and shoot people down at . . . the main courtyard and people will die."

Aside from the courtyard, that's how it played out.

The father of the family he was staying with normally drove him to his adult education course, but that morning, the killer said he didn't go to school on Valentine's Day. He put on a Junior ROTC polo shirt. All the ROTC kids wore them on Wednesdays. He packed the AR-15 into a softback carrying case, and extra magazines into a backpack. He told the Uber driver he was going to music class, leading the driver to mistake the big bag for a guitar case. In the back of the car, the killer texted with the friend he was staying with, who was inside the school. It was normal chitchat. The final text came at 2:18 p.m.: "Hey yo, hey whatcha doin?"

They arrived one minute later. He walked briskly to the freshman building, entering at 2:21. He walked down the hall, entered a classroom shooting, and then repeated that four more times. He killed eleven people in just two minutes on the first floor. At 2:23, he reached the far end of the hallway, just past the bathroom, and climbed the staircase. He spent just one minute traversing the second floor in the opposite direction, including brief stops to shoot up two more classrooms. No one died there. He climbed the next flight, to the third and top floor. By now, smoke from all the gunfire had set off the fire alarms. People were responding to the apparent fire drill, and the murderer encountered them both in the stairwell and in the third-floor hallway. He opened fire in both locations, killing six. At the end of that corridor, he tried something different. Although he had not pulled the fire alarm, he tried to take advantage of it. He had an optimal sniper position. Kids were pouring out of every building. He tried to break out the glass, but it was hurricane resistant and he failed. At 2:27, just six minutes after entering the building, he dropped his rifle and backpack, then ran down the stairs and out the exit.

He had killed seventeen people: fourteen students and three staff. Seventeen more were physically injured by his gunfire.

No police engaged him. The school resource officer, sheriff's deputy Scot Peterson, was branded a coward for taking cover outside in the melee. He said he was unclear where the shooting was coming from, and believed it was outside. Peterson would resign eight days later.

The mass murderer walked to the Walmart half a mile away, and bought a drink at the Subway inside the store. That was rare. Few perpetrators escape mass shootings alive. Police officers arrested him there about an hour later, at 3:41. They took him to a hospital, where he was checked out and released back into police custody.

Broward County sheriff's detective John Curcio questioned him for several hours, and he made a full confession. But he blamed a "demon" voice in his head that instructed him and said, "Burn. Kill. Destroy." He described himself as "worthless," "stupid," and a "coward." He repeatedly said he wanted to die.

4

Social media exploded that evening. Classmates took to Twitter, Facebook, and Instagram, pouring out their ordeals and demanding that we, America, "do something!" But what?

David Hogg didn't have the answer—but he could picture one of the tools. So he got to work on his documentary, to help survivors enact some plan. The next morning, in that first CNN interview, Alisyn Camerota asked David how he had the presence of mind to begin a documentary while awaiting possible death.

"When you're in these situations, you can't really think of anything," he said. "You're kind of just frozen there, kind of like—Anyways, I was really thinking about, 'What has my impact been, what have any of our impacts been?' And I realized I hadn't really had one. I thought to myself: 'If I die today, I want my impact to be— If I die, I want to tell a good story. I want to show these people exactly what's going on when these children are facing bullets flying through classrooms. And students are dying trying to get an education. That's not OK. That's not acceptable. And we need to fix that.'"

Camerota returned to the documentary. "It's so graphic, we can't play it right now."

———————

For Jackie Corin, the movement started with a Facebook post. It was hard to get her mind off her friend Jaime Guttenberg when she sat down at her computer that night. Jaime was an aspiring ballerina, a younger version of herself, whom she had grown close to on the dance competition team. Jaime was still dancing and still a freshman, and she had been in the freshman building. She was now officially "missing," that horrible euphemism for "probably dead."

Jackie's Facebook post began, "Please pray for my school," worked up to a call for stricter gun laws, and ended with, "MAKE IT STOP."

"The end of my little message was that we need to make a change," she said later. "I obviously didn't know how. I had no idea."

Cameron vented on Facebook, too, starting with "I'm safe." He wrote that on the ride home, to his mom's home, with his dad, Jeff Kasky. Jeff didn't live there, but was determined to ensure Cam got home safe. It was a friendly divorce, and the Kasky boys live with their mom, Natalie Weiss, and her husband, Craig. But Natalie and Craig were on a cruise vacation.

During the lockdown, Cameron called his dad, and then Natalie on the ship. Natalie had gone to the ship's spa, she said. "I came back like all on cloud nine and then he said, 'You have to sit down,' and I just started saying 'No no no no no no no,' and then he told me 'active shooter,' and the nightmare just didn't stop until I saw him again."

Cameron said he had to go and then Jeff called, and then the FBI, and they had all sorts of questions, like "Was your child there?" "Whom can you reach?" "Whom can you speak to?" and she didn't know anything. She kept thinking, "Whenever you get hurt, you fall, you're a kid, you want Mom." So she was failing as a mom. She couldn't shake the thought, until something scarier occurred to her: "I'm so far away, but all [the parents] are too far." She thought about dads she knew who would have run recklessly into the school. None of them could have helped. "I feel like it has to be forgiven. We had moms that were at work, moms that were at home, and nowhere was close enough."

Natalie said all this three months later, in a leisurely interview in her living room, and it seemed like she had mostly forgiven herself. That day was so fuzzy. She wasn't even sure where she had been. Somewhere in the Caribbean. When the call came, her surroundings evaporated. "It was like a book slammed shut. When he said 'active shooter' and 'I'm hiding in a closet with Holden,' everything else was surreal."

They would not be home until Saturday. Natalie was desperate to hug her boys. She was trapped on a boat. They searched for a faster way back, but couldn't find a way. "There was so much guilt," she said. "Should I be put on a helicopter? Can I afford a helicopter? What do I do? I knew he was safe. I knew he had his dad. But as a mother, it was like torture."

She had been going to therapy since the shooting— made sure the whole family went. "You need it now. If you don't do it, you'll just need it ten times more in the future. We made that a priority."

Cam got home with his dad, got right to a computer, and began posting on Facebook. He summarized the carnage, anxiety, and false rumors in one long, horrifying paragraph. And then he got political: "There are two less obvious awful things here. First of all, [Marco] Rubio and [Rick] Scott are about to send their thoughts and prayers. Those guys are garbage and if you voted for them, go to hell."

He added several more thoughts, and concluded: "Please don't pray for me. Your prayers do nothing. Show me you care in the polls."

His next post lamented not thanking his teachers enough. He offered eternal thanks for all they did, and then singled one out by name: "Driscoll, if you're reading this . . . thanks. Everything my little brother and I ever do in the future is pretty much completely because of you. We almost slipped through the cracks. We almost kept walking. We almost went right into the danger."

He created a Twitter account. He tried to sleep. He got up. "Can't sleep," he posted, again on Facebook. "Thinking about so many things. So angry that I'm not scared or nervous anymore. I'm just angry. And a little confused. Trying to get the word out and talk to people. I don't even know what I want to say necessarily. I just want people to understand what happened and understand that doing nothing will lead to nothing. Who'd have thought that concept was so difficult to grasp."

And then he did something so simple, but so vital . . . the single most significant moment of the movement. He asked for help. He gave out two more social media handles—Instagram and his new Twitter account—and asked people to message him. "I want people talking about this. I can't let this die like all the others. I need this to be the end. Everybody needs this to be the end. Talk to me."

Then he got some sleep. And messages poured in.

5

Jaime Guttenberg, Jackie Corin's fourteen-year-old ballerina friend, was not "missing." She was dead. She was one of the seventeen memorialized Thursday evening at a huge candlelight vigil. Florida congresswoman Debbie Wasserman Schultz attended and met up with Jackie afterward. A family friend had forwarded the Facebook message, and Wasserman Schultz wanted to help. By now Jackie had ideas germinating, and her instincts were to make something happen immediately, which meant Tallahassee, not Washington. Passing something in the Florida legislature was merely implausible, not impossible. So Wasserman Schultz connected Jackie to Lauren Book, the state senator representing Parkland.

Book was instantly on board. She encouraged Jackie to think big. They started brainstorming Friday, and began to hash out a plan. They had to act fast, because Florida was about to enter week six of a nine-week annual legislative session. "We have about ten days to craft really important legislation," State Representative Kristin Jacobs explained a few days later. "Because it's a whole year before the legislature comes back together, and the momentum will be completely lost." The ticking-clock scenario could be a blessing or a curse. But the stall tactic—a cynical maneuver that had shut down every previous movement after every previous tragedy—was off the table.

Jacobs was a Democrat and represented Parkland in the Florida House. While Jackie organized the event with Book, Jacobs was quietly working behind the scenes with Book and the Republican leadership to craft a bill. If they somehow struck a deal, the bill would go to Governor Rick Scott, a Second Amendment warrior with an A-plus NRA rating. "Honestly, I can't see any of us going home now without something," Jacobs said. The biggest danger was they would agree to something "so weak that it's just a 'Oh, we passed something,'" she said. "This is not going to be an easy lift. This is going to be Democrats on one side not liking it and Republicans on the other side not liking it and a whole bunch of us in the middle dragging them in. It's a very delicate environment right now."

Jackie was only vaguely aware of the particulars, but she could feel a tipping point. "I just wanted to do it immediately," she said. "Because I knew that the news forgets. Very quickly. And if we were all talk and no action, people wouldn't take us as seriously." They could not wait a month, as with the big push too long after Newtown.

Jackie first visualized waves of students descending

on the capitol from schools around the state. She put the word out, and messages came pouring in from lots of schools eager to get on board, but the organizational hurdles were overwhelming. "So I brought it down to one hundred Douglas kids, and even that was just very difficult," she said a week later. "I couldn't even imagine what my original idea would have taken." Tallahassee was at the north edge of the state, 450 miles away. She had to charter buses, transport, feed, house, and chaperone a hundred minors for . . . how many days? Two? It would definitely take two days. And they had to convince top state officials to meet with them, or what was the point?

State Senator Book set her staff in motion, especially Claire VanSusteren, a senior aide. The three of them worked through the details all weekend. It was intimidating at first. "I was terrified," Jackie said. "I'm a seventeen-year-old calling a Florida state senator. That's just not normal." But she got over her skittishness pretty quickly. "You have to remember that every single person we talk to is also a human, and we all have families, and we all have emotions. I just forget that sometimes. I got so lucky with them. I call them my fairy godmothers."

State Senator Book worked the phones, cajoling her colleagues. As the yeses grew, the logistical concerns multiplied. Jackie had pictured a town hall format in a big chamber, but the unexpected response opened fresh possibilities. "Claire was like, 'We were going to have dozens of meetings,' and I was like, 'What? That's a lot.'"

But Jackie came to love the plan. She had asked for volunteers by text and social media, and was getting flooded with yeses of her own. She hit her hundred max quickly, and it was tempting to keep expanding, but Jackie wanted buses rolling by Tuesday. The logistics were daunting already. So Jackie sorted the hundred into ten groups, which would rotate around the capitol throughout the day, meeting officials in intimate sessions. Senator Book compiled a profile on each official, which Jackie matched to students based on interests and personalities—"Strong students with hardheaded legislators," she said.

Housing changed a couple of times. Could the kids sleep on the floor? Of course, Jackie said. "At one point we were supposed to sleep in the Senate building on the twenty-second floor," she said. "That was the plan." But then Florida State University offered space in an office building nearby: two big rooms, one for girls and one for boys. Jackie put the word out to bring sleeping bags and air mattresses, and very little else.

Claire handled all sorts of things Jackie would never

have considered, including two permission forms that every parent had to sign. Local and national media were getting on board fast, so they allotted several slots on the buses for media to ride along. Those slots were gone by Sunday, so the rest of us planned to caravan behind.

Funding fell into place too. Uber Eats donated lunch, and private individuals covered two dinners and breakfast. Senator Book insisted on paying the $12,000 to rent the three jumbo coach buses—not out of campaign funds but personally. She had survived sexual abuse beginning at age eleven, and her fight for victims' rights drove her entry into politics. She saw a younger version of herself in Jackie.

"Lauren [Book] understood how taking action in the wake of something so traumatic can really help your healing," Claire said. "Taking action, leading marches, getting laws changed, and really speaking out to create this change really was what helped Lauren make the transition from a victim to a thriving survivor. Anything she could do to help Jaclyn and the other students in their journey, she wanted to do."

In the midst of all this, as they were really getting rolling late Friday, Cameron called.

3

#NeverAgain

1

Cameron Kasky first tweeted #NeverAgain on Thursday. He would delight in telling the *New Yorker* that the hashtag came to him on the toilet, in his Ghostbusters pajamas. Wasn't "never again" a Holocaust phrase? his friends asked. Yes, but so what? They brushed it off and went with it and #NeverAgain was born.

Cameron's late-night plea to "talk to me" had worked. He woke up to reams of messages, and then friends started showing up. CNN had seen his posts and asked him to write an op-ed, which they posted that day. That led to a lot of national media, including appearances on NPR and *Anderson Cooper 360°*.

Cam and his friends went to the vigil Thursday evening and came home with more kids. Cam's living room—technically, his mom's; she was still making her way back from the Caribbean—would morph into the headquarters of a nascent movement.

The response had to be huge. A march on Washington—the whole country pouring into the capital to demand gun reform. A massive show of force to demonstrate the national will backing their demands. Demands—they would need some demands. They would get to that. They had to do it fast. Speed was paramount, no Newtown mistakes this time. But they had to be realistic. This couldn't be done overnight. And they didn't want to peak too soon.

They needed more brainpower. They issued a Twitter invitation for anyone to join. And they needed a meeting place, a virtual space, for a movement. "Working on a central space that isn't just my personal page for all of us to come together and change this," Cameron posted. "Stay alert. #NeverAgain." They gave themselves a deadline, their first, to have that space created by midnight. They made it. A Facebook page: NeverAgainMSD.

They kept at it well into the night. Much more social media, Instagram accounts, Twitter, and Snapchat. They were all on some platforms already, but realized they had to maximize all channels. They helped each other create accounts and get up to speed. And they started setting down ground rules: this had to be bipartisan. That meant backtracking a bit, and a new edict: no more singling out Republicans. No endorsing any candidate, just ideas. There were a lot more Democrats on their side, but all the more reason to reach out to Republicans.

And with every post they made, the clearer it became that they needed one voice. Internally they could debate fiercely, but consensus ruled and then they had to present a united front. Contradict each other or bicker by Twitter, and the powerful gun lobby would rip them to shreds. It might anyway.

Friday came early. None of the kids could sleep much. "Good morning," Cameron posted. "Our voices are being heard. People care. People feel the way we do. Anderson Cooper's eyes are even more beautiful in person. More coming today, but please know—this is only the beginning for us."

Hour by hour, his sprawling living room grew fuller. Some of the kids were active in the school's TV news program: Ryan Deitsch and Delaney Tarr, and a smart, articulate friend of Cameron's whom he recruited too. Emma González was a striking sight: full lips, piercing brown eyes, sparse makeup, and a shaved head. She had lopped off her hair a week or two before senior year. "People used to ask me why, and the main reason is that having hair felt terrible," she later explained in the *New York Times*. "It was heavy, it made me over-heated, and every time I put it up in a ponytail (and I looked terrible in a ponytail) it gave me a headache. And, it sounds stupid, but it made me insecure; I was always worried that it looked frizzy or tangled. What's the best thing to do with an insecurity? Get rid of it. It's liberating to shave my head every week."

Her parents had not approved. "The more my parents said no, the more I wanted it," she said. "Actually, I even made a PowerPoint in order to convince them that I should do it. I figured I would look really good with it, and I do."

Cameron had no idea what an impact Emma González would have.

"For me, it started with Emma," David wrote in his memoir. "She was friends with this kid from the drama department named Cameron Kasky." David knew him just slightly, from a single class in common, though he had noticed Cameron's "sly, kind of edgy sense of humor."

"Emma was the link that brought us together," David wrote. She coaxed him to Cameron's house on

Friday, and his first impression was, "Wow, these guys are extroverted." A house run amok with right brains. So many talented creatives, but who did they know with a knack for getting stuff done? They needed an implementer. They needed a Jackie Corin. Cameron called her.

"It was so late," Jackie said. It was nine thirty. "My bedtime is usually so early, I go to bed at like eight o'clock." But she couldn't sleep, so she came right over. Cameron laid out his plan. "Then I told him I was taking kids to Tallahassee," Jackie said. "He was like, 'You're taking kids to Tallahassee?'" She thought that's why he had brought her in. He was incredulous. "He was like, 'I just thought you'd be perfect for this,'" she said. "The things we were working on just collided perfectly."

2

A march on Washington: What would that entail? What would it cost? Most of the core team was assembled now: Cameron, Jackie, David, and Emma, plus Alex Wind, Delaney Tarr, Ryan Deitsch, Alfonso Calderon, and several more. They brainstormed, and researched. The Women's March on Washington the previous January provided an upper-end template. It had drawn nearly half a million people to the capital, but the real story had been the sister marches. A detailed academic analysis of 653 reported sister marches around the nation estimated a grand total of 3.3 to 5.2 million participants, with a "best guess" of 4.2 million. That translates to 1.3 percent of the population and would make it the largest single-day demonstration in recorded US history. So that was the top end. The Women's March had set a fund-raising goal of $2 million, with big-ticket line items for bus parking, outside security, and a massive supply of Porta Potties. They didn't quite make it. Eleven days out, they were at only $849,000, but a huge rush of money poured in in the final week. On march day, they stood at $1.8 million, ten percent short, but the march was an unqualified success.

Two million seemed ambitious. One? A million dollars seemed audacious for a tiny group of high school students. But attempting this on the cheap and putting on a massive fiasco would reinforce the stereotype the Right was throwing at them: that these were children, in way over their heads.

A million it was. They would announce it on the morning shows, and try not to flinch.

How soon? Five weeks seemed like the sweet spot: potentially doable, but such a mobilization that the organizing would create its own story, and provide a month-plus metanarrative to sustain the interest they had already established. They would convert the narrative of angry kids to one of proactive kids, taking control of their destiny. And if it did get huge, it could jump-start . . . whatever they came up with next. They would start working on that highway once they built the on-ramp.

Still, five weeks. It felt borderline reckless, but it had to be. They set the date, March 24, and a name that captured what they were feeling: the March for Our Lives.

3

Saturday came early. Still more kids, but most of the team was assembled now: nearly two dozen MSD students, and five recent graduates, who had been close to them in drama club. They were good friends from high school—a little older, a little wiser, and had some distance from the horror, which could be a good thing. Two of them were film students, and another one was in communications; they were going to need those skills. And Pippy—legally Kaylyn Pipitone, but nobody called her that—was a born mom, and man, could they use one of those right now. They all had moms, but moms didn't always understand. Amazing to have a make-believe mom, who was one of them. "I was the mom when I was in drama club too," Pippy said. "I just took everyone under my wing." Eventually the group would be open about the recent grads, but in the early days, they had them keep a low profile. They were getting pummeled by attacks alleging that they were pawns of adults, agitators, and the Democratic Party, which must be helping them behind the scenes. Their childhood friends who had gone to school and collaborated with them the past two years hardly qualified, but it was a touchy subject.

It was a big group for a living room, but what a living room. Like most of the other kids, Cam lived in a gated community, lush with palm trees and succulents nestled around a web of inland waterways and a pond with a waterspout. The living room featured a grand piano and walls of windows that seamlessly blended the indoor/outdoor living spaces out to the pool. A tiny little finger of the Everglades stretched right up to the edge of his lawn. Frogs, marsh rabbits, and whitetail deer roamed the area, along with an occasional great egret or alligator. "Parkland was just the most stereotypical white suburban, rich, perfect place," Alfonso said. Parkland's median income topped $130,000, double the national average, with the median home price nearly triple, at around $600,000. It had tiny pockets of poverty, just 3.5 percent of its population below the poverty line, and 19 percent of its students eligible for free lunches. The wealth was visible in the big houses and in the small details. The Porta Potties for the spontaneous memorials in Pine Trails Park didn't smell. They were spotless, odorless, and plentiful, and the basins gleamed. Outside, there were two handwashing stations, double sided, for a total of four sinks, with full soap dispensers and pristine bottles of hand sanitizer too. There were water bottles everywhere, pallets of them, free for the taking.

Parkland is a pastoral four-stoplight community that most of South Florida had never heard of. It hugs the Everglades, fifty miles north of Miami, on the periphery of the metro area. A chain-link fence along the edge of town marks the border of the Everglades preservation area, but that's a political distinction—technically, scientifically, the town sits atop the Everglades, its homes on a series of tiny peninsulas constructed along its edge.

For several thousand years, Parkland gurgled within the Everglades, which the writer and activist Marjory Stoneman Douglas famously called Florida's River of Grass. But twentieth-century developers were busily draining the wetlands to "reclaim" new tracts for sugarcane farms and housing divisions, aided by the Army Corps of Engineers. Stoneman Douglas began fighting to preserve the wetlands in the 1920s, when they were Florida's only fresh water source. But it was her landmark 1947 book that woke the public to a coming crisis, with the Everglades on a trajectory toward extinction—wiping out a vital, complex ecosystem, and threatening the drinking water of the millions of new residents flooding in. The battle raged for decades, but when the dust settled, Stoneman Douglas was hailed as a visionary who averted ecological catastrophe. But she couldn't stop the creation of Parkland.

Developers created it by dredging up tons of sand and piling it into craggy finger peninsulas, surrounded by deeper canals, until the map looked like a suburb of cul de sacs, with blue waterways in place of the lanes. In 1963, Parkland was incorporated, and cane farms began to rise from the swamp. In the 1980s and 1990s, the farms were carved up and paved over, to create an outdoor wonderland dotted with high-end homes. The town's original charter demanded 2.5 acres per dwelling, a requirement relaxed later, but that set the tone.

Parkland remains a cozy bedroom community, with 23,000 residents as of the last census, but still just a handful of shops, restaurants, and gas stations, mostly on the perimeter. It has several spacious parks, where coyotes, raccoons, bobcats, and iguanas roam among the scrub oak, Australian pine, and numerous varieties of palm. Pine Trails Park was just expanded the past decade, with baseball, football, and soccer fields; basketball courts; children's playgrounds; and the outdoor amphitheater for live shows. The town is young and vibrant, with 30 percent of the population too young to vote, and less than 11 percent old enough to retire.

It's not cheap to live in Parkland, but there are affordable neighborhoods close by. Douglas High draws a big chunk of its student body from Coral Springs, a larger commercial town across the Sawgrass Expressway whose median income is about half that of Parkland. Ethnically, the Coral Springs kids brought MSD into almost perfect alignment with the country: 59 percent non-Hispanic white, 18 percent Latino, 12 percent black, and 7 percent Asian—within a point or two in every category. (Parkland was 13 percent Latino and 6.5 percent black.) But Douglas families were still far more affluent than most Americans, with 22 percent of the school's students eligible for the free or reduced-price lunch program, versus 52 percent in the United States as a whole. Successful families were drawn to Parkland for the nature, fishing, and outdoor recreation, and above all, the schools. *U.S. News & World Report* recently ranked Douglas in the top 7 percent of high schools in Florida and the top 12 percent in the United States.

It was 1990 when Parkland had drawn enough residents for Broward County to erect a high school on the former swampland. The residents named it after the champion of the Everglades, whom they now held dear. Marjory Stoneman Douglas lived to 108, and had turned 100 that year. It's a suburban legend that Stoneman Douglas rejected the honor or even demanded that construction be stopped. But her biographer was never able to confirm how she felt about it, and said she "had always thought it was a bit of an insult."

Stoneman Douglas lost the Parkland battle, but the "developers'" encroachment ended there. The high school named in her honor, or dishonor, stands as a marker to what transpired, and an outpost against the perpetual threat. When a gunman struck, the Parkland kids saw poetic justice in the long arc of history, recasting their school so eloquently in the image of its namesake. They had also lost a horrible battle at Parkland, with a human loss this time, but like Stoneman Douglas, they were resolved to mark Marjory Stoneman Douglas High School as the final outpost in a generational war.

The kids worked feverishly Saturday morning, while Cameron's mom raced in from the airport. Finally, she could wrap her arms around her boys, the hugs of a lifetime, and . . .

"When I got home someone put a camera in my face," she said. "I just wanted a moment alone with my kid. Just to celebrate. There was like a room full of students and there was Cam. It kind of took away the intimacy."

Quick hugs, then they were on the move. They had to drive to Fort Lauderdale, for a rally there at one o'clock. It had a clunky title: "Rally to Support Firearm Safety Legislation." They could do better. It was the first political rally most of them had attended, so how crazy that many of them were going to speak. It was organized by multiple groups, mostly moms: Moms Demand Action, Women's March Florida, the MSD PTA, etc. It wasn't a huge crowd, several hundred people, but the news vans would supply millions.

Cameron, David, and Delaney all gave speeches, and all were enthusiastically received. But that rally will always be remembered as the moment Emma González called BS.

4

Emma had been thinking about gun safety legislation Wednesday afternoon, before the shooting. She had been thinking about the NRA. She was taking AP US government, and the lesson that day had been the role of special interest groups. They discussed how lobbyists use money to influence politicians toward their agendas—good agendas, like Sierra Club, Emma thought, and gross ones, like the NRA. She hated the NRA. An hour later, she was in lockdown in the auditorium. That night, she discovered that several kids she knew were dead.

Thursday, she went to the vigil. That was painful. "I just wanted to see everybody," she said. "It was a day full of tears, but really good tears in a way." Her friend David Hogg was burning up the airwaves all day, and Anderson Cooper's producers had booked him for the show Thursday night. They asked him to recommend other articulate students, so David texted Emma, and she said yes. Adulatory texts started streaming in soon afterward. "Wow, people are listening to me," she thought.

The organizers of the Fort Lauderdale rally noticed the texts, and asked her to speak. "I started writing it at eight o'clock last night and I didn't stop writing until I got out of the car this morning," she said later that afternoon. And then she gushed about other big things in her life. "I just got my license, I just got into college." She was thinking a lot about college. A small liberal arts school, New College of Florida, had offered her admission and reached out immediately after the shooting to see if she was OK. That impressed her. "I'm like two seconds away from accepting," she said.

Emma stepped up to the podium in a black spaghetti-strap top, black bra, half-a-dozen wristbands of assorted shapes and textures, and no hair. A paper flyer stating THE TIME IS NOW! was taped to the podium, and three microphones were clamped on top, one securing an American flag. A woman stood beside Emma holding a fourth, watching her intently throughout the speech, biting her lip as it began.

Emma tapped a stack of papers, and then held them up with a big smile: "I know this looks like a lot, but these are my AP gov notes." Everyone there should be home grieving, she said. "But instead we are up here standing together because if all our government and president can do is send thoughts and prayers, then it's time for victims to be the change that we need to see." She raised her hands to mark air quotes around "thoughts and prayers." And with that line, Emma drew the first wild cheers of her young activist career.

Since the Second Amendment had been written, she argued, "our guns have developed at a rate that leaves me dizzy. The guns have changed but our laws have not." Then she quoted a teacher: "When adults tell me I have the right to own a gun, all I can hear is, 'My right to own a gun outweighs your student's right to live.' All I hear is mine, mine, mine, mine."

Every country had troubled teens, and mental health issues, yet mass shootings were such a uniquely American problem. As she pointed out, Australia had one mass shooting, in Port Arthur in 1999, then passed sweeping gun laws and had not had one since. She went on to say, "Japan has never had a mass shooting. Canada has had three and the UK had one and they both introduced gun control and yet here we are."

Emma described a chilling interview she had watched that morning, in which a survivor was asked whether their child would go through lockdown drills. Adults seemed resigned to that fate, but her generation said no way. They were sick of studying inaction—they'd been studying it their entire lives. Her AP government class had conducted three debates on it already that year, and it raged on in closets on Wednesday, while students hid from the gunman killing their friends. If students learned anything, "it's that if you don't study, you will fail," she said. "If you actively do nothing, people continually end up dead."

She castigated Republican senator Chuck Grassley for sponsoring a bill preventing the FBI from performing background checks on people adjudicated as mentally ill. She decried the NRA's influence on politicians. "To every politician who is taking donations from the NRA, shame on you!" She was eight minutes into the speech, still wiping away tears with the backs of her hand, but her sadness was dwarfed with a rising and fierce resilience. The crowd was behind her now, chanting back repeatedly, "Shame on you!" Emma waited them out, rubbed the back of her head, and smiled for the first time since she had begun.

"The people in the government who were voted into power are lying to us," she said. "And us kids seem to be the only ones who notice and are prepared to call BS. Politicians who sit in their gilded House and Senate seats funded by the NRA telling us nothing could have been done to prevent this, we call BS." She raised her fist and pumped it to each syllable, to wild screams: "*WE! CALL! B! S!*" As she repeated the chant, the audience yelled it with her: "They say tougher guns laws do not decrease gun violence. We call BS. They say a good guy with a gun stops a bad guy with a gun. We call BS. They say guns are just tools like knives and are as dangerous as cars. We call BS. They say no laws could have prevented the hundreds of senseless tragedies that have occurred. We call BS. That us kids don't know what we're talking about, that we're too young to understand how the government works. We call BS." She waved her notes in defiance at that last one, still wiping away the tears. Then she called on the audience to register to vote, to call their congresspeople, and to "give them a piece of your mind!"

It had been eleven minutes and forty seconds. Emma knew she had struck a chord with the hundreds assembled there, but had only the slightest conception of what she had just accomplished. "I had no idea that my speech was going to be broadcast nationally," she said later. "My mom killed her battery trying to film it 'cause she didn't think it was going to be anywhere."

Emma had been to political rallies. She had heard great speeches and used them for inspiration. She also had done some creative writing and had ideas of her own. "I knew I would get my job done properly at that rally if I got people chanting something," she said. "And I thought, 'We call BS' has four syllables, that's good, I'll use that. I didn't want to say the actual curse words. This message doesn't need to be thought of in a negative way."

CNN carried the speech, and it instantly went viral. By nightfall, Emma was a national sensation.

5

After the rally, everyone went back to Cam's house. They chose five kids as leaders and chief spokespeople: Cameron, Emma, David, Jackie, and Alex Wind. But there was no question the first three were the media stars. "We are the three voices of this," Cameron told the *New Yorker.* "We're strong, but together we're unstoppable. Because David has an amazing composure, he's incredibly politically intelligent; I have a little bit of composure; and Emma, beautifully, has no composure, because she's not trying to hide anything from anybody."

Emma put it more succinctly: "All these kids are drama kids, and I'm a dramatic kid."

Cam's mom, Natalie, helped them settle in and let them have their space. "The first person that I didn't know that made an impression on me was Emma," she said. "Her beautiful, giant eyes. They look right into you." Most girls give you what they want you to see, she said: their makeup, their hair. "But she just gives you her eyes. She had this nymph-like lightness, like a dancer, the way they almost don't hit the floor, they just tinker." Emma was often fond of thrusting her arms up and out, in imaginary dance moves. "She never met me before and she just gave me this big hug, like, 'Thank you for opening up your home,'" Natalie said.

They had their plan, and the Sunday-morning news shows seemed like the place to unveil it. So many choices: *Meet the Press, This Week, Face the Nation, Fox News Sunday.* They booked them all.

Most of them slept over at Cam's. The media dubbed the weekend the Slumber Party. Some of the kids bristled at that: the only relationship it bore to a slumber party was that hardly anybody slept. Eating was an issue—remembering to. TV news crews were filming nonstop, and started bringing them food, which reminded them to eat. "I saw this ice cream, and it looked *so* good," David told me Sunday. "And then I realized I hadn't eaten breakfast, I hadn't eaten lunch, and it was five o'clock."

They had a modest website running by showtime Sunday, with a GoFundMe page to accept donations. They would need to set up a foundation to manage the money, which meant attorneys, accountants, and paperwork, but all that could wait. Raising the money could not. They had a tight window—saturation media coverage of the worst tragedies lasted three to five days, and Sunday was day five.

Sunday morning, the five leaders ran the network gauntlet. Their plan was out there now, and nobody laughed at them. Even the hosts seemed to take it seriously. All they had to do now was pull it off.

4

Tallahassee

1

Monday. Jackie had a day and a half to get her buses on the highway. "The hardest part of it was honestly getting together the one hundred kids," she said. "They have parents that are concerned—they're letting their child go on a trip with only a dozen chaperones to the state capitol. I was on my phone the whole weekend, just making sure all of the students' parents were comfortable sending their child seven hours away."

Most of the kids were dressed up at the organizational meeting in Pine Trails. They had come straight from a funeral. "Two, in fact," one girl said—for Luke Hoyer and Alaina Petty. It was a big crowd, well over a hundred, because many moms came by—to show their support or to make sure the kids felt comfortable, or both. Many said they had volunteered to chaperone, but their kid had vetoed that.

Jackie started the meeting. Her thin voice didn't carry, so she hopped up on a chair to shout over the crowd and gently chastise serial chatterers in the back. It's not easy to quiet a mob of boisterous teens, particularly without offending them, but it was the first of countless times over the coming months that I would watch Jackie pull it off.

She outlined the basics of the trip. Expect media everywhere, she said. Several TV cameras were trained on her as she spoke, and cell phones were raised high. Any random student could expect to be dialed into two or three lenses at any given time. It was day six.

Jackie asked the media to be respectful: If a student doesn't want to talk, let him be. She asked if everyone knew which Publix grocery store they were meeting at—"the one by the Walmart." (She didn't mention that it was the same Walmart the killer had walked to after the attack. Everyone knew.) She called for questions.

"Attire?"

Oh, right. She'd meant to hit that. It had been a big topic with Lauren Book and Claire. Lots of the kids assumed they should dress up, but that felt all wrong. As soon as you start dressing up, you tend to match your speech and manner to that: formal and unnatural. The trip was about giving voice to high school students, so they should look like and speak like students. Jeans and T-shirts, Jackie said—no dresses, no ties, definitely no suits. And pack light: just toiletries, a fresh T-shirt, maybe a towel. There were shower facilities, but not much time to use them. Wake-up time was already predawn. The Red Cross had just come through with a hundred cots, so air mattresses could stay home.

The governor's office called that night. Governor Scott was in. Dream fulfilled. The question was, where to fit him in? The schedule was packed, right up to five p.m., and if they got the buses rolling promptly they were already looking at one or two a.m. to Walmart, even later to their homes. But it was the governor offering two hours, in groups of a few dozen, rotating in and out. They added him to the schedule from five to seven p.m. It would be a very long night.

Jackie said the enormity of it began to dawn on her that evening. Not because of all the kids hushing each other to hear her, or a bank of cameras trained on her, following her every step. It was Google. "I used to google my name and nothing would come up," she said a few days later. "I was just a little kid and nobody knew who I was. And now google even 'Jaclyn,' and 'Corin' is like next to Jaclyn Hill's name."

2

The Publix lot was mobbed by noon Tuesday. Cameron came to juice the crowd, though that hardly seemed necessary. Jackie was besieged by kids and moms lining up with last-minute concerns. Jackie's mom, Mary Corin, shadowed her, frequently dispatched by Jackie on quick errands, and often turning to her for advice. Her daughter was clearly in charge.

The crowd swelled to hundreds, with parents, onlookers, and media. It was so much louder than the meeting: the buses were running, diesel engines lumbering, and a helicopter buzzed overhead. Jackie had to announce team assignments, so kids could link up with chaperones and board the right bus. They had no megaphone, no way to be heard. They needed a plan B, and they needed it fast.

"Let's hop on a car," Cameron said.

Jackie gaped. "You're joking, right?"

While Jackie was assisting a mom, Cameron had found the owner of a big black SUV, asked if they could use it, and was already clambering onto the roof. Jackie followed him up. "I was terrified," she said. "But whatever."

Cameron, a natural, threw his whole body into his delivery. He lurched so far forward, I was afraid he might tumble onto the asphalt. When he hopped down, sweaty, those kids were ready to storm the Bastille. Then he turned it over to Jackie for the mundane practical stuff. Ten teams: first she called the chaperones, who raised their arms, then the kids, who gathered round.

Back on the pavement, kids were already lining up with new issues. Most were fixable, just relentless. Some kids just wanted to switch groups, to hang with friends. "No," Jackie said softly. "Get on your bus."

A school board member was chaperoning, and I caught him for a quick interview just as he was boarding. He stood in the doorway answering my questions with one foot on the first step, until Jackie whisked by, addressing a different issue. "No more interviews," she whispered, without slowing down or looking up. He apologized, sheepishly, and turned to find his seat. She was never mean, just firm.

A CNN producer approached Jackie about switching buses. This time she looked peeved. I'm sorry, she said, no changes. The producer persisted, and Jackie was incredulous. Hear me out, the producer insisted: they weren't asking for a better bus, their team had inadvertently been split up. They were set to livestream segments to CNN, HLN, CNN International, and CNN.com, but they couldn't pull off any of that from separate buses. Oh. That was legit. Jackie would find someone to swap, and she did.

Jackie must have settled a hundred minor issues in that last hour, all of it filmed, even the trivial stuff, often by five or ten devices at a time. I asked her later if the spotlight was intimidating. "You get used to it real quick," she said.

Jackie's dad, Paul Corin, watched Jackie manage the chaos in disbelief. She'd always been a go-getter, he said, but this? "I'm in awe," he said. "Of my own daughter. I want to take her when she gets back to get her DNA tested, because I saw her come out of my wife, but I'm not sure I could produce this."

He described her as brilliant and emotional. "But she's not showing it *now*, because she's laser focused right now."

Last-minute glitches kept mounting. Jackie worked through them, but the clock ticked past one p.m. She had no margin for error. They were scheduled for a late arrival, then pizza with students at Leon High School a mile from the capitol, and a late-night crash course, sort of Lobbying 101. Most of the kids admitted they had little idea what the term meant. The air-conditioning had gone out on one of the buses, and the driver couldn't get it fixed. It was sweltering in there already. The bus company gave up and dispatched another bus, which would take another hour. Jackie ordered the other two to head out. They waited. "It really flattened the mood," Jackie said.

Jackie's driver said the delay would force him to work overtime. He demanded Jackie pay for his Tallahassee hotel room. "He got out of the bus and started walking away," Jackie said. "I was a mess. I was crying. I kind of had a breakdown. 'I have so much pressure on my shoulders—you cannot be doing this!'" She agreed to pay, and he agreed to drive.

3

They expected Tuesday to be eventful. It began with a team meeting at Cameron's to run through everything before heading to the Publix. Most of the team was headed to Tallahassee, but key players had to stay back. A huge CNN town hall was scheduled for Wednesday night in Boca Raton, where David, Cameron, and Alfonso would be key speakers. Alfonso would attend most of the Tallahassee event and then fly down to make it. David was off to L.A. taping *Dr. Phil* and would also get back just in time. And then there was the primary objective, the march; no time to waste.

The Women's March had provided a template, kindred spirits, and plenty of allies. Deena Katz, one of its organizers and a *Dancing with the Stars* producer, got on board quickly and filed the permit application for the National Mall early that week. It projected student speakers, musical performers, and half a million marchers. It proposed a fifty-foot-wide stage, twenty tents, twenty generators, fourteen Jumbotrons, and two thousand Porta Potties.

The kids also recruited Emma Collum, a South Florida attorney who had handled transportation and logistics for the Women's March. She described an exhaustive labyrinth of regulations dictating everything from march routes, bus parking restrictions, and petty rules on Porta Potties.

Could they pay for all this? Apparently. They had five weeks to raise a million dollars and were closing in on $1.5 million in two days. That was double the Women's March haul in its first two months. Then George Clooney and his wife released a statement:

Amal and I are so inspired by the courage and eloquence of these young men and women from

Stoneman Douglas High School. Our family will be there on March 24 to stand side by side with this incredible generation of young people from all over the country, and in the name of our children Ella and Alexander, we're donating $500,000 to help pay for this groundbreaking event. Our children's lives depend on it.

Later Tuesday morning, Jeffrey and Marilyn Katzenberg announced they were matching that pledge. Steven Spielberg and Kate Capshaw quickly followed. They applauded the kids for "demonstrating their leadership with a confidence and maturity that belies their ages."

All afternoon, the three buses snaked up the Florida Turnpike carrying Jackie's hundred Douglas emissaries to Tallahassee, with a caravan of news vans trailing behind. At four p.m., NPR's *All Things Considered* took the air, and led with the story of the journey; they hadn't even gotten there. Right about the same time, Sean Hannity's radio show was playing on another Florida station, running a gun promotion. At 6:36 p.m., Oprah tweeted a fourth half-million-dollar pledge, which drew nearly half a million likes. "These inspiring young people remind me of the Freedom Riders of the 60s who also said we've had ENOUGH and our voices will be heard," it said.

The two-million-dollar celebrity windfall came with a price. Conservative critics took it as confirmation the kids were pawns—and added Decadent Hollywood to the list of puppet masters. "Crisis actor" charges leapt from right-wing websites to mainstream media. A growing conspiracy theory contended that school shootings were hoaxes cooked up by the Liberal Media as a pretext for a government gun-grab. It escalated when The Internet discovered that David Hogg had been photographed thousands of miles away in summer 2017. David's friend got into an argument with a lifeguard at Redondo Beach, California, and David was interviewed about it on local TV news—"proving" he didn't even live in Florida. That was airtight evidence for the fringe Right. They scoffed at the explanation: the Hoggs moved to Parkland from Torrance, California, in 2014, and David returned to spend most summers with his friend there. Sometimes, they went to the beach. The conspiracy sites howled. Crisis actor, *obviously.*

Marco Rubio actually tweeted in support of the kids Tuesday evening, labeling the charges "the work of a disgusting group of idiots with no sense of decency."

"Thank you," David tweeted back.

His friends responded with humor. Wolf Blitzer asked Cameron about the crisis actor charges live on CNN. "Well, if you had seen me in our school's production of *Fiddler on the Roof*, you would know that nobody would pay me to act, for anything," Cameron said. Wednesday morning, he tweeted: "@davidhogg111 is smart, funny, and diligent, but my favorite thing about him is undoubtedly that he's actually a 26 year-old felon from California."

The kids also responded with the facts, and assurances. The first $1.5 million came from more than 18,000 individual donors. "Donations will be used to pay the expenses associated with the March for Our Lives gathering in Washington, DC, and to provide resources for young people organizing similar marches across the country," a spokeswoman said. "Any leftover funds will go towards supporting a continuing, long-term effort by and for young people to end the epidemic of mass shootings that has turned our classrooms into crime scenes."

They even used their parents. The kids rarely sanctioned that, because they understood the power of images. Parents at the microphone would undercut their message that this was all them. But they faced a countervailing narrative: Should two dozen high school kids really be handling $3.5 million, an amount growing by the day? And they did need help—not in planning, but in execution. An excellent *New York* magazine piece a few weeks later captured it well: "To handle the logistics alone, the kids desperately need grown-up help—even as they guard the specifics of what help they're getting." They had their guard up about that. I was constantly astounded about their candor in just about everything: what they were doing, how they were grieving, breakdowns and screwups and their own privilege. But one thing they were consistently cagey about, straight through summer and into fall: adult assistance. The only time I ever felt a smarmy talking point thrown at me was on the Tallahassee trip, while they were most sensitive about the issue and still new at handling their roles. Every time I asked about outside support, kids repeated the line "This is for kids, by kids." That lasted only a few days. They despised talking points, and corrected the error quickly. After that, when they didn't want to answer my question, they just told me so. It didn't happen much.

Clooney mostly texted with the kids directly. But he also spoke to their parents on Tuesday, to allay concerns on all sides. The kids let Cameron's dad, Jeff Kasky, make a statement. "These people putting their money in—not a single one of them has said anything along the lines of 'I'll donate but you have to listen to what I say.' Nobody is pulling the strings for these kids," he said. "I have to make clear: [Clooney] is not directing them, nor is anybody."

He also said Clooney had hooked them up with attorneys and admin help, and, crucially, the powerhouse PR firm 42 West, which represented major entertainment talent. Jeff Kasky said the March for Our Lives Foundation would be set up that week to oversee the handling of all funds.

4

It was a wearying ride to Tallahassee, with three rest stops and lots of bladder issues. At the stops, kids said the elation had subsided in the first hour. No one was sure what they were in for. They were excited to meet their representatives, but fuzzy on what that would look like. And what should they say? Many were taken aback by the media whirlwind. They had expected us to move on by now, not follow them up the turnpike.

"I don't think any of us thought it would get this big so quickly," Daniel Duff said. Daniel was a skinny freshman with curly brown hair and braces across an irrepressible smile. He could be Central Casting for the sidekick's handsome little brother in a high school rom-com. Governor Scott was one of the few officials he was familiar with—"Mostly because he looks so much like Voldemort."

Daniel was fourteen, from a fervently Republican

family, and had never paid much attention to politics. He was very into it now. Tallahassee sounded exciting. He was really eager to talk to officials—but how blunt should he be? Was someone going to guide them? He wasn't aware of the training ahead, but would find it a godsend.

The lead bus pulled into Leon High School around 9:30 p.m. The kids were tired, hungry, and ready to crash. The campus was built on a hill, with a grassy ridge and a staircase leading up to the school. The grounds were lit, and hundreds of students lined the ridge. The kids staggered off the first bus to rapturous cheers and a hug-brigade of local officials lined up beside the door. As they mounted the staircase, adoring Leon students pressed in from both sides. A bank of TV cameras were positioned to capture it all, with the caravan of more rolling in. The kids felt like astronauts returning from the moon landing. No one had foreseen this. Daniel Duff wondered who was hugging him, and was visibly overcome. All those kids stayed at school till ten o'clock? "I didn't know that we were that big," he said. "To meet some kids who have a voice?"

Several Parkland kids stepped up to the microphone at the top of the stairs. Impassioned speeches recaptured the mood from the Publix lot, until a technical glitch took out the speakers. They wrapped it up and went inside. Some of the Leon kids joined them, but the bulk remained outside to repeat the process. The second bus got a similar welcome, but when Jackie's bus pulled in an hour later, they had given up and gone in for pizza with two-thirds of the Parkland contingent. Jackie's group was ushered in quickly with little fanfare.

It was very late, but the legislative training went forward. It was vital. Claire VanSusteren gave an overview. This is a conversation, two ways, and it demands respect, she said. It's OK to be emotional with officials, but if you get angry or contentious, meetings will be canceled fast. She said that had happened to a group of activists earlier that month.

Several speakers repeated her warning, but Representative Jared Moskowitz went a different route. "You need to make this real for them," he said. "You've got to put them in that school."

"You are the epicenter of the earth right now," Senator Book said. "You are what is going to change the world. And the most important thing is that we *not let people look away!*"

Daniel Duff was relieved. He got it now. They all did.

Senator Book and Claire VanSusteren spent the night with the girls, in sleeping bags on the Red Cross cots. Conversation bounced among normal teen topics, the speeches they were planning, and memories of the shooting. Some were sharing stories for the first time. "After three o'clock, I could not stay up one more minute," VanSusteren said. She suggested everyone get some sleep.

"We don't really sleep anymore," the kids told her. She shuddered. Then she wandered off to try.

5

At five a.m., the doors swung open for the *Good Morning America* crew. The kids walked to the capitol groggy but exhilarated. But disillusionment crept in fast. Sessions seemed to take one of two frustrating paths. "For the most part, the people we talked to already agreed with us," Daniel Duff said. That was the biggest complaint, because so many of the yeses had come from allies. Alfonso's group had been paired with more hard-liners, who seemed primarily intent on merely placating them. More thoughts and prayers. Either way, all minds seemed to have been made up long before they arrived. So why talk, if no one was actually listening? Of course, legislators had thought about this—and voted on it—that made sense, though only in retrospect for many of the kids; they hadn't really thought about it before. Or they assumed the officials' own kids getting gunned down might make them rethink things. They might be receptive to hear what they had to say. No sign of that.

The House chamber was gaveled to order and began with a tribute to the Parkland kids, and a reading of the seventeen names. Senator Book's team was hoping for some real floor debate, and the kids packed the balcony hopefully, but it was generic speechifying. Claire advised them to move on quickly, and they did.

Most of the meetings were conducted behind closed doors, at the legislators' insistence. The kids then filed out and described them to the media throngs. And they were not happy. Senate president Joe Negron opened his session to the media. He was joined by two other Republican Senate leaders. The senators were respectful and engaging, seemed genuinely concerned, and answered every question—but most of them evasively. The questions were dignified, as instructed, but the reactions were spontaneous and blunt.

"Why should anyone have an assault rifle?" a boy asked. "That's an issue that we're reviewing," Negron said. The students groaned.

One student asked for a simple yes or no answer on raising the purchasing age of an assault rifle to twenty-one, and Negron offered a long-winded dodge. The grumbling grew louder. Then Senator Bill Galvano poked his head to the microphone and said simply, "My answer is yes." Applause broke out and shouts of "Thank you! Thank you!"

"I'll take two more questions," Senator Negron said. "This young lady, and the young man in the red tie." When his turn came, the red-tie boy stood and spoke more sternly than his peers. "You said you would look at things closely. Are you willing to actually act on anything? Yes or no?"

Senator Negron gave a long, meandering answer: he was proud of the senate, they were working on mental health . . . No real answer.

Alfonso Calderon wore a bright red tie over a crisp blue dress shirt with a rainbow lapel pin. He was the only kid who dressed up. In the hallway afterward, I asked if he'd gotten the memo.

"Yeah, I have a problem with rules," he said. But then he laughed and said it was actually strategic. Ties are catnip for adults—they'll always call on you. It had worked with the senator, and with me and countless other reporters, who had lost most of the students we wanted to follow up with in the mad hallway jumble. The red tie made it easy.

His crazy mop of black curls, piled high and flopped over to the right, sides buzzed razor short. It was quite a look, but he pulled it off. High cheekbones, deep dimples, intense brown eyes, and a mischievous smile helped. He was cocky, but self-deprecating—he definitely saw life, including himself, as a comedy. It took only moments with him to see he shared Cameron's wicked sense of humor. They turned out to be close friends. Alfonso was one of the Never Again leaders who handled most of the group's Spanish-language TV. We spoke briefly and he promised to circle back, but his friends were waiting, and were looking on expectantly. He resumed his position at the center of his pack.

Just outside the building, it felt like a different world. Throngs of students and teachers and PTA members had marched on the capital to support them. Demonstrators gathered instead beneath the six soaring Doric columns and the wood-and-copper cupola atop the adjacent old capitol dome. Several different rallies had been in the works, by different groups on different days, but they had merged to rally behind the Parkland kids. Thousands already filled the granite steps, the lawn, and the Apalachee Parkway, when the final contingent from Florida State University rolled in.

Seventeen placards were positioned on easels up and down the steps, each one bearing the contents of one of seventeen bills that had failed in the last several years—failed even to be read in committee. "Seventeen bills that could have saved seventeen lives," a mom told me, a senator told me, aides told me, and the incoming president of the Florida PTA told me. They had their talking point.

A whole lot of students had come, but they were not the majority of the crowd, not by a long shot. There were moms, so many moms, and grandmas. Dads too, but three-fourths of the crowd was female, many of them in red Moms Demand Action T-shirts. They had been fighting for this so long, they said, and many had lost hope, until they saw David Hogg on Thursday morning, the leader they had been waiting for—and then Emma called BS on Saturday, and really blew them away. The signs were all hand-painted, with phrases like AM I NEXT?; PROTECT KIDS, NOT GUNS; and CHILDREN SHOULDN'T DIE FOR YOUR HOBBY. There were elaborate artworks of acrylic paint on ten-foot tarps, supported by poles along each side. One said BLOOD ON YOUR HANDS, with bright red palm prints, and dripping blood. Another featured a giant blue clockface labeled

NEXT MASSACRE COUNTDOWN CLOCK. And of course WE CALL BS signs everywhere.

The speakers were powerful, and the mood euphoric. With the Parkland kids leading them, they were convinced they could break through this time.

But almost none of the Parkland kids were feeling that. Their introduction to their government had filled them with disillusionment. Officials had turned the rotunda over to them for most of the noon hour to address the public, via the press. Jackie had organized about a dozen kids to deliver short speeches, in quick succession.

Alfonso started slowly and graciously, thanking officials for having them, describing his life just a week earlier: his biggest worries about what show to watch at six p.m., when to do his homework, study for a math test, and fit in theater rehearsals for a show at an elementary school down the road. "We are just children," he said. And there he took a sharp turn. "A lot of people think that that disqualifies us from even having an opinion on this sort of matter. As if because we've been through a traumatic experience, that we don't know what we're talking about and that we're speaking irrationally. We know better than anyone. We understand what it's like to face a gun, to lose our friends, to return to school, to look at an empty seat." He faltered there. "And you know that that empty seat is because— Because someone's— Because someone's dead." Parkland was a beautiful town he said, a safe town. "And it's now ruined!" He packed so much revulsion into that word. Alfonso was the first Parkland kid I heard enunciate that. The Columbine kids had fought so hard to reclaim the word as the name of the school instead of an atrocity, but they had lost. When they went off to college, other kids named their high schools while they said Colorado, or Denver, or anything to avoid the pity and awkward silences.

Alfonso said he wasn't ready to go back to school in a week. "I don't think anybody here is ready." He had been to grief counselors, but they needed more than counseling. "What we need is action." The precise action—they were still working that out. But they would not be fooled by platitudes or spin. "We are old enough to understand why someone might want to discredit us for their own political purposes. Trust me, I understand. I was in a closet, locked, for four hours with people who I would consider almost family, crying and weeping on me, begging for their lives. I understand what it's like to text my parents, 'Goodbye. I might never, ever get to see you again. I love you.' I understand."

They demanded action, and were prepared to sacrifice, Alfonso said. "I am prepared to drop out of school.

I am prepared to not worry about anything else besides this, because change might not come today, it might not come tomorrow, it might not even come March twenty-fourth, when we march for our lives down in Washington, but it will happen, in my lifetime, because I will fight every single day—and I know everyone here will fight for the rest of their lives—to see sensible gun laws in this country and so that kids don't have to fear going back to school. Thank you."

6

Jackie continued fielding problems and herding strays. She conferred with Book in her office, and savored a few minutes of downtime, playing with Book's one-year-old twins in their drool-soaked DOUGLAS STRONG T-shirts. The babies briefly defused the pressure and reminded Jackie whom they were fighting for. Would those babies still fear gunmen in their high school? The Columbine students were old enough to be Jackie's parents. They had never thought to fear for their own kids. We knew better now.

Jackie looked exhausted. Was all this good for her own recovery?

The angry cloud hovered through most of the afternoon. "I'm extremely, extremely angry and sad,"

Alfonso Calderon said. "I don't know if I'm going to have faith in my state and local government anymore, because what I saw today was discouraging."

But shortly after five, the first group cycled out of their meeting with Governor Scott, and many of them left his office beaming. None of them wanted to talk right off, because dinner had arrived and they were ravenous for their box meals. Once they had eaten, many described the governor as listening, responding, and asking probing questions. "I feel like he really heard us," sophomore Tanzil Philip said. "I sat right next to him and he was writing down everything we were talking about and he put checkmarks next to the things that were really important to us." That sure contrasted with the legislators, he said.

There were many dissenters. Daniel Duff complained that Scott never even uttered the words "gun control." Still, all the students seemed glad they came. "Oh, a hundred percent," Daniel said. He looked forward to organizing the Washington march, but also considered attending a local one. "I haven't talked to my parents about that," he said.

They boarded the buses spent, and arrived home around four a.m. A car was already waiting in front of Jackie's house. After a quick snooze, it whisked Jackie and her mom to the airport for their flight to Los Angeles to tape *Ellen*.

7

On Friday, Governor Scott defied the NRA and proposed a modest gun bill. Two weeks later, he signed a variation of it into law. It banned bump stocks, raised the minimum age for buying a gun to twenty-one, and added a three-day waiting period for most long gun purchases. It did not address assault weapons.

The kids had discussed those ideas throughout the trip, and most of them derided them as minor no-brainers. The country would still be awash in guns; a tiny fraction of attackers would just have to work a little harder to get a certain deadly type. "Some people know the baloney that politicians feed us," Jackie said. But she saw a marathon. The gun safety team had lost ground relentlessly, year after year, state after her state— nothing but losses, her entire life. And a prominent Second Amendment warrior had just broken, publicly, with the NRA. No one had seen that coming. Finally, the momentum had flipped to them. Jackie Corin gave her movement something it desperately needed. She gave it a win.

5

Spring Awakening

1

Cameron Kasky was always different—different from everyone, but different from his brothers from the start. The Kaskys had three kids, all boys, two and a half years apart. Cameron was the middle child, but the dynamics changed when his little brother, Holden, began to show signs of autism. "It's not like it made Cam the youngest, but it's almost like his childhood was kind of rushed because his brother's needs took over," his mother, Natalie, said. But Cameron never hurt for attention. When Cameron was a young boy, they went on a Norwegian Sky family cruise. "Jeff and I walked into one of the adult nightclubs, and [Cameron] was performing. He had left the kids' camp—I don't know how, because you're not supposed to; maybe his leaving was how the cruise lines eventually changed their policies. Jeff and I walk in, and he's up there making all these off-color jokes. The entire audience is hysterical."

They were howling. You can watch it on YouTube— Jeff posted it before the shooting. It's "Jokers Wild" open-mic night, and the room has an industrial Vegas prom decor: exposed beams, corrugated metal ceiling tiles, lights reflecting every foot or two off its gleaming polyurethane wood floor. In the middle of it, a microphone stand, lowered to minimum height, is aligned with Cam's wisecracking mouth. His dress shirt is oversized and untucked; khakis spill over his dress shoes, and curly locks onto his collar. He is completely at ease, working each bit like he's hamming it up with his grandparents, owning the room. A man watching far behind him doubles over.

Natalie recalls a rush of pride, and an inability to breathe. "This is what a real comedian's mom feels like. It's a mix of horror, nerves, and pride." And almost immediately, one clear thought occurred to her: "This is going to happen so much. Whenever he gets a live mic, he's going to be entertaining adults. He was seven or eight."

"He's taught himself everything," she said. "He's taught himself to swim, he taught himself the ABCs, he taught himself to read—this thing about not need-ing parents is not new." She reconsidered. "It's not that he doesn't need us, he needs support." Natalie and Cam seem to have a cozy relationship. Cam didn't need parents charting the movement, but he needed a sanc-tuary. "I want to be home and protect Holden and stay out of things," Natalie said.

Swimming was Natalie's most vivid early recollec-tion of discovering who her boy was. She took Cam to the pool as a toddler and tried to get him started on floating. "Resist, resist, resist." And one day he was jumping up and down in the pool, then tried it at an angle, a tighter angle, and pretty soon he was swim-ming. "He didn't want or really appreciate the need to reach out. It's like, 'I can do it myself.' Just the way he was built."

Reading was more gradual, but more revealing. She sent Cam to Montessori pre-K, and redecorated the long hallway to the boys' rooms with alphabet wallpaper at eye level, to make learning fun. "He couldn't wait for them to come down," Natalie said. He loved pre-K, reading was exciting, but this "fun" business—he saw right through it and resented it. God, did he hate to be patronized. He didn't have the vocabulary for that word yet, but the concept was infuriating.

By pre-K he was reading, and in kindergarten it

really took off. By first or second grade he was plowing through chapter books. "I couldn't keep him in books—it was just like flying out the door." And when he was seven, Jerry Seinfeld did a comedy book for kids, *Halloween*— "And if you ever checked it out, you'd be like, 'Of course Cameron was into this.'"

That's also the period when politics got ahold of Cameron. "About in third grade, I started to notice the undeniable political mind," Natalie said. "He was very pro-Obama." He was going to Pine Crest Elementary School, a prestigious private school in Boca Raton, and Barack Obama was facing off against Mitt Romney for reelection. Cameron told her a lot of the kids' parents were less liberal, and he was getting a lot of pushback. "Basically, his teacher would say he was on a soapbox and didn't know the appropriate time and place—that eventually, he would have to turn the audience over to the teacher for the day. So there were a lot of those phone calls before the election."

That went hand in hand with his interest in theater, she said. Mrs. Blakely was the drama teacher, "and she could tell right away that this energy needed to go somewhere. I think everyone kind of agreed, this energy needed to be after school."

Pine Crest had a strong drama program for an elementary school, but Cameron outgrew that quickly, and moved on to community theater. *High School Musical* stood out, and *Seussical*, in which he played the Cat in the Hat. Music became a passion: first the cello, then the upright bass, but eventually Cameron decided his voice was his true instrument. For a while, politics took a back seat. "Because he felt the world was a safe place with Obama," Natalie said. It came roaring back in 2017, when Trump was inaugurated—"And everything started to be really, you know, ugly? He just felt like he needed to tune in a little more."

They sent Cam off to Starlight Camp when he was very young, and he was very excited. His older brother, Julian, had gone there, and his cousins too, and for two years they had raved about it. "There were periods, you followed your exact bunk to your exact activity, and he hated it," Natalie said. Camp was supposed to be fun, and that wasn't Cam's idea of fun. So they tried French Woods, a performing arts camp, and Cam was in heaven. He returned, enthusiastically, for seven years. "The kids were in charge of their own schedule, you didn't have to be with your bunkmates the entire time, you got to be with like-minded people. That was so important to him."

They were putting on shows: ventriloquism, magic, circus. "And the most important thing that he kept saying: 'We get to do it ourselves.'" Natalie said. "'They trust us. They let us walk alone.' And he was young."

Pine Crest was formal and rigid, and his older brother, Julian, loved that, but Cameron chafed. Just before he reached the upper division, he said he wanted to transfer to public school, with the regular kids. "I panicked," his mom said. She saw him losing out on an elite education; Cam just saw a nightmare of rules. He was not unruly, selfish, or disrespectful—just contemptuous of dumb rules that had outlived their usefulness.

Natalie got comfortable with public school when she realized they had been here before. An instant replay of the summer camp debacle. "I was wrong about school and I was wrong about camp," Natalie said. "And then I just released it and I let him do what felt right. I just have this pattern on hearing what he has to say, having my own thoughts and breathless moments, and going with ultimately what he thinks." He's highly intuitive about what will work for him.

2

A month before the attack, Christine Barclay had a problem. Barclay ran a performing arts studio at the Boca Black Box theater in nearby Boca Raton, where she taught young actors and staged student and semi-pro performances. She was casting a slate of spring musicals: *Seussical, Legally Blonde,* and *Spring Awakening.* She had plenty of talented girls, but boys were a problem. Her flamboyantly out tech assistant, Spencer Shaw, who had transferred from Douglas a year earlier, waved off that problem.

"I can get you boys," Spencer promised. "Don't worry about boys."

He posted a story on Snapchat and Cameron showed up the next day. Cameron and Barclay hit it off instantly. He returned with more boys day after day, and by the end of the week, Barclay's small studio was packed with talented young actors. "Where are all these boys coming from?" she asked her assistant. Cameron. He gathers, he draws, he organizes; it's what Cameron does. "I had this amazing foundation of a company," Barclay said. "This Cameron Kasky kid comes in and fills all the holes."

Cameron had his eye on two shows, but *Spring Awakening* really grabbed hold of him. It was based on a seminal nineteenth-century German expressionist play about teen sexuality and neglectful, pious parents—a toxic combination. Cameron was after the male lead of Melchior, a radical freethinker and something of a pied piper, whose naive girlfriend dies from a botched abortion. His best friend also commits suicide, and the play climaxes in a graveyard scene in which Melchior pulls out a razor in despair and argues with his friend's ghost about slitting his throat to join them. Broadway heavyweights Duncan Sheik and Steven Sater had been so distraught by the Columbine massacre in 1999 that they adapted Frank Wedekind's play, subtitled *A Children's Tragedy*, as a rock musical. They retained the period setting and costumes, but reimagined it with much more heart, and juiced it with a rock score.

"Wedekind was writing a sort of scathing social critique about the moral imbecility of adults," Sater said. "He was certainly empathetic to his younger characters, but not so focused on their inner worlds. I always wanted to remain faithful to Wedekind, but we found that by introducing songs to the narrative, we grew more invested in those young people—we had access to their hearts and minds and all their unspoken desires. And so we began creating heroes' journeys for our three main characters." So Sater added a classroom scene, in which Melchior stands up for his troubled friend Moritz. "And that made us care more deeply about Melchior, it helped us root for him." Sater elaborated: "Melchior has an entire song, 'Touch Me,' in which he imagines how sexual pleasure must feel for 'the woman.' So, it only made sense, from the perspective of who he'd become, that what had been a scene of rape in the original play evolved into a love scene," with the character Wendla embracing her own urges. "Again, we didn't want Wendla to be just a victim," Sater said. He wanted her to have a journey of her own, one in which she embraces her sexuality, and the love she's felt, and that finally "she embraces the new life within her, just before it's taken away from her."

They pushed other elements to be even edgier, adding two masturbation scenes and rousing songs like "The Bitch of Living" and the gleefully bittersweet showstopper "Totally Fucked." Melchior opens the song:

> *There's a moment you know*
> *You're fucked.*
> *Not an inch more room*
> *To self destruct.*

But then he embraces his fucked-up fate and the full cast belts out the chorus:

> *Yeah, you're fucked all right and all for spite*
> *You can kiss your sorry ass goodbye.*

Despite sweeping the 2007 awards season with eight Tonys and all the major "best musical" awards, including the Olivier in London three years later, the show is too risqué for most high schools. When Barclay asked her kids what shows they wanted to do, they begged for *Heathers*, *Rent*, *Avenue Q*, and *Spring Awakening*. "Edgy shows about conversations people avoid having," she said. "We're all thinking we're so progressive, but these kids are still desperate to do these shows. Why? Because they're not being allowed to do them at their schools. I'm not at the school, I don't have a principal, I don't have a school board breathing down my neck," she said. "I'll be the place that does those edgy things. Someone has to be the place to go out on a ledge and let the kids be dark and be upset and be angsty and sexual. Or there's no outlet for it. We're perpetuating exactly what's happening in the show."

The cast was having a ball. "These kids have been waiting for an opportunity to sing 'I'm totally fucked!' at the top of their lungs. I didn't choreograph that number, I said, 'Now jump off that stage,' and that's all I had to say. They were ready for it. They took off their own clothes. Cameron does that froggie jump, he shakes his butt and slaps his ass all on his own. I didn't tell them to do any of that."

Casting Cameron had been dicey. Sawyer Garrity, another Douglas student, had an angelic voice and had landed the female lead of Wendla. Cameron's voice was passable, but he would never get to Broadway on a song. But the rebel, the magnet, the pied piper—Cameron *was* Melchior. And he exuded the frenetic sense of the show. "Cameron's always been like a champagne bottle that's been corked too long," Barclay said. "He would interrupt himself in conversations with me, before even getting to the end of the sentence, and then we're on a different conversation. He was a live wire, ready for something in life."

They had a frank talk about his voice. He got it. Cam agreed to an hour of voice lessons a week—intense and one-on-one. Barclay couldn't make him a songbird, but he was born to play this role.

Cameron threw himself into the part. When he cared about something, he had only one speed. He was bitten by the drama bug, and was eager for more, more, more. Had she found enough boys for *Legally Blonde*? he asked.

She cast him as the Ivy-Leagued Warner Huntington III, the male lead. Then he brought Holden and schmoozed her for a part for him. Then he offered his Chihuahua, Brutus, for the production. He also landed a role in MSD's spring musical, *Yo, Vikings!*, and assisted on its direction, and was directing the school's one-act performance of *Coney Island Christmas* for the statewide drama competition. He was hoping to win districts for that in February, and go on to the state competition in Tampa in March. Cameron liked a full plate.

But it was Melchior that consumed him. And he couldn't get enough coaching from Barclay. "He kind of immediately became an adopted teen son of mine," she said.

"It's like magic between the two of them," Cameron's mom, Natalie Weiss, said. "They just understood each other right from the start, as so many relationships are like in the theater."

Barclay was ambitious too. She had moved down from Manhattan and begun the program two years earlier, and it was suddenly gaining traction. She cast her spring slate eight months into her first pregnancy, and scheduled herself straight up to her due date, which was Valentine's Day. She would leave the staff and the kids on their own for a month of maternity leave—deliciously ironic, given the show—and then six frantic weeks till opening night on May 3. Four months of hoofing for two shows, three hundred seats a night. They could do it, but everything had to go just right.

3

The baby missed her due date. "When Valentine's Day happened," Barclay said, "I immediately texted Cam, because Cam was like the ringleader of my MSD crew." *How was he? Where was he?*

Cam reported that most of this crew was locked up in the drama room. Barclay's musical director, Ed Kolcz, was with them, because his day job is musical coach at Douglas High. Barclay was driving in to her studio for *Seussical* and *Legally Blonde* rehearsals, also packed with Douglas kids. "Every time my phone was dinging, it was Cameron confirming that another kid was alive in our cast," she said. "So it was just like: 'Heard from Kirstin, she's OK.' 'Heard from Ethan, he's OK.' Finally, we got up to the full cast, and I was like, 'OK, I didn't lose any of my kids.' And then it all started to lift off."

Barclay was already a mentor to Cameron, but with his mom struggling to find a way home from the Caribbean, he leaned on her especially hard. "He started to get all these interviews. He started to call me before them. 'OMG Christine, What do I do?' He was like, 'What do I say to Anderson Cooper? His eyes, I'm going to be distracted by his eyes!'—like making Cameron jokes about it.

"My advice to him—which, I'm not the loudest voice chirping in his ear—was to not be a pot stirrer, not preach to his own choir," she said. "The problem in our country right now is people are only really willing or able to talk to people who already agree with them." She said, "Cameron, you're a child. Because you're a kid, maybe through the eyes of a child, preaching to both sides, maybe people will listen."

Saturday, around the time Emma was calling BS, and Cameron's mother was getting back from the Caribbean, Barclay went into labor. When Caroline was born Monday, the kids had already done their press gauntlet announcing the Washington march, and were gearing up for Tallahassee the next day.

Cameron disregarded Barclay's advice Wednesday night. CNN had invited the Parkland kids and the NRA to its town hall, so anticipation and ratings ran sky high. The NRA was smart enough not to send its CEO, Wayne LaPierre, who was predictably bombastic. He would have come off as the crazy old white guy with no compassion for these kids. It deployed its wily secret weapon, Dana Loesch. She was just as ruthless, but exceptionally nimble. Loesch ultimately never gave an inch, but appeared to in the moment—so calm and understanding. She listened to her adversaries, acknowledged their position and their pain, while gently laying the groundwork for the case that they were perhaps misguided, and she really had their best interest at heart. And she commanded any stage with fierce resolve and striking beauty: straight black hair, a Kennedy jaw, and brown eyes that smote her opponents even as she smiled. Cameron had not come for her. He had come for Marco Rubio.

The NRA was an easy target—but also slightly off target. The NRA was their sparring partner; they would never defeat it, and why should they? It had a right to exist. The problem was politicians in its thrall, and the goal was to break that connection, remove the NRA boot from their necks. If every politician in America began voting their conscience, this would be solved tomorrow, Cam's team believed.

The target was Marco Rubio: Cam's Exhibit A in the NRA-Congress connection, his representative on the NRA dole. The NRA had donated only $4,950 to Rubio directly, but donations were not its primary MO. It liked to create its own ads, buy the airtime, and control the message. The NRA had spent $3.3 million on Rubio's behalf over the course of his political career, making him the sixth-largest NRA beneficiary in the US Senate. If Cam could shame Rubio, or scare him politically, into severing that bond—who knows what dominoes might fall.

Also, Cameron was still seething. His classmates were murdered, his senator seemed complicit, and Cam wanted to take him down. Humiliate him, if possible.

The moderator, Jake Tapper, introduced Cameron, and he laid right in. "Senator Rubio, it's hard to look at you and not look down a barrel of an AR-15 and not look at [the killer], but the point is you're here and there are some people who are not." He asked his friend, Douglas senior Chris Grady, to stand. "This is my friend who is going into the military," Cameron said. "I need you to tell him that he's going to live to make it to serve our country."

Senator Rubio calmly buttoned his blazer while assuring them that Chris would live to serve the country and have a voice in changing its laws.

Cameron took a moment to call for bipartisanship. "Guys, look, this isn't about red and blue. We can't boo people because they're Democrats and boo people because they're Republicans." He said anyone ready to change was somebody they need on their side. "So Senator Rubio, can you tell me right now that you will not accept a single donation from the NRA in the future?"

The crowd erupted, and leapt to their feet, applauding. It went on and on, and Senator Rubio waited them out with his hands clasped behind his back, sidestepping back and forth, over and over. Cameron fought back a smile and overreached, lamenting twice that he really wanted to take on "the NRA lady"—how she can look in the mirror . . .

"I'm sorry, what was that?" Senator Rubio asked.

"I don't freaking know," Cameron said.

"That's OK."

"The question is about NRA money," Tapper said.

Rubio started out coherently, saying he'd been consistent over time, and then grew rambling and confused: "Number two—no. The answer to the question is that people buy into my agenda. And I also support . . ." By the fourth concept he cited supporting— "The things that I have stood for and fought for"—the crowd was beginning to jeer, and Cameron cut off the filibuster:

"No more—no more NRA money?" He tried to brush that off, and Cameron kept repeating it. "More NRA money?"

Rubio, notoriously flusterable, started stammering (and this is how the official transcript punctuated it): "I—there—that is the wrong way to look—first of all, the answer is, people buy into my agenda."

"You can say no."

"Well—I—I—the influence of any group—"

He had totally lost the crowd. The jeers were louder and relentless now, and Cameron turned to the crowd to call them off. "Guys, come on, be quiet. We're gonna be here all night."

Rubio continued insisting that the NRA was irrelevant: "The influence of these groups comes not from money. The influence comes from the millions of people that agree with the agenda . . ."

Cameron kept pulling him back: "In the name of seventeen people, you cannot ask the NRA to keep their money out of your campaign?"

"I think in the name of seventeen people, I can pledge to you that I will support any law that will prevent a killer like this from getting a gun," Rubio said.

"No, but I'm talking about NRA money." Cameron then suggested maybe they could raise enough money for Rubio to replace the NRA contributions, and then circled back: "Are you gonna be accepting money from the NRA in the future?"

"I—I've always supported—I will always accept the help of anyone who agrees with my agenda. But my agenda is—I'll give you a perfect example . . ." He rattled on until the segment was used up. He'd spent all of it running from the question, and never advanced a coherent point.

The reviews for Rubio were withering. He was the butt of comedy sketches and late-night monologues for days.

Dana Loesch faced off against Emma González a few minutes later, and Loesch came prepared—not just to debate, but to emote. She tried to disarm Emma by praising her bravery and then recasting it entirely as a mental health failure.

After the town hall event Wednesday night, Cameron called Barclay from the airport around two a.m., about to board the red-eye, giddy about taping *Ellen* in L.A. "Just an excitable kid," she said. She chided him, half-joking, "Did you bring your script? Are you going to go off-book by the time you get back? Are you drinking water, because your throat sounds like shit right now—you've literally lost your voice."

"Then he's calling me crying because he's getting death threats," Barclay said. "It was really taking a toll on him. From the physical exhaustion, the emotional exhaustion, the death threats—on him, on his friends that he now felt responsible for, because he had started this movement. The stress about trying, I think—it's what every celebrity kid goes through. It's like, 'OK, do I leave my life? How much of my real life do I abandon? How much do I give up? How much do I try to save?'"

Way too much for a seventeen-year-old boy. And the last thing he needed was an out-of-school musical, with a suicide onstage, a gun blast, and that graveyard scene mourning his two dead friends, with his character leaning toward killing himself.

About a week after Tallahassee, and a lot of texts with Clooney, Barclay called him to talk. Her staff was keeping an eye on him, sending her daily reports, and it was getting worse. He had an awful time at rehearsal that day.

"I was trying to relieve him of the part," Barclay explained. "I said, 'Cameron, is this just going to be added shit for you? Not even just lines learning and being in rehearsal, but emotionally?' At first, he took offense, like I was kicking him out. I was like, 'I'm not trying to take this from you. I'm merely asking you if this is something you are able to do.' He wouldn't give it up."

Barclay agreed, but he couldn't phone it in. "You're going to figure out how to work this all into your schedule, because I have an obligation to the theater and to the rest of the cast. He said, 'Just let me get through the March for Our Lives. I probably won't be too present in March, try to do all the other scenes around me, and if you can do that then I'll be there, I'll do it."

She said OK, but he had to give up *Legally Blonde*, "Because I just said, 'Dude there's no way.'"

4

When Barclay returned early from maternity leave, the kids were just back to school and in rough shape. She gathered the cast, crew, and staff in the theater for a long talk. "Now these kids that I'm looking at are a completely different group of kids than they were the last time I'd seen them," she said. They talked for two and a half hours. "I said, 'OK, are we going to do this? What do you guys want to do? And they all said they wanted to do the show. Every single one of them. They all felt like they had to. 'We can't let that person take one more thing from us. They've already taken so much.'"

That is a pervasive feeling with school shootings. At Columbine, the one major issue that pitted students against families of the victims was the library, where most of the killing took place. The parents were adamant it be torn down—no one should ever set foot in there again. The students were overwhelmed with a sense of loss—their friends, their name, their identity—and did not want to surrender one more inch, literal or symbolic. Any fragment of their life they could salvage felt like a victory.

Barclay said she would prioritize security: police cruisers stationed during rehearsals, and metal detectors for the shows. OK, she said finally: What do you want to do now?

"Totally Fucked." They wanted to do "Totally Fucked."

Barclay said OK. "We turned on the music and we all stood onstage and we all just scream-sang through 'Totally Fucked.' Some of them were stoic and some of them were ripping it out, but we did it."

With that out of their system, they wrapped around each other and sang "I Believe," the tender song, sung over the love scene that will do the teens in. It was a different kind of love that day. Sawyer and Cameron laid down center stage hugging; Cam fed her Dunkin' Donuts while the cast swayed around them, arm in arm, singing:

I believe
There is love in heaven
I believe
All will be forgiven . . .
I believe
I believe
I believe

"And I cried, and they cried, and it was like watching soldiers go to battle," Barclay said. "It was like the walking wounded, and they just weren't going to let someone take it away from them. The kids who had been through it, the kids who hadn't been through it—they were like, 'We're going to be anchors for you. We're going to hold the fort while you're traveling all over the world. We're going to understudy for you . . .' And they did."

6
Back to "Normal"

1

On Valentine's Day, Daniel Duff's parents and brothers feared the worst. They kept texting him like crazy—no response, but the messages showed delivered. "I was like, 'Fuck, his phone is on!'" his brother Brendan said. "I was figuring a lot of people turn off their phones, and that happened with a bunch of my friends, so that means something."

Brendan had graduated two years earlier, so he knew where all the classrooms were located. He didn't know Daniel's schedule, but he watched a newscaster talking to a kid in the drama room in the middle of rehearsal, which meant that Daniel would be there. And there was so much misinformation flying around, some of it incorrectly pointing toward drama kids. The whole family was texting Daniel, and it looked bleak.

Daniel's iPhone battery had been running low. In a brief lull in the melee, he had decided he'd better charge it. He'd set it down, but panic resumed, and he'd run off without it. He hadn't even had time to plug it into the wall. But it had enough charge to misdirect his loved ones all afternoon.

Daniel was in the drama room, along with most of the kids who would become March for Our Lives. All the leaders were juniors and seniors. All the kids had lost someone they knew, but the upperclassmen were less likely to have lost someone close to them. Daniel was a freshman. He lost seven friends.

As in all these tragedies, a weird hierarchy of victimhood reared up. Often it was about loved ones lost—how many, how close—but months later, Daniel's dad described another aspect. "Some of Daniel's friends have taken the attitude 'Wait, you weren't even in that building!' There's kind of a hierarchy of who was closest."

That prompted Daniel's mother to describe a moms' therapy session she had just gone to. "I was the only mother there, of five women, who didn't have a child in the building, so I kind of felt guilty. The woman next to me, her son still has a bullet in his arm, and shrapnel—they were very upset. She said he has like a tic now, he doesn't speak. I almost feel guilty saying, 'Daniel seems to be OK.'"

Psychologists discount that sort of reckoning—especially since trauma is etched into the psyche at the moment of terror, by the perception of terror. The norepinephrine flooding the brain is just as toxic whether the killer is five feet away or five miles—so long as the victim believes he might arrive momentarily. Actual danger is irrelevant. Rationally, most survivors realize this, but try telling that to the guilt center of your brain.

Daniel looked like a young Corey Haim, down to the brown curls, though he let them fall naturally and didn't tease them out. He had looked up to Cameron since he was little. Cameron was tight with Daniel's older brother Brendan, and when the Duffs went on vacation, Cameron looked after their dog. Brendan had graduated from Douglas in 2016 and was studying PR at Elon University in North Carolina. He had rushed home to look out for Daniel, and quickly landed at Cameron's house, advising the group on media strategy. Brendan was a major player in Never Again behind the scenes. He helped the kids understand early on that the message was the mission, and they would get one shot at a public persona.

"Brendan was one of our great friends," Cameron said. "So when his brother Daniel started high school, we said he had to join drama. He doesn't really know what he's doing there, but he's trying."

Daniel agreed and enjoyed it, to a point. The night before the shooting, he had had a long talk with his dad. Drama wasn't for him. Cameron and Alex were so passionate about it. His loves were music and photography. He would finish out the year, but that would be it. (MSD offered a variety of different theater classes, and like most of the Never Again kids, he had it as a class as well as an extracurricular activity.) His dad was fine with his decision; he had given it a good shot. But what a fortuitous turn that he had connected with the group. Never Again felt like his therapy. It seemed to be getting him through.

But recovery is different for everyone, and activism can also serve as avoidance, a way to sidestep dealing with the fears, either intentionally or not. "I am so proud of them, but worry that it will be very hard when they settle into their grief and trauma recovery down the road," said Robin Fudge Finegan, who led victims' advocate teams at Oklahoma City and Columbine, then served as a senior FEMA official. "One cannot go end around grief and trauma."

Exactly two weeks after the attack, MSD classes were set to resume. Most students were eager to get back but apprehensive about stepping inside. So the school set up an open house on the Sunday afternoon prior, and dubbed it "campus reunification." Building 12 would be closed off as a crime scene for months, so many classes had to be moved. The rest of the campus was open.

After eleven days watching his campus on television as a crime scene, Daniel discovered that's how he thought of it. Changing it back to his school was way trickier than expected. The helicopters didn't help. He lived within walking distance of the school, and the choppers kept hovering for several days. "I would walk outside, look up and see the helicopters, walk back in, look at the TV, and see the footage the helicopters were capturing," he said. Helicopters were triggers for him, and so were any sort of *bang* sounds. He described walking with a group of friends, and a car engine "kind of went *pop pop pop*, and we all started hyperventilating."

But Sunday, he reunited with all the kids he had gone through it with, and that was a huge relief. He'd known they were all alive, but somehow it took seeing them to feel fully safe again.

Wednesday, February 28, school resumed. Reporters were everywhere. Daniel was annoyed. He was happy to talk to them, but not to be inundated with them. The drop-off line was monstrous that first morning. "Obviously, parents didn't want to leave their kids alone," Daniel said. His mom wasn't afraid of a repeat shooter, so she drove around toward the back gate, which was farther away—but still so many reporters! Daniel was navigating the press gauntlet when a reporter asked if he had a minute to talk. No time, he said—he was trying to make an appointment with another one. They both erupted in laughter.

Class schedule began that day, but not really class. "So much Play-Doh, and so many comfort dogs," Daniel said. "I don't know what kind of meeting they had before, but every classroom had Play-Doh," he said.

Daniel was getting restless. "I did use the Play-Doh one time—I was really bored," he said. "I didn't really make anything. I kind of just squished it around in my hand." The comfort dogs, though—those were great. He was eager to get back to work—not full speed, but something. But some of the kids were still in shock, not ready for any stress, so they had to take it slow.

And sometimes he needed it slow—especially in the classes he had had with Jaime and Gina. "I was really good friends with Gina, so sometimes I'll look over and see the empty chair, and I know I talk about that a lot and I know a lot of people talk about that a lot, but that's one of the things that hits me the worst."

Daniel was excited to have a diversion—both from his grief *and* his activism. "Something to be a part of that isn't political," he said. "To be a kid again. I'm wearing a March for Our Lives shirt right now."

And he was still looking to do something creative with his life. He reflected on his artistic ambitions, seriously considering photography. But just mentioning it dredged up a painful memory. "I was so mad at all the photographers at the vigil the day after the shooting," he said. "The moment of silence, I just heard camera shutters clicking the whole time. My friend Emma was like bursting crying and she was hugging me for support and there was a camera in my face taking pictures of me."

Four weeks later, it still burned.

2

Jackie had some rough moments returning to school, too. "Normal" would never be the same, but a key first step is resuming a normal schedule. Hard to get back on track for five AP tests when you've got your hands full fomenting an uprising. That first Sunday, she went to "campus reunification" with her parents. A car ran over a water bottle, the cap popped off, and it made a bang. "I legitimately freaked out," Jackie said. "I had an anxiety attack, and started crying. And I wasn't even the one to hear gunshots, but I'm terrified. So if it affects me that much, I can't even imagine the people that were actually in the room."

She had no empty desks to acknowledge, but she had an odd surprise her first day back in precalc. What was Alfonso doing there? "He was in my math class all year and I did not know him," she said. New friends: the silver lining.

Jackie Corin will never command a stage like Emma González, match the fire of David Hogg's Twitter feed, or keep the faithful giggling like Cameron Kasky. But while they lit up the Internet, along with Delaney Tarr and Sarah Chadwick, Jackie was the driving force behind the scenes. Movements are born from hope, but they are built brick by brick. Jackie had been laying the foundation for MFOL before she knew it existed.

Jackie is an implementer by intuition, but a natural leader as well. She has a quiet charisma that doesn't project from a stage or transmit through a TV set, but is powerful in the room. She knows what to do, takes charge, and then she's relentless. Cameron's mom had noticed it that first Saturday, when she returned from the cruise to find the team organizing in her living room. Among all the silliness and horseplay, Jackie seemed on a mission. "My first impression was she was like super-intensely trying to organize these buses," Natalie said. "And I was like, 'Of course she's class president. She's organized. She's capable. She's a leader.'"

Jackie was never political, not even a little. The sharp turn in Jackie's trajectory is captured in her Instagram feed: all activism post-Valentine's, not a whiff of politics prior. So many chummy girlfriend poses and scenic vistas before the attack: tie-dyed shirts at Camp Blue Ridge, fluorescent face paint at a Miami Dayglow concert, wading the Chattooga River with big American flags. Even the aesthetics flip: the before side is all choice lighting, cropping, and color saturation, carefully curated to present a vibrant, digitally enhanced life. Dingy grays and muted colors after, hastily documented cinema verité style. And dividing them, that stark post, a plain white background with the small silhouette of an AR-15 beneath three huge words, the last in red, MAKE IT STOP. It would be months before Jackie would return to the carefree poses of "normal" life.

Two weeks into the struggle, Jackie had identified a new enemy: fear. Politicians were afraid of the NRA and its supposed political omnipotence, which would crush their careers if they dared step out of line. Reasonable gun owners were afraid of making modest concessions that they actually agreed with, because ceding the momentum would supposedly ignite a wave of dizzying defeats ending in the abolishment of the Second Amendment and the end of deer hunting. The NRA preached "Never give an inch." Don't support measures you agree with; support holding the line.

"I think people are scared to make such a big change," Jackie said. "Even though maybe their moral compass is saying it's right. Just like the civil rights movement . . ."

Never Again was facing a bit of a branding issue. They were using two names regularly, and interchangeably, drifting slowly toward MFOL. They were keeping rather quiet about why for a while.

And there was a problem with the march. The DC mall was not available. The conflict involved a small student group filming a video on some of the same grounds. The park district followed a strict first-come, first-served policy. They suggested Pennsylvania Avenue. That would require permits from the city for the streets and from the federal park service, which had jurisdiction over the sidewalks and parks along Pennsylvania Avenue.

So the kids had a choice: move the date, or move the venue. Easy, Jackie said. "We were told it was already booked, so we were like OK, Pennsylvania Avenue, even better. It's in front of the Capitol."

The changes also meant actual marching would be figurative. Instead of a march to a rally, it would just be a rally. But that would be enough.

It was already enough. Coni Sanders's father, Dave Sanders, was the teacher killed saving students at Columbine. Coni had become a prominent champion of gun reform, waging a relentless struggle; the activists seemed to lose every skirmish on every front. I got a gushing message from her around that time. "I am in awe of what is happening," she said. "It's working, Dave. All these years and it's working."

PART II

Building a Movement

Nonviolence seeks to defeat injustice, not people.

—MARTIN LUTHER KING JR.'S
THIRD PRINCIPLE OF NONVIOLENCE

7

Peace Warriors

1

The Parkland generation was raised on lockdown drills—responding to tragedy by learning to hide better. Tragedy: a word we've grown so sick of, but we employ it selectively. Year after year brings a fresh crop of devastated kids—most of them affluent, telegenic, and white. It's horrifying, yet safer than enrolling in an inner-city school. In February, seventeen died at Douglas High, along with 1,044 others in America. In the first six months of 2018, over 1,700 kids were killed or injured by guns, heavily concentrated in the inner cities. Where were the tears for them?

The disparity is partially an adult affliction: shrugging our shoulders at the urban violence, wishing we could help, but flummoxed how. We don't understand the nuances of their neighborhoods or experience their pain. But paralysis is a learned response, and kids are often still appalled. The MFOL kids were.

"We know that the reason that we're getting this attention is because we're privileged white kids," Delaney Tarr said. "If you look at Chicago, there's such a high level of gun violence. But that's not getting the attention that this is getting because we're in such a nice area."

They were determined to change that. They made their first move right out of the gate: Don't frame the problem as school shootings. They were fighting gun violence, for all kids, not just them. But they didn't know much about urban violence, either. Time to start talking to city kids.

2

Arne Duncan had served eight years as Chicago's schools superintendent and seven more as Obama's secretary of education. He lives in Chicago, ground zero in the urban gun wars. Duncan saw a chance for a powerful connection. He reached the Parkland kids through their school superintendent, and then got in touch with Father Michael Pfleger on the embattled

South Side. Father Pfleger is the pastor of Saint Sabina Catholic Church, Chicago's largest African American Catholic congregation. It has become a beacon of hope in the Auburn Gresham neighborhood ravaged by gun violence. He runs the BRAVE (Bold Resistance Against Violence Everywhere) youth group there, organizes the annual Peace Marches, and mentors young activists of color across some of the city's most violent neighborhoods. The pastor recruited a few kids from BRAVE, and more from the Peace Warriors group on the embattled West Side.

The Parkland kids were all over it. It came together on a Friday night and Emma agreed to host a meeting at her house the next day. They didn't want another weekend to go by.

D'Angelo McDade was the executive director of the Peace Warriors, a professional position intended for an experienced full-time adult. D'Angelo was a high school senior, struggling to avoid violence and get to college. Months later, asked if he recalled how he got the invite, he answered without hesitation. "I was called at 11:26 on March 2. At 11:26 p.m., I called and texted Alex. I called him at 12; I texted him at 1."

Alex King is a fellow Peace Warrior—a big, stocky guy with a generous crown of cornrows and a close-cropped beard. He's a really smart kid with a sly sense of humor, constantly taking people by surprise. Alex has spent his life around guns, and has a lot to say. "I've been shot at, I've had guns pulled on me—really, I've had it all," Alex said. His first time getting shot at was at age fourteen—he thinks; they run together. The first time he encountered a gun was at age eight; he just stumbled on it in a closet.

Duncan bought the plane tickets, and early Saturday half a dozen kids, plus two parents, were drinking in the Florida sunshine. It was freezing when they woke up in Chicago, snow still on the ground from a brutal storm two weeks earlier. Felt good to take their coats off—they would be swimming in a few hours. How crazy to be cranking the AC! All these palm trees waving along the highway. They really had those, even at the airport; they were everywhere. How cool to finally see them in real life.

They pulled up at Emma's. "It was a gated community, and I thought it was a hotel resort or something," Alex said. "I was like man, she *lives* here! And then when we pulled up to her house, my first reaction: Should I step on the grass? Should I go straight to the sidewalk?" Emma's mom rushed out to greet them, and she walked straight up the lawn. "So I just followed her," he said. "And then I saw the house—it was like this big glass window that was also a door and I was like, 'Wow, OK.' And I also thought, 'Should I take my shoes off before I step in?' But when I actually got in there, Emma came around the corner running, hugging everyone—it was just like happy faces all around the room."

That's the thing about Emma. I've asked hundreds of people to describe the Parkland kids, and with the others I get a description, but with Emma they tend to describe the feeling after she enters. They describe tranquility. Sometimes they portray it radiating from her, settling over her surroundings, other times it's her little body absorbing the tension, drawing anxiety out of the air. Her smile is often mentioned, but more often the smiles in the room.

About a dozen MFOL kids were bouncing around Emma's spacious living room. Big relief, ice broken, now what? "Honestly neither side knew why we were there," Alex said. "It was like, put Parkland and Chicago together and hey, let's just see what happens. And we got to connect right off the bat."

They ate pizza on the lanai, and chicken wings. The food just kept coming. They played a lot of icebreaker games, splashed around in the pool, and spent time just being kids together. "We became friends before we went into the deeper conversation of what we have to do to change this," Alex said.

They went back inside, piled onto the puffy off-white couches, pulled in dining chairs, and shared their terrible stories. Alex described his nephew DeShawn Moore getting gunned down the previous spring. May 28, 2017.

"It was a Sunday afternoon, I believe. He was on the porch with his girlfriend at her house and this car was circling the block and one time when they came around the block again, they started to shoot. He pushed her in a panic into the house, he tried to run home but— He tried to run away from the shots, but it turned out he was running towards them, and when he turned around trying to get away, it turned out he was shot twice . . . once in the back of the head and once in the back."

Alex learned his nephew was dead on Facebook. Was that common? Yes, pretty common. Alex had lost several family members to gunfire, but losing DeShawn was the one that sent him reeling. He leaned forward on Emma's cozy couch to recount that story, then confessed his plunge into self-destruction, and his road out.

Self-destruction, the Parkland kids hadn't seen that coming, but Alex's buddy D'Angelo McDade had a similar tale. D'Angelo is even taller than Alex, with a similar big frame, a high and tight haircut and chin-strap beard. He's a bit more serious than Alex, and a natural orator, with a preacher's cadence when he gets going. He sat back from the circle a bit, on a dining room chair, directly across from Jackie and Emma, who leaned in intently. D'Angelo spiraled downward after he got shot in August 2017. He was hanging out on his porch with his grandfather and a dozen family friends, when a man they'd never seen before came walking down the street and opened fire. "I was shot in my left leg, one from the left side and one from the right side," he said. "The left side, it went in but did not come out; the right side, a bullet ricocheted off a doorframe and hit my leg. I was on crutches for six weeks." His grandfather and another relative were also hit. Everyone survived. "And to be clear, we don't have drug dealers in our houses—gangs, or anything," he said. "It's literally just an old-time place with old folks and children."

The shooter was caught and released multiple times, and D'Angelo believes he will likely get away with attempted murder—three counts. "There is an assumption that if your house is being shot up that you are a drug dealer and/or gangbanger," he said. So getting shot was another strike against him; he could feel the thud of doors slamming shut in his future. Victimization of the victim.

"I had a really bad attitude," D'Angelo said. "I had

this attitude of, 'You can't tell me anything.'" Then he found the Peace Warriors. Violence is woven so deeply into these kids' lives, and the Peace Warriors seek to unravel it, one strand at a time. But the key step is stopping violence at the source. The Peace Warriors call themselves interrupters. "Interrupters of nonsense," D'Angelo said. "We associate nonsense with violence, whether verbal or physical. If two students are engaging in horseplay and then begin showing verbal aggression, our Peace Warriors immediately step in. Mediating that situation to make sure that conflict does not rise to a pervasive or worse problem."

That required a whole lot of bodies to be present when it mattered. Their goal was to amass a quarter of the student body, or 125 Peace Warriors at North Lawndale College Prep High School. They were at 120.

The Peace Warriors taught him humility, D'Angelo said. Alex concurred. A way to redirect anger at the real adversary—which is complicated. Guns are killing his people, but they are the last link in a cycle: "the school-to-prison pipeline." The first step to combating gang violence is getting honest about why kids join gangs, and then creating realistic alternatives. Gang life is alluring—let's be straight about that, they said. Lawndale kids who take up arms are driven by economics. Crime pays; drugs pay. Gangbangers are decked out in some hot shit, all the tech gadgets and bling. But there are deeper emotional draws. The gang offers a sense of connection, an extended family, with a name that carries weight. Members feel confident and respected. In the short-run, they feel good. That's a hell of a draw. It preys on kids feeling hopeless, disconnected, and bleak. Alex and D'Angelo had both felt the lure. When you're humbled by violence, that's when you're most vulnerable to embracing it.

The Peace Warriors have to match what the gangs offer at every level, and come through with it, legit, D'Angelo said. "If you're looking for employment, we have it. If you're looking for a sense of family, we have that." When a kid is tottering on the gang bubble, you have to reach him on his terms, spoken and unspoken, before you inspire him to join the bigger cause. Not every kid's going to tell you that his home life is a shambles and he feels like shit. But few kids grow up in that environment feeling good. The Peace Warriors' big agenda—rescuing their neighborhood by rescuing its high school kids, one at a time—appeals to a lot of students. But first they have to survive.

The Parkland kids were amazed. Not surprised, exactly, but enlightened. This was new. But it wasn't that hard to understand.

It became clear quickly that suburban kids feared

violence inside their school—once in a lifetime, but horrific—and the Chicago kids feared violence getting there. At the bus stop, on their porch, walking out of church. It could happen anywhere, and it did.

They played more games, took breaks, and chatted in small groups. D'Angelo was talking to Emma about suffering, and the power of converting pain into action. That sounded a lot like principle 4. D'Angelo reached into his pocket and drew out a collection of dog tags, each a different color, translucent and stamped with a different number, one to six. He found the blue one. It said PRINCIPLE #4, with a peace sign—that was it. OK—Emma had no idea what that meant. Martin Luther King Jr. had preached six principles of non-violence, D'Angelo explained. The Parkland kids were embarking on number 4: "Suffering can educate and transform." And MLK singled out a particular kind of suffering: "Unearned suffering is redemptive and has tremendous educational and transforming possibilities."

"Oh wow, can we do this all together?" Emma asked.

The full group reconvened. "We taught them the principles, and they taught us about policy," D'Angelo said.

8

Strategy

1

Jackie had gone to Tallahassee with an emotional appeal. "It didn't really work," she said a few weeks later. "Rick Scott did defy the NRA, so obviously it meant something, but it's just like a Band-Aid on a wound," she said. "It's not going to do anything."

They had to counter with credible demands. For two weeks, they had been demanding gun reform, but what exactly? Some of them were short on specifics; others, like David, were deep in the weeds. They all had different ideas. No consistency—big problem. It was vital that they speak in one voice—or they risked not being heard.

A subtler issue was also surfacing—tone. They were taking some withering abuse, and they knew better than to turn vicious in response, but where were the lines? Twenty-plus personalities were their strength, but they needed boundaries on aggression. It was awkward to start imposing rules on each other. The incoming attacks were all over the map.

The Peace Warriors arrived at just the right moment. They helped shape the MFOL policy agenda and the tenor of their approach. They all kept talking: by email, phone, and text. The Parkland kids peppered the Peace Warriors with questions about the six principles, and then burrowed deeper on their own. The more they learned, the more they found it was like listening to themselves—a better, wiser version of the selves they were fumbling toward. How liberating to discover Martin Luther King Jr. had already done all that work. Brilliantly. He had drawn from Gandhi, and it was amazing how well the principles stood up across time, space, and cultures.

They were most influenced by principle number 3: "Nonviolence seeks to defeat injustice, not people." Gun violence is the enemy, legislators blocking solutions were a problem, and those legislators were adversaries, not enemies—and that was a clear distinction, not just a grammatical point. Even if they had been corrupted by NRA money, none of those people were evil, and none of them deserved to be treated as if they were.

The Parkland kids loved the spirit of the principles and their practical implications even more. Politics in America had grown deeply polarized and personal, and that was benefitting no one. It sure as hell hadn't led to sensible gun laws. Demonizing your adversaries just sealed off ears. Right about that time, David Hogg identified the hardest part of their fight: "People mishearing what we're trying to say. Like, do we want an assault weapons ban? Yeah, we do, but, we don't want to take the Second Amendment away. We want responsible owners to be able to own guns. A lot of people have said that we're like Nazis trying to take their guns and stuff—we fucking aren't. We're kids that are trying to save lives, and put reasonable gun legislation in place, where if you're a mentally unstable individual or somebody with a criminal history, you can't get a gun. And if you're a criminal, we're gonna come after your guns. I think we all can agree on that. But it's these fringe arguments that so many of these people push that become the issue."

David Hogg struggled with principle number 3 more than anyone on the team. He was a born debater, with a short fuse. He slipped past the boundaries frequently, but it helped to have a team drawing him back.

————

Less than a week after creating her Twitter account, Emma would surpass a million followers—about double that of the NRA. By the summer, Cameron would amass 400,000 followers, David twice that, and Emma at 1.6 million towered over them all. America was listening, eager to do something, supposedly, and turning to these teenagers to be led.

About a week after the powwow at Emma's, Father Pfleger flew the Parkland kids up north for more meetings, adding a group of young Latino activists from the gritty Brighton Park neighborhood, and white kids from the North Side. "We kind of put together this black, white, brown, West Side, South Side, North Side group," Father Pfleger said. "They're very different, you know. The Parkland kids are afraid in school; our kids are afraid to go to and from school." They all spent the day together, and walked the neighborhood, to get a sense of where they lived and how they lived. That sparked much deeper conversations than they'd had at Emma's house—about how they felt about those conditions, and what they had done to try and change them. The Parkland kids loved that: fresh perspectives and fresh inspiration. They were a few weeks into this struggle—the Chicago kids had been born into it.

Chicago is battling a gun violence epidemic, but it's generally seen by outsiders—even in affluent areas of Chicagoland—as a South Side problem. The Peace Warriors lived on the West Side. So did the Latino kids from Brighton Park. Each neighborhood was unique, with varying cultures and systemic hurdles. Individualized projects work best, but organizers are much more effective working together. The Parkland powwows actually helped solidify local ties. "We've had several meetings trying to build this coalition here in Chicago," Father Pfleger would say a few months later. But the real goal was a unified coalition across the country, especially one uniting cities and suburbs. "So it's not just Chicago doing their thing, Parkland doing their thing," Father Pfleger said. "How do we begin to connect these dots and unite the youth around America?"

The biggest hurdle was getting white America to reengage with the inner cities and try to help them out. It wasn't a lack of caring; more a lack of hope. I grew up in the Chicago suburbs, and most of my family is there. I return regularly, and I rarely encounter people who are OK with the devastation going on nearby. Just as rare, though, are people doing anything significant to help. The problem seems too overwhelming and too intractable. We don't really understand what's going on there, or see any way out. So mostly, we turn away.

The Parkland kids copped to the same ignorance before they were attacked. They had no clue what the kids in Chicago, Baltimore, or Compton were going through, or how to help them. But they were astonished how easy it was to learn. Two days together, a trip to one of their neighborhoods, and a lot of follow-up texts, and they had a pretty solid foundation. It wasn't that hard.

They also found it refreshing to see what an impact the Peace Warriors and the BRAVE kids were having on their neighborhoods and their schools. Some projects were failing miserably, others having tremendous success. But even the successful ones had one tragic element in common: virtually no financial support. America saw all these places as gaping holes of hopelessness and despair. Even locally, few suburbanites had ever heard of the Peace Warriors or any of the successful groups. Fund-raising was nearly impossible, because media coverage was nonexistent. So promising projects remained small and lacked basic resources—which hampered their ability to prove themselves sufficiently to draw more funding or exposure. A vicious cycle.

Could the MFOL kids change that? They had a megaphone. They were eager to share it, but what if they could do better? Could they merge their movement with this huge existing urban network? It might be invisible to white America, but these folks had infrastructure, proven methods, voters, and a just cause.

Despite all the work they did with groups like BRAVE and the Peace Warriors, MFOL still took a lot of flack in some circles for being a bunch of white kids. This criticism was most painful when it came from other Douglas students. At first, it had felt like the group had the diversity issue covered. MFOL was male, female, straight, gay, and bi, and had lots of Latinos. They were not trying to exclude anybody, they were just working with the kids they knew. There were plenty of other Douglas groups representing other demographics. Did they have to check all the boxes? Yes, came the reply from some quarters. Lots of other groups were active, but MFOL was sucking up 99 percent of the attention. And the bulk of donations. If they were going to speak for not just this school, but this generation—*especially* if they were going to represent the urban black struggle—they had to be more inclusive within their ranks.

2

Time for demands. Solutions had to be specific, and far reaching, but reasonable. Above all, they pledged to keep their hands off the Second Amendment. They didn't want to cause trouble for hunters, gun collectors, or gun enthusiasts—although they didn't think hunters had the right to a howitzer or an M16.

Matt Deitsch, one of the recent grads, led the research project. The kids had returned to school, but he was going to withdraw from his college semester. He plowed through reams of studies and articles to create a syllabus, and then circulated the best material among the group. They read, discussed, argued, went back to do more research, and finally settled.

They quickly developed five demands—and they called them that—(1) universal, comprehensive background checks; (2) a digitized, searchable database for the ATF (the Bureau of Alcohol, Tobacco, Firearms, and Explosives); (3) funding for the Centers for Disease Control to research gun violence; (4) a ban on high-capacity magazines; (5) a ban on semiautomatic assault rifles. Not one of them was specific to mass shooters or schools.

Professor Robert Spitzer weighed in on their agenda. Spitzer is an expert on gun politics. He is chairman of the political science department at the State University of New York College at Cortland and has written five books on gun policy and gun politics, and written about it for the *New York Times*. "I think it's policy smart and it indicates a very shrewd eye to how they would like to proceed," he said. That didn't mean candidates could drop them right into their stump speeches. The movement actually requires two agendas, Spitzer said: one for policy and a variation to run on.

"If I were running for office on the gun issue, I probably wouldn't organize it around these particular items," he said. Demands two and three were too boring and inside-baseball for voters presented as policy. But they could be powerful for a candidate and a movement that summarized them conceptually as plugging all the holes in a pathetically leaky system. And they could get much more mileage by driving home the message of why the background check system is so ineffective: it was deliberately undermined by the NRA. "I'm sure very few people are aware of the fact that the ATF still does its background checks from paper records located in a building in West Virginia," Professor Spitzer said. "They were barred from computerizing their records back in the 1980s by pressure from the NRA written into legislation. When I repeat that now, reporters are kind of shocked, asking, 'Is that really true? How could that be true? No computers?'"

Voters don't understand this, Spitzer said. They will be outraged once someone demonstrates that effectively.

The same concept applies to demand three, Spitzer said, though its potential is somewhat less explosive. It's hard to find people against studying an issue. Of course most voters would support study, and be disgusted to learn that was forbidden—though it won't bring them out to the polls. It's vital that it be written into legislation, though, so that as the movement succeeds in passing legislation, the system can be studied as it evolves. Various changes will prove more and less effective than anticipated. The ability to study what we're doing will be critical for long-term success. That's pretty obvious—unless your goal is undermining that success.

The sticky item on that list was banning semiautomatic rifles, Spitzer said. "It's a pretty hot gun issue to touch. There is support for it, candidates have campaigned on it, including some former military candidates. But . . ." That one really depended on the district, he said. You could run on it in urban areas, but it would be tricky in a lot of swing districts. Candidates really have to read their district on that one. There was movement on semiautomatics, though, Spitzer said, even before Parkland. "Right now there actually is majority support for restricting or banning assault weapons and that was not the case ten years ago. That's kind of a marker of the outer edge of policy ideas that can win majority support."

Background checks were the no-brainer, Spitzer said. "It's low-hanging fruit. Ninety percent of Americans consistently support uniform background checks, as do eighty percent of gun owners. So it's practically universal support. It's hard to get ninety percent support for anything in America."

Spitzer had a few suggestions for candidates beyond the MFOL demands. "I would talk about a terrorist watch list. I would talk about doing a better job of getting information about people who have mental illnesses, because that's been a big problem. And that's also something that everybody agrees on, and it's something you can explain. And that would be plenty. I think those three things alone would be plenty in a campaign."

MFOL had an agenda now, and was sizing up its adversary. The NRA closely guards its membership data, but it claims nearly five million members—"And David Hogg is three of them," Jackie took to telling audiences later. "Lots of people like to buy us memberships." They doubted the five million figure, but if accurate, it represents just 1.5 percent of the population. Yet the NRA has succeeded by turning out reliable single-issue voters to swing close elections, with no countervailing force. Sizable majorities favor gun reform, but progressives never vote on guns. That asymmetry allows a tiny minority to consistently defeat huge majorities, or to convince politicians they will. The NRA's aura of invincibility goes largely untested, because officials so rarely risk opposing it, even on trivial matters. Every "wrong" vote, even for legislation backed by solid majorities of gun owners, chips away at a legislator's NRA score, which can energize a primary opponent.

MFOL had to be that countervailing force. They had to demonstrate they could match the NRA vote for vote. Optimally, exceed it. They set their sights on November, to prove to an audience of 435 that it's riskier to oppose them than the NRA. They saw the number one battleground as the House of Representatives. They had to overturn some seats.

3

Most of the MFOL kids were too young to vote. They couldn't even check into a hotel room, and a parent or two had to chaperone them on every trip. There were a lot of trips. Jackie Corin estimated she had logged thirty thousand miles or more that spring, meeting with school groups, legislators, academics, and activists, traveling as far as a conference in Kenya. She wasn't even the most frequent flier—that would be David, though a dozen of them were practically living on the road. They were soaking up so much out there: organizing techniques, messaging, what was working, what was falling flat, what kids out in the trenches really needed, and how their tweets were rippling out into local communities in unforeseen ways, good and bad. Time to change the fear dynamic. All that local contact crystallized their phase two strategy long before the march: Leverage all that enthusiasm. Organize it.

Young voters have long been a sleeping giant of American politics, because most of them stay home. If they ever turned out in percentages to match their older counterparts, they could swing most elections. Trouble is, they never do. Millions of students were answering the call but were unsure what to do. Most of them were new to all this. The message from MFOL was simple: Get started. Start small. Grab a clipboard, grab a friend, start a sibling march in your community. A prominent link on the group's website spelled it all out. They were stunned by how many visited the site.

Every event, big or small, modest or glamorous, came with one demand: voter registration—a table or booth or preferably a clipboard team hitting up the venue and the parking lot. David Hogg was frequently seen working the crowd. They had to walk the walk, demonstrating the imperative "You can't vote, if you don't register."

All those local kids would have to shoulder the long, hard grunt work of sending teams through their neighborhoods to register voters, and staffing booths at their schools. They would have to continue connecting and recruiting and expanding their networks, every day until Election Day, to keep excitement high and turn out the vote. MFOL provided guidance, structure, publicity, and talking points. Local organizers from half a dozen states whose groups had been jump-started by MFOL were radiant. Often the biggest things the Parkland kids brought was validation: most kids didn't believe they were qualified to do these things until the Florida activists paved the way. Early on, the Parkland kids noticed something significant: every high school visit required a student to invite them, to win faculty approval, and recruit classmates to execute the event. The simple act of visiting these schools was activating young leaders and giving them a first taste of organizing. MFOL couldn't hit 435 US House districts. They could not hit hundreds of thousands more state and local electoral regions. The kids they connected with could. The MFOL kids brought attention, excitement, talking points, and a template. A network was taking shape in their wake.

4

The NRA had lain low after the shooting. That was its MO. A *New York Times* story called it "a well-rehearsed response": keep as quiet as possible until the gun control conversation cools down. But it always cooled down quickly. What if Parkland was different?

NRA leadership stuck to the plan. No public statements, and they pulled way back on Twitter. In the two weeks before the attack, @NRA posted about twenty original tweets a week. For the five days immediately after, that dropped to zero. But then it roared back: more than thirty each of the next two weeks. This signal to resume attack came eight days after the shooting. Wayne LaPierre, the NRA's CEO, broke his silence at the Conservative Political Action Conference (CPAC), where his name was initially kept off the program to mute protest. He carefully avoided attacking MFOL directly, but hammered "elites" and "socialists" who "don't care not one whit" about saving kids. "They care more about control, and more of it," he said. "Their goal is to eliminate the Second Amendment and our firearms freedoms so they can eradicate all individual freedoms. . . . They hate the NRA, they hate the Second Amendment, they hate individual freedom."

The Twitter account followed the same rules, for

months afterward, generally training its fire on media stories about gun safety. There was not one tweet attacking David Hogg by name until August 4, and still nothing tagging Emma as of early fall. But to the NRA's own tight audience, it was a very different story. The *Times* described a furious debate that first week on NRATV, the organization's online video channel. Hosts of its shows "spoke chillingly of leftist plots to confiscate weapons, media conspiracies to brainwash Americans," the *Times* reported. "With broadcast television–quality production and three dozen original series, NRATV has the ability to reach millions of people through the channels that distribute it like Apple TV, Roku and Amazon Fire TV." NRATV had deep resources, as part of the NRA's $35 million membership support program.

For its first big salvo, the NRA struck strategically: March 4, Oscar night. While the ceremony was underway, NRATV released a slick sixty-second video of spokeswoman Dana Loesch eviscerating "every Hollywood phony" and everything Hollywood stood for. She sat beside an hourglass in a black dress against a black background to deliver a scathing tirade against politicians, late-night hosts, athletes, and "every lying member of the media"—all the supposed puppet masters pulling the MFOL strings. It ended with Loesch appropriating the Me Too movement's #TimesUp by saying,

"Your time is running out; the clock starts now," and flipping over the hourglass. NRATV tweeted the clip with the #TimesUp and #Oscars hashtags. It scored 4.4 million views that week.

Sarah Chadwick posted a parody response video the next day, one of MFOL's first videos. It clocked 1.2 million views in the same week. They had some catching up to do, but the kids didn't have $35 million or three dozen TV series with established audiences. Not bad for the first time out.

Meanwhile, they were expanding their website, with a new logo, new swag for sale, and a toolkit for kids around the country to use to start their own local marches. The sibling marches were gaining way more traction than they had ever dreamed.

5

They were constantly trying out fresh tactics, but an underlying strategy was maintaining the megaphone. Weeks after the tragedy, David Hogg explained why he thought they had finally broken through. "The immediate choke hold that we placed on the news cycle, to make sure that people would not be able to look away from this," he said. Five weeks to the march was always a risk, but they couldn't take on another megaproject till they pulled off that one. They could use a little juice, though, and lots of other groups were sprouting up as well. Families of the fallen created Change the Ref, Meadow's Movement, and Orange Ribbons for Jaime. Fellow students started Shine MSD, Parents Promise to Kids, Societal Reform Corporation, and others. Shine MSD was the most prominent, growing out of the anthemic song about the tragedy written by students Sawyer Garrity and Andrea Peña. They recorded the song and released it on iTunes, and it became a hit. And a huge momentum boost would come from the two National School Walkouts. They dovetailed perfectly with MFOL and they coordinated closely—to the point that much of the public assumed it was all a single effort—but mercifully, each walkout was organized and implemented by its own local team.

Before Valentine's Day had ended, Lane Murdock had decided to convert her horror into action. She would stage a walkout. Murdock was a high school sophomore in Ridgefield, Connecticut, just twenty miles from Sandy Hook. She posted her idea as a Change. org petition before she went to bed that night. She had a powerful date in mind for her walkout: April 20, the nineteenth anniversary of the tragedy at Columbine that set this horrible wave in motion.

When MFOL announced its march on Washington that weekend, Murdock adapted her walkout into an all-day affair. The nonprofit group Indivisible helped Murdock's petition take off. Soon it became a national movement.

But Murdock's idea took a little while to gain national attention, and by then a different walkout had built a huge head of steam. The youth branch of the Women's March, EMPOWER, announced their own plan two days after Valentine's Day. It set its sights on March 14, the one-month anniversary of Parkland.

So there were the National School Walkouts in the works, organized independently, and benefiting from shared publicity.

But was it all accomplishing anything? How much were they affecting the gun debate? *The Trace* studied media coverage after the last seven major mass shootings. They all drove gun control into the conversation briefly, but peaked in the first two days, constituting around 2 percent of all news stories. Coverage then dropped off drastically, even after Orlando and Las Vegas. Parkland's coverage actually rose after two days, peaking at 4 percent. It held near 2 percent for a solid month. Then one month out, something unprecedented in media would happen. The first National School Walkout would draw so much coverage, it would hit 5 percent of all news stories, eclipsing even the immediate aftermath of the attack.

Elise Jordan is a Republican political analyst and a *Time* magazine columnist. She has been participating in an ongoing series of focus groups around the country for the Ashcroft in America Research Project since 2016. She was astonished by the responses from conservative Republican focus groups in Jackson, Mississippi, and Memphis, Tennessee, in March.

"They wanted commonsense gun reform, and everyone at the table owned a gun," Jordan said. These people had fought gun control their entire lives. They were not ready to embrace the entire gun safety agenda, but were ready for something new.

"Can we knock it after we've tried it?" one voter asked. Another one said, "I think enough people see these stories and think, 'I might not agree with it, but if you think you're doing something to prevent that from happening, give it your best shot, because I'm tired of watching those stories.'"

Jordan had spent much of her life with these people. She grew up in a small town in Mississippi, surrounded by guns in her home. She called herself a Second Amendment absolutist until Parkland. Then she had

had enough. She was taken aback to see how many of her fellow Mississippians had, too. "I think the NRA is out of step with gun owners," Jordan said. "Gun owners are all for commonsense reform; they don't want to see their children mowed down in schools."

9

Change the Ref

1

Ten hours after the Parkland shooting, Manuel Oliver lost his temper. "Tell us something!" he yelled. It had been a horrible day.

Manuel Oliver and his wife, Patricia, were repeating a ghastly process first improvised in 1999, improved through repetition, yet still horribly inadequate. When a SWAT team rescued hundreds of Columbine students, school administrators had to wing it. They loaded the kids onto school buses, drove them to nearby Leawood Elementary School, and announced the rendezvous point through the local media. Leawood was mobbed by frantic parents, siblings, aunts and uncles, grandparents, and neighbors—complete chaos. So they directed everyone to the auditorium, and marched the kids across the stage. That was great for the kids whose families had arrived, greeted by ecstatic screams from the crowd, and groups rushing forward to envelop them in hugs. It was deeply retraumatizing for the lonely kids who walked the stage to silence. Vital data collection was also haphazard. Police had no triage procedure for questioning or sorting survivors. Astute officers questioned some kids fleeing Columbine, and ran promising leads over to lead investigator Kate Battan, but most fell through the cracks. Battan was racing to establish the killers' identities while drafting search warrants. The killers' homes had to be locked down immediately. No telling if more bombs, weapons, or coconspirators were still on the loose. Both lives and evidence were at risk.

So, like everything else in the school-shooter era, smarter protocols were devised, and every cop and administrator in the country got training. In 2018, the Heron Bay Marriott, five miles from Douglas High, was chosen as the rendezvous point in case of an emergency. The first bus arrived about 4:30 p.m. As kids stepped off, they were greeted by a cop who logged their names and birth dates on hotel stationary, and asked if they had witnessed the shooting. Nos were sorted to the huge conference room, where anxious parents waited. Yeses went to smaller rooms, where FBI agents waited to question them, then on to the reunion area. Many families had reunited elsewhere, but it allowed investigators to gather in a systematic way a great deal of information missed at the crime scene.

Inside, the process had come a long way too, but it was still brutal. In tragedy after tragedy, when the last bus unloads and the stragglers stop arriving, everyone looks around, counts the remaining families, and does the math. This is the moment where parents from prior tragedies described praying for a critical injury, or bargaining with God. The death count is usually public by this time, and it gradually aligns with the family count. The last best hope is that their child is coming out of surgery in some hospital, and miraculously calling out their name.

By seven thirty, the buses were long gone from the Heron Bay Marriott, and the reunion room had that sparse feeling of desperation. Miguel and Alex Duque translated fresh intel into Spanish for their parents, and an eight-year-old boy stepped up to translate into Chinese for Peter Wang's family. Around eight, several prayer circles formed: an African American family, a Jewish family led by several rabbis, and Joaquin Oliver's family saying the rosary. At 8:40, Sergeant Rossman appeared to ask the families to email photos to match against bodies still in the school. That was grim. For Columbine families, it was a request for dental records, because no one had cameras on their phones then. They had to run home to get them, something constructive finally, in an afternoon of feeling impotent, devastated about not having protected their child. Of course no parent failed that way, but most of them will tell you that's what they felt.

At Parkland, it was a quick task: flip through your phone, or bounce around social media. Then, nothing. Hours of nothing. Positive ID is a painstaking process, and the police never want to risk a mistake. But they tend to leave families in the dark. Loved ones crave information, anything, even an overview of the process, what stage they are at, or how long it might reasonably take. Cops rarely divulge that sort of thing. They are trained to withhold information until the process is complete. What makes sense in routine cases can be inhumane when mass casualties arise.

At one point, Manuel Oliver got down on his knees to pray. Twenty minutes to midnight, Manuel finally blew. "Where the fuck is my son?!" he shouted.

Prayers stopped, heads turned. Manuel was pacing in front of a sheriff's officer standing guard. "Let us know what's happening," Manuel pleaded. "Let everyone know what's happening."

Finally, word came. At 12:02 a.m., Sergeant Brown entered, flanked by additional officers. "Please excuse the delay," he said. Then he outlined the procedure. One family at a time would be escorted to the adjacent room to learn their child's fate.

"It's been ten hours!" Manuel Oliver screamed.

It took another ten minutes for the process to begin. A pair of agents in the familiar navy FBI jackets, with the three yellow letters emblazoned in back, approached the first family and led them out.

It was glacial. The entire deceased list was complete, but the notification process dragged on past three a.m. The agents reappeared every fifteen to twenty minutes, and the waiting families often cried, held hands, or tried to change the subject. Then they braced for the reaction from the next room. "The screams and cries of some pierced through the walls, while others didn't make a sound at all," Univision reported. It's hard to believe this was the protocol perfected. By one a.m., most of the families had moved out into the hallway, where the screams were less audible. Manuel and Patricia Oliver and their family were escorted out at 1:41. Joaquin was dead. No shouts were heard.

2

His friends called him Guac, for "guacamole," because some of them had trouble pronouncing his name. Joaquin Oliver was seventeen. He was born in Venezuela, emigrated with his parents at three, and earned his US citizenship just a year before he was killed. He never lost his admiration for the Venezuelan national soccer team, and took part in a South Florida protest against President Nicolás Maduro. Guac was shy until middle school, when he suddenly turned into a colorfully exuberant kid. "He kind of went from a caterpillar to a butterfly," his sister, Andrea Ghersi, said. Andrea had looked after him as a toddler, and they were very close.

Guac was a huge sports fan, first baseball, then basketball, his true love. His hero was the Miami Heat star Dwayne Wade. He dressed his first Build-a-Bear as Wade. Frank Ocean was often booming through his earbuds, and Ocean's *Blonde* album inspired Guac to bleach his hair: long and blond on top, short and black on the sides, sometimes with a full black beard and mustache. His funeral was held at a huge mausoleum, with at least a thousand mourners, many of the boys in sports jerseys with "Guac" on the back in masking tape, and their hair bleached blond on top and shorn on the sides in solidarity.

College was on the horizon for fall, but Joaquin hadn't settled on a school yet, or a major. Marketing maybe, like his dad, who ran a successful business fusing branding, marketing, and original art. Guac had just begun honing his voice as a poet and writer with his creative writing teacher, Stacy Lippel. "His writing always had such depth and emotion in it," she said. "That talent was in him the entire time." He was quite the social butterfly now. "If he wasn't there in my class one day, it was very strange, very quiet," Lippel said. Guac's muse was often his girlfriend, Victoria González. He told his sister that Victoria was his soul mate, and wrote a poem about wanting to live forever, as long as it was with her.

3

Manuel Oliver knew he had to do something different. He was awed by the MFOL kids—they called him Tío (Uncle) Manny, which he asked to be called. He threw his voice behind them, but needed to be more than an echo. He was a successful artist, so he went for something creative.

He began with a mural. He started at an art exhibit in Miami called Parkland 17. It was headlined by Guac's hero Dwayne Wade. Manny painted a twenty-foot mural on drywall before a live crowd. It featured a stunning likeness of Joaquin's head and shoulders, six feet high, black and white, with a yellow background and graffiti-style block lettering: WE DEMAND CHANGE. Then he picked up a sledgehammer. He slammed a huge hole, straight through the drywall, tore it back out and repeated that sixteen more times. "The sound of the hammer . . . boom, it's like a bullet," he said. The sound is jarring, the violence is jarring—that was the point. Tío Manny would paint many more walls, and vary the image each time, but seventeen holes would always be struck. Every audience shuddered. And then for every wall, he slid yawning sunflowers into each hole, because the seventeen blasts were horrible, but not the end of the story. Life bloomed again.

He chose sunflowers because the night before the tragedy, Joaquin had asked him to pick up some flowers for his girlfriend for Valentine's Day. Manny's last image of Joaquin is him holding the sunflowers as he hopped out of the car at school that morning, saying, "I love you, Dad."

Tío Manny said it back, and added, "Dude, you make sure you call me back." He wanted to hear Victoria's reaction. "And he never called back. But I do know that Tori got the sunflowers. So, he had time to give them to Tori."

Tori split the flowers in half, sealed them in epoxy, and made a necklace each for Patricia and Tío Manny, which they hold dear.

Tío Manny called his murals Walls of Demand. He planned seventeen. They were the first major initiative of Change the Ref, a nonprofit Manny and Patricia created in March "to raise awareness about mass shootings through strategic interventions that will reduce the influence of the NRA on the federal level."

The name came from a basketball incident in the last days of Guac's life. Gauc got called for a foul by a ref he felt had a grudge against him. Guac argued and the ref threw him out. He came back to the bench, where his dad was coaching, and asked for help. Manny contested the call and got thrown out, too. Guac thanked him on the ride home. Manny said, Don't worry about it. That wasn't just a bad call; it was a weird call. You can't win with that ref. All you can do is change the ref. That's what we need to do here, Tío Manny said. So many politicians getting so much money from the NRA. You can't win if the ref is paid off. Change the ref.

The second wall went up in Los Angeles, a month later, and this time Tío Manny was ready to push it. He wasn't sure how Patricia would feel about it, or Andrea. Were they really OK with any of this—their son and brother's face appropriated, six feet high, the face of a political movement? So the day before the L.A. painting, they all sat down and struck "an emotional deal."

"If any of us is not OK with it, then we stop doing it," Manny said. "And that included everything. If I need to stop doing walls right now, you just let me know."

They were on board. Joaquin would be proud. Tío Manny knew that was so. He pointed to a post Joaquin had retweeted in December. It cited the fifth anniversary of Sandy Hook, and it said that if you believe mentally ill people should have access to guns, let alone AR-15s, "then you need to realize the NRA has you brainwashed." It wasn't a one-off, Tío Manny said—they were close, and Joaquin was committed. "Sometimes I use this as an example that tweeting and retweeting is not enough," Tío Manny said. "Me and Patricia are all the way for the rest of our lives and will not only tweet and retweet but also create and find untraditional ways to make statements."

The next day, Tío Manny went for it. The L.A. mural featured four separate images of males of various ages. The first three are similar: young boys in backpacks, innocently walking down various streets. The oldest, in the center, Joaquin, is checking his phone, and all three are unaware of the giant gun scopes encircling their bodies, bull's-eyes over their chests. Then Tío Manny painted a big crimson splotch over each boy's point of impact. The fourth image was different: no target; a young man facing the other three, crying out in pain. Manny raised the sledgehammer, and drove seventeen bullet holes, one through each of their hearts. WE DEMAND 2 STOP THE BS, he painted around the boys.

He sped up the pace. Every few weeks Tío Manny painted another mural at a strategic moment. All were livestreamed. May 5, the NRA's annual convention began in Dallas, and Tío Manny painted his mural a block from the convention hall. President Trump and Vice President Pence were both featured speakers, so Tío Manny expanded the scope, and featured Trump dressed as a circus ringleader and Dana Loesch as a clown clutching an AR-15. Joaquin was in the gun sights again. That drew lots of national media.

The murals were left as permanent markers, but the third wall, in Springfield, Massachusetts, was destroyed by vandals after three days. "We don't actually really care that much," Tío Manny said. That was part of the message, documenting the resistance, the anger, the attempts to silence Guac's voice. "Someone destroys your good points just by showing power," Tío

Manny said. "It's a reflection of what's going on with the conversation."

4

Change the Ref launched a second big initiative in April, one even more creative. They partnered with the ad agency Area 23 to create a site that would convert Tweets or Facebook posts into letters to congresspeople in Guac's handwriting. Users could then print them from the site, or let it handle delivery.

The idea was based on the Congressional Management Foundation's finding that personalized postal letters were the most effective means of influencing congresspersons' votes. Guac's handwriting added a special poignancy, for both the sender and receiver. "We are giving a voice to Joaquin," Tío Manny said. "So he can talk."

Thousands of Guac letters were submitted to Congress in the first few weeks. David Hogg and Emma González were two of the first correspondents. The project won three awards at the Cannes Lions International Festival of Creativity, the most prestigious event in the advertising and marketing worlds.

Through it all, Tío Manny worked closely with

the MFOL kids. Same cause, different strategy. "We think it's more powerful if we do separate things," Manny said. They coordinated, publicized, and reinforced each other, and they appeared together at key moments. The kids wore Change the Ref buttons and wristbands, making sure they were prominent in their photo shoots—to honor Guac, and to spread the word. Emma began embroidering a great big Change the Ref patch, stitching it onto the bomber jacket she would wear at the March for Our Lives, right across her chest, just above where the podium would rise, so millions of eyes would catch it in every shot. Tío Manny added MFOL logos to many of his murals, and wore a March for Our Lives wristband on his left hand, his painting hand, so that all the close-ups would capture their bond. Each group understood branding and cross-promotion. They wanted to convey how deeply they supported each other—to the public, and to each other.

The kids adored Tío Manny. They even waived the no-adults policy at their meetings for him. Even their parents were forbidden, no exceptions, except for him. "I just got a call from Cameron, asking me to come over today to have some pizzas with them," he said during an interview. "That's the kind of relationship we have.

Patricia and I feel better by believing that Joaquin is one of them. 'My kid is right here, fighting along with you guys, making a big noise. . . .' And Patricia and I feel honored as parents of one of the kids who is leading the movement."

10

Exhausted

1

David Hogg was angry. Everyone agreed on that. Media profiles were popping up everywhere on the kids now, almost exclusively on the big three, and journalists had typecast them quickly. Cameron and David were assigned clichés: class clown and angry pugilist. Emma was unique: some sort of tiny, fiery truth god, exposing bullshitters with the intensity of her brown eyes. *The Outline* ran a big piece headlined "David Hogg Is Mad as Hell," over a photo of him grimacing. "His anger was palpable from the moment he walked into the room," the author said. "He said 'fuck' so many times during our interview that he jokingly said he hoped it wouldn't be televised." *The Outline* piece was well reported, and generally perceptive, but that take on David—true?

It was tough to reconcile with the bubbly, playful David I had chatted with that first weekend. He was equally joyous and agreeable on follow-ups that week. But when I interviewed him in mid-March, David was spitting fire. "Politicians have been allowed to become corrupt, abused their power, and kept their power, to allow the slaughter of their citizens," he said. "These politicians have shown that they want to be on the wrong side of history and that's absolutely fine—we'll be sure to smear them in our history textbooks that we write, and that will be their legacy and how they will be forever remembered, as the cowards that many of them are—that want to take money from special interest groups instead of putting their constituents' lives in front of their political agenda."

He peppered random answers with allusions to his Twitter accusers, spitting out terms like "libtards," "Nazis," and "crisis actors." The digs were getting to him. He was angry at the system rigged against young black boys, repeatedly decrying the "school-to-prison pipeline." That was a signature phrase of the Peace Warriors, and while David had missed the meeting at Emma's house, the concept quickly permeated the group.

David kept saying he was an angry person and a nihilist. His mother rolled her eyes. He was never an angry person, Rebecca Boldrick said. Now, though, he's like a pit bull. If David were a comic book character, he would be Bruce Banner, appearing in public as the Hulk.

The anger was new, but David's obsessiveness went way back. "Oh my god, like he will get really into something like drone photography, and for like three months he's just maniacal about it," Rebecca said. "And then something else comes up and he's just totally into that."

She ticked through several obsessions, all visual. "Like making movies, and editing things."

David was doing interviews constantly, calling himself the de facto MFOL press secretary, so the anger never cooled. And there was another factor: living beside Lauren. "I couldn't stand to be around my sister in this same house with her crying incessantly and knowing that I couldn't do anything to help her four friends that had died," he said. "That was one of the hardest things for me, because whenever I would call my mom, my sister would pick up and she couldn't even speak, she would just be crying, for like four days straight, she could barely even speak. And as cowardly as it is I couldn't stand to be around her knowing

I couldn't do anything." So he threw himself into the movement nonstop. "That's my way of dealing with it."

And it was helping, he said. It helped to channel his rage into something constructive, and it helped to engage with all these creative new friends at MFOL. "It's kind of like our own therapy group," he said. "We're all kind of misfits. Oh, we are absolutely huge fucking misfits. Like you hear the square peg in a round hole, we're like a fucking mutated octagon trying to go in there."

David was pursuing a career in words, but often thinks in shapes. "Did you know David's dyslexic?" his mother said. "I always like telling people that. I am, my dad was, it runs in the family." Rebecca had watched David struggle, failing to read until fourth grade. Teachers wrote him off, he said, "telling my parents I would amount to nothing, like I was some kind of broken toy." Rebecca wants other kids to know that dyslexia doesn't have to stand in their way. She is as fierce and stubborn as David, and they butt heads constantly, but she was amazed by what he had done. David also inherited her quirky sense of humor. He said he had no time for laughter anymore, but he confessed that John Oliver was still getting through. "Just cause he's, like, fucking hilarious. That's my dream job right there, working to expose the ridiculousness and corruption and just how frankly stupid these politicians have become."

Little things amused David. He paused midrant to chuckle over the name of a Norwegian interviewer, Fjord. That got him on a roll. "The French always talk very slowly with the French accent"—he amused himself briefly, tossing out various French words like "croissant," then flipped right back—"and I'm like, 'Get the message through, man! Like I want to fucking talk to you, but I can't if you take so damn long."

More than once, David grew irritated at me lingering on a topic and snapped, "Next question!"

2

The kids were on a wild ride, and their parents were buckled in with them. At home the kids were often uncommunicative. That left the parents feeling rudderless.

Parents had been invited to an early meeting, and the kids said it took three times as long: concerns about everything, *I have an issue with* . . . The kids had heated discussions of their own, but they were on the same wavelength, with their own silly process that moved along at their own pace. So parents were banned.

Since the parents had been banished from the kids'

meetings, they were holding some of their own. Mostly just to compare notes, make sure the kids were all right. The parents were often thrown together on the kids' relentless touring schedule. Rebecca got to know Jeff Kasky on a cross-country flight to Los Angeles, and she could definitely see where Cameron got his sense of humor.

David's mom, Rebecca, described her life as "a whirlwind," which was an improvement on the "shitstorm" she experienced in February. David's remarkably calm father, Kevin Hogg, was a retired navy pilot. He had then served as an FBI special agent at Los Angeles International Airport until he was diagnosed with early-onset Parkinson's disease. He retired again with disability benefits and moved the family to Florida, where the cost of living was lower. David transferred to Douglas in the middle of freshman year, and it took two years before he felt like he fit in.

Kevin had kept his diagnosis private out of embarrassment, Rebecca said. The concept of privacy was laughable now. The TV cameras were trained directly on David, but the Internet was obsessed with his dad. "FBI special agent" was catnip for conspiracy theorists, even with a "former" in front of it. Wild stories abounded, and no secret from his past was too obscure for a meme.

Retirement simplified chaperoning duties. David was on the road constantly, and they never let him travel alone. Rebecca worried about the pressure on David—but Lauren was her big fear. At least Lauren's pain was visible. David's trauma was hard to read. Anger blacked out everything.

All the parents worried about what their kids had taken on. A twenty-year national crisis loaded onto the shoulders of traumatized kids? It seemed to be helping them—but it seemed like a lot. "I'm terrified," Emma's mother, Beth González, said. "It's like she built herself a pair of wings out of balsa wood and duct tape and jumped off a building. And we're just, like, running along beneath her with a net, which she doesn't want or think that she needs."

Rebecca worried about packages. Every week a huge new stack of letters showed up at school, and some came directly to the house. Their address was out there; that was unnerving. Most of the mail was positive, but the bad ones were threatening.

Mail delivery was Kevin's favorite part of the day. David could be harshly contrarian and rebuffed all of Kevin's attempts to help, but he had conceded the mail. It piled up fast, and what a nightmare to process it all. When would David have time?

That's a common problem. Shooting survivors often

describe unforeseen guilt. Public support means everything, but it quickly becomes a burden too. Even when
it's 98 percent positive, it's the vicious 2 percent you remember. You never know which envelope will be toxic,
and they go right for the jugular. Columbine principal
Frank DeAngelis said he let thousands of letters build
up, and he felt obligated to at least read them all. So
he assigned himself a quota of twenty-five a day, but
that was overwhelming. "My counselor said that was
putting me in a bad place," he said. So he boxed them
up and put them away for a few years. (That story had
a happy twist. He finally pulled the boxes out in 2002
while going through a divorce. One of the letters was
from his high school girlfriend. They reconnected and
they're now married.)

Kevin foresaw some version of this. Plus there
were checks in there, and random bits of cash like $5
bills—not to mention heartfelt wishes from people who
deserved a reply, or at least a read. Kevin devised a little system, sorting everything in an old cardboard box.
The tricky part was sometimes discerning where the
money should go. Most of the writers were clear—for
David's college fund, or for the movement, or to treat
himself to something nice—but sometimes Kevin
had to make a judgment call. David could make some
choices later, but at a minimum, every contribution

would get a thank-you, no matter how small. It was the $5 donors who could probably spare it least.

Working his box made Kevin happy. David would thank him some day.

3

Misfits. David kept calling them misfits—and theater geeks, drama nerds, and journalism fanatics. He loved the image of the misfits fighting back. "I think it's very true," his mom said. "They're used to being outliers and they don't care about being different."

Some of the other MFOL boys were using the misfit label too. A few days later, I met three of them for a long group interview. As I tossed out some of David's phrases, Alfonso and Ryan Deitsch giggled and agreed. Daniel Duff looked a bit taken aback. Finally he spoke, hesitantly. "Are we? Misfits?"

Ryan let out a howl. "We are totally misfits!"

"The fact that you asked that question proves you're a misfit," Alfonso said.

Ryan kept riffing. "You have to ask if you're the weird guy on the bus."

Daniel decided to go along. "Yeah, we're like the drama club and the TV club."

"Can we be honest? Those are not the popular clubs," Alfonso said. "Although, me, I was an exception. I feel like that's all I have to say." He said it with a big smirk, and then let out a hearty laugh.

But I sensed Daniel had it right. We have all seen our share of teenage misfits, and it's hard not to wince. These kids had huge circles of friends, and Alfonso was constantly trailed by a pack of girls. I bounced the idea off Jackie and she was incredulous. "Who's a misfit?" she asked. When I mentioned Alfonso, she laughed. "Come on. Those boys were overplaying it." They were comedians, so they had fun with themselves. The real outcasts weren't laughing.

Jackie was battling different stereotypes. She was blond, petite, and pretty, a deadly combination. "I've gotten the dumb blonde," she said. It reared up often on Twitter. She avoided feeding the trolls, but she was touched when friends defended her. Her friend Adam was irked by a post saying she obviously hadn't paid attention in class. "Adam Alhanti tweeted that comment and was like, 'Actually, Jackie's class president, has an SAT score of 1510 and a GPA of 5.2.' And I was like, 'Oh my god, Adam.' They'll go after everything they can to demean me, but it's not working."

4

David Hogg was exhausted. He couldn't even find time to schedule all his interviews—mine had been double-booked with *60 Minutes,* and then frantically rescheduled thirty minutes prior. The National School Walkout was set for March 14, the one-month anniversary. He was planning to walk out for seventeen minutes and walk back in. He was thrilled to see it happening, but grateful not to be in charge this time. David had been crisscrossing the country on a month-long tear. So many interviews. "Probably over a thousand," he said—on every conceivable network, in every language, on every continent. "I've done Venezuela, Colombia, Norway, Germany, Sweden. . . . I've done about ten in Australia alone."

"Is it getting any easier?" I asked.

"Nah. It's just as crazy. I'm just getting more tired."

"Are you sleeping at all, or eating much?"

"No to both."

"Is there any end in sight? How long can you keep that up?"

"I can keep going till the day I die."

Although . . . his body had other ideas, he admitted. The pace had just taken him down. "I was sick for the past four days. Sinus infection. And that just knocked me out, so I just laid in bed for like three days and didn't answer anyone."

It was one p.m. on a Monday, and he wasn't in school. "I woke up late and was just like, eh, whatever. So I've kind of just been moseying around, cleaning up my room finally because it hasn't been cleaned in like a month." He liked order, hated a mess, but everything was on hold. He had put one thing in order, when he was too weak to do anything else.

But he was plowing ahead with interviews, defiantly presenting indefatigable David. Scheduling was a nightmare. David was better with concepts than keeping track of things. He later met Michael Bloomberg and asked how he does it. "He was like, 'I have a scheduler,'" David said.

He finished an hour with me and hopped on his bike to race to the other interview. Ten million people would see a boisterous and assertive David on *60 Minutes* that Sunday. No clue that he had just collapsed.

Several of the kids were showing early signs of burnout. And David wasn't burned *out*, just down. He had plenty of fight left in him long term. He knew he was in a marathon, but kept sprinting anyway. Pacing himself, that just wasn't in his character—or not a trait he had developed yet. He was seventeen.

Jackie was a year behind David, but had developed that skill years earlier. She was self-aware, set realistic goals, and kept a constant eye on pace. Her eight o'clock bedtime was out the window now, because sleep wasn't coming anyway. Most of them were still struggling with sleep. So Jackie found other ways to pace herself.

"I'm not getting burnt out," she said. "Honestly I'm kind of jumping on stuff more. In the beginning, I was exhausted because I was nonstop going going going and now it's slowing down and I'm like, 'What now?'" She had just gone to the Seventeen Families art exhibit, where Tío Manny had done his first mural. "I posted pictures of it on Twitter, and I kind of like broke down," Jackie said. "I hadn't thought about why I was fighting for a few days and it kind of came back to me. It kind of gave me another motivation. I think everyone's getting even more into it now. In the beginning, we all weren't friends." Most of the kids were friends from drama club or news, or both. She and Sarah Chadwick were the only two from neither, she said. "Like I knew Cameron and Alex but I didn't know anyone else. I was scared, I didn't know who to talk to, I was a ball of stress. But now that I'm friends with everyone, I can actually talk to them."

Most of the kids were outgoing, and they bonded

quickly. A few in the group were reserved and took longer. David. David took the longest.

Jackie laughed pretty hard at the notion of David as an angry kid. Alfonso also had an angry TV persona, which was even more absurd. "They're so opposite!" she said. She hunted around on her phone for silly videos of David from the group chat. "They're hilarious." She found one of David doing something like a Zoolander impersonation, high-stepping down the hallway at the secret MFOL office, mugging at an imaginary camera. She replayed it for me several times, howling each run, but wouldn't forward it. "I can't. He would kill me." Another contrast to his public persona; David was a very private person.

Jackie wasn't surprised by David's image, though. "I just met that side of him," she said. It was mid-March. "We actually had a conversation—he said that he didn't like me at first either, because I come from the side of the school—" She considered how to put it. "My friends are kind of crazy. I'm in the student government kind of group—it's like parties and stuff like that. And David's like a TV production person, so he didn't like SGA. A lot of people don't like SGA. I personally am not really friends with them anymore because they kind of dropped me after this. So he always thought I was like a stereotypical annoying girl, and then he realized I wasn't, and then I realized he wasn't a serious person all the time."

5

Alfonso hardly ever sounded serious. He could riff on anything. "Alfonso's really on all the time," Ryan Deitsch's brother Matt said. "It's hard being on all the time." Alfonso made it look easy, and he could flip from silly to serious and back midsentence. An astute *New York* magazine feature had described Alfonso as "comparatively conservative." Many of the kids had Republican parents, but few of the kids were, so I asked Alfonso if that was accurate.

"Yes, surprisingly."

"In what way?"

"You know how when you're this age, everyone's like, 'I'm a Republican; I'm a Democrat'—there's no actual thought. In general I say I'm pretty center. Like on social issues I go pretty liberal, and on fiscal issues, sometimes I'll go conservative."

He dissed both parties at length. "So both are evil entities, let's get that out of the way. One of them tried to use me for political gain, and then the other is just showing their face because if not the country would hate them because we're kids who honestly did survive a school shooting and I'm joking a lot now, but—"

He was thinking out loud, really, and he plunged ahead awhile longer and then asked to clarify: "What I mean by using us is, first, we are using [the Democrats] to our advantage. Realistically, they're giving us a very nice platform, they're letting us speak to their leadership which are people in power. Before this, I would've probably never voted for that party, and now I'm considering it, I'm really thankful that they at least reached out to us, like we didn't have to jump so many hoops to speak to them, like the Republican Party. And the Republican Party, generally, I don't feel agrees with our viewpoint, so it's understandable that they don't want to talk to us."

That was becoming a problem. By March, nearly all the MFOL kids were bringing it up nearly every interview. They were eager to work with both parties, and knew that lots of Republicans quietly supported them but couldn't risk the association. Ryan Deitsch commented on that danger that same week: "When you take a selfie with a bunch of kids that went there to speak their minds and have their voices heard and then it's like, 'I was just with Never Again—vote for me next election—'"

"We have not endorsed political candidates nor shall

we ever," Alfonso said. "That is a rule we have made. That's why we've spoken to both leaderships—I mean as much as we can, because one of them doesn't want to talk to us as much, and we're trying to work with them. Honestly, if a Democratic senator and a Republican one asked me to talk to them at the same time, I'd probably speak to the Republican."

6

Daniel Duff was planning to walk out, and excited about it—and tickled that he was going to lead the walkout at a distant school, thirteen hundred miles away. His cousins in Pennsylvania had hatched a plan. Colin and Kyleigh Duff were students at Parkland High School (no connection), and Daniel was helping plan the walkout there. Colin and Kyleigh asked Daniel to record a short video, saying who he was, why he was walking, and why it mattered. Colin and Kyleigh's classmates were over the moon. One of the kids leading the national movement was personally involved with their walkout. The school administration got on board. "So they're going to meet in the auditorium, watch me, and then they're going to walk out," Daniel said, still a bit incredulously. It was a big school too—about three thousand kids. Daniel wasn't a leader at the MFOL meetings, more of a foot soldier. But he would be so much more for these kids. "I'm going to be like the voice of a walkout, I guess," he said.

Daniel described the plan gleefully, while still scripting it. Two days later, he was morose. He had stayed up way too late on rewrites and recording, and hated the result. "I was so tired, and I had my March for Our Lives shirt on and everything," he said. "And I watched the next morning, and I was like, 'I look way too tired and you can clearly see me reading the script.' So I'm going to redo it once I get home."

The walkout was in two days, and his uncle would have to edit it, but he was going to record it over. He had to get this right.

11
Walkout

1

This was turning into a huge deal. Twenty-five hundred schools had organized school walkouts, in every state, and the media was all over it. But in Parkland, the school administrators had erred on the side of caution, and decided it would be a quiet affair.

That's not what happened. Kids disobeyed their faculty. They moved fast, busted out of school, and merged several protests on the fly through shouts and texts and social media. The change came suddenly. At 9:59, one minute to walkout, few of the thousands who would flood into Pine Trails Park within the hour had any idea they were headed there.

Here was the plan: Each school participating was

asked to walk out and observe seventeen minutes of silence on Tuesday morning at ten a.m. local time: one
minute for each of the fallen at Douglas High. How they
conducted it, and what might follow, was up to them.
Every school had to deal with its administration, and
the responses ran the gamut across the country. Many
administrators threatened detentions or suspensions
for the insubordination. Others supported the kids and
worked with them, but safety was a big concern. At
Douglas, the plan was to walk out to the football field;
play "Shine"; hear a short speech by Ty Thompson, the
principal; observe the seventeen minutes of silence;
and then file back inside. The entire event would take
about half an hour. Everyone would be safely sealed off
behind the tall chain-link fence, still festooned with
flowers, brown and crumply now. The press, a constant presence and a growing irritant, would be kept
at bay.

Other local schools were even more restrictive:
walking "out" to the corridors inside. But all these
plans suffered from the same glitch: most of the kids
hated them. What was the point of limiting the protest
to seventeen minutes? And reporters could be super
annoying, but wasn't this exactly the wrong moment to
shut them up? This was a show of force—why seal off
the messengers?

Susana Matta Valdivieso, a seventeen-year-old Douglas student, decided to do something bigger, even if her classmates couldn't participate. She spent weeks organizing a multischool rally at North Community Park in Coral Springs. She lined up kids to speak from several schools, and coaxed Rabbi Melinda Bernstein to offer an invocation and lead a moment of silence. Bernstein was also bringing a microphone and portable speaker set. Angel Lopez helped publicize it on his @browardstrong Instagram account. Angel was a recent graduate of Coral Gables Senior High in the neighboring suburb, who began organizing after the attack. The site was a short walk from Douglas, whose students had been warned not to set foot off the campus. Violators would be locked out and marked truant for the remainder of the day.

Not good enough. A small rebellion was brewing. Lauren Hogg first got wind of it on Instagram that morning. A Snapchat message was flying around during first period that read: "After the 17 minutes, please march with us to Pine Trails. 17 minutes is NOT enough."

It was unclear how many students were ready to test the administration. They liked Mr. Thompson, and they had been through a lot together. Most kids later said they had been undecided, waiting to see if it amounted to anything. As they filed back in from the football field, no one seemed to be making a break for it. But everything changed when their young siblings made a move just down the street.

Westglades Middle School abuts the Douglas campus just beyond its football field. Its students were grumbling too. "We had organized a walkout," said eighth-grader Christopher Krok. "The school said OK, but they put us in the field—which we thought wasn't enough. That won't show anything." He and his friends hatched their own plan, which was also flying around social media that morning. "I didn't think anyone would actually do it," eighth-grader Justin St. Piere said. No one did. Only the four organizers were on board, and they were pretty iffy. That was so far fewer than at Douglas, where the rebellion was faltering—but these four actually walked.

It started with Christopher Krok, who led the rebellion in full military uniform—US Army dress greens. Christopher was the young commander of Westglades' Junior ROTC program. He said they had been plotting all morning, but he wasn't sure they would go through with it until "about two seconds before it started." He nodded at his friends around him.

"Ryan, Spencer, me, and my sister here, we were like, 'Let's just walk out.' We got stopped by security and the principal and we just said, 'No, we're going.'"

They made it past the principal, out to the street, where they expected to be on their own. Back inside, there was a standoff. The hallways were full from the walk in, so hundreds had watched the four escape. The principal was furious. Kids were afraid to follow, but then a few bolted. Another stare-down, another burst. The kids were still intimidated, but growing nervier by the second, and the breakouts got bigger, the intervals shorter, until the dam burst. A wave of students poured onto Holmberg Road, and the staff gave up.

The kids ran down the street until they reached Christopher Krok, who was extolling the need for stricter gun laws to the assembled reporters while making his way down Holmberg Road toward Douglas High. Dozens of boys in army uniforms followed, many twelve and thirteen years old, and under five feet tall. They wore various ROTC rank insignia, and were talking to reporters nearby too, demanding a ban on military assault weapons and passionately describing sensible gun regulations—focusing on the "well-regulated" militia authorized in the Second Amendment. They said there were about fifty-five students in their unit, and they believed virtually all of them walked out.

They kept walking down the street, and the pace quickened as the wave caught up with them and they realized this was really happening, the whole freaking school, it looked like—and then some kids started running, soon everyone was running, laughing, no idea where they were headed, but they were really going there!

Reporters kept asking where they were going; kids kept shrugging.

"I honestly have no clue," St. Piere said. "I'm just following the group."

Finally, a kid at the front of the pack yelled, "Pine Trails!"

None of them actively tried to signal the Douglas kids. They did not plan to rev up from a leisurely stroll to a stampede right in front of Douglas, just as its students were retreating back inside. It just worked out that way. But the Douglas kids noticed.

At Pine Trails that afternoon, Douglas kids confirmed that it was the excitement beyond the fence that sparked their sudden decision to go. Their little brothers and sisters had taken to the streets to support them—that was the spark. And just as at Westglades, it was suddenly a wave. They followed the Westglades pack to Pine Trails. Seemed right, among the memorials. They hadn't been there in a while. Nearly two miles away, but they didn't mind.

The memorials were all still standing, but weathered and withering, the teddy bears, soggy and a little smelly after days of relentless spring rains. Each victim's name was hand-painted on a sign, faded now, and Peter Wang's was torn loose, lying on the ground. Freshly printed signs posted everywhere announced that everything soon would be collected for long-term preservation.

When the kids arrived, there was a lot of milling. No one seemed quite sure what to *do* now that they were there. But Susana Matta Valdivieso was ready. She had made a split-second decision as she watched her classmates bolt. She hit social media: Reroute! Angel Lopez and others helped spread the word. She chose a position in front of the angels and started her first speakers. Early arrivals walked over to see what was happening, and a crowd formed. The rabbi threw the microphone and speakers into her car, raced over, and hooked them up. Then it seemed official. That was the remarkable thing about the Pine Trails rally. It was spontaneous—organized, reconfigured, and expanded on the fly via Snapchat and Instagram, but with seeds sown long before.

Angel Lopez made it, frustrated that so few from his own school had. "The kids that were daring jumped the gates," he said. David and Lauren Hogg arrived and held up an improvised sign. David said he had first gotten wind of it when he saw students heading for the doors. He was going to skip it, because he was so behind in school, but needed to cover it as a journalist. And then the fever grabbed him, and he was coaxed to the microphone and delivered the second-most-memorable speech of the event.

As the rally progressed, a little girl burrowed her way to the front, where I was holding out my phone to record the speaker. She wore a maroon JUSTICE sweatshirt, big white headphones around her neck, and red cat ears on her head. She rose just a little higher than my waist. Her name was Aarayln Hughes. She leaned in meekly to whisper to me. "Excuse me, sir. What if I want to speak?" She thought I was in charge. I wasn't yet sure who *was* in charge, but Susana seemed to be directing people to the microphone, so I nodded toward her. Aarayln looked distraught. She had already summoned all her courage. I leaned down and encouraged her to scoot past me. I bet she'll let you speak if you ask, I said.

A few minutes later, Aarayln Hughes took the mic and wowed the crowd. "It hurts for me to see all these kids crying," she said. "No kid should be going through this. I want my voice to be heard because no other sixth grader is doing this. I want this generation to make a change for everyone: big, small, teenagers, adults—even if you're eighty years old, I don't care, make a change. These gun laws need a change!"

Her applause was even louder than David's. Aarayln Hughes had found her voice. She was not meek now.

2

Jackie was thrilled. What an amazing day in Parkland, and gun safety was dominating the national conversation again. And they hadn't had to organize this one. That helped. The march in DC was ten days away.

One reaction had left her with a sour aftertaste, though. This is her account of the following day.

Jackie walked into math class that morning, AP calculus AB. Her teacher asked, "Who's walking out today?" All the hands went up. "I bet half of you don't know why you're walking out," he said.

Jackie was stunned. He knew she and Alfonso were in the class. "I wasn't going to let him do that," she told me.

I know why I'm walking out, she told him.

Why, Jackie?

For disaffection for current gun legislation.

Do you even know current gun legislation?

I actually do.

"And so we basically got into that for a little bit," she said. "And he proceeded to call me immature and said I would never understand the complexity of this issue until I'm an adult. But he actually didn't say it like that. He didn't say 'the complexity of this issue.' I just made it sound smarter—he just sounded dumb."

"I think I happen to be more mature than more than half the adults in this country right now," she said.

I beg to differ, he said. But we don't have to get into that.

"And then he started teaching math but as he was writing on the board he continued to say, 'This walkout won't accomplish anything. You're just going to walk out to get out of class.'"

This is a statement, she said. People have been protesting for centuries and it's the largest message. Look at Selma, look at the Little Rock Nine. It made a statement and it made history.

"He's just stuck in his own world," she told me. "He actually just got a cell phone for the first time after the shooting. So he's clearly stuck a hundred years back. He doesn't understand. We were actually arguing for twenty minutes and the entire class was silent."

I asked how old he was.

"Probably in his sixties. He's the one who doesn't understand the complexity of it. He hasn't heard enough of our side, because he won't listen to us because he thinks we're just kids. As do a lot of adults."

"Are you getting that from a lot of adults?"

Not so much in person, she said. "On Twitter. The random old dudes will have like three grammar mistakes in their tweet and be like, 'You don't know what you're talking about.' But there's an overwhelming amount of love from adults. The only people obviously giving hate that I'm aware of, other than the people on Twitter, are the kids at school because they think I'm doing this for attention."

"Really? How many are you getting that from?"

"It happened to be my old friend group. It's a good assortment of fiftysome-odd kids. I just had my study hall and was crying. People weren't talking to me, because people just don't talk to me anymore. They shun me. I sat alone during lunch today because I couldn't find Emma. I'd rather be by myself than with people who talk bad about me behind my back."

"And how are you getting wind of it?"

"Oh, there's people that still support me that are telling me who's saying stuff. And I appreciate them telling me. I made a lot of new friends out of this. They

make me so happy. I genuinely haven't been this excited to be with a group of people in years. So that's
what's been going on—it kind of sucks. Especially in
school, because I have all my classes with them, but
when I leave school—like I'm going to the office after
this [interview]. Every time I go there, it's kind of like
a sanctuary. I love everyone there."

Losing all her friends? This was the second time she
had mentioned it in the past few weeks. I clarified what
she meant by "old friend group": pre–Valentine's Day?
Yes. Her friend group from before Valentine's Day
was gone. Then she corrected herself: they had been
her friends until her Twitter follower count took off.
"It sucks, but it's happening to all of us. Which is how
we're rising above it—with each other's support."

Falling out with one close friend can be devastating
for a high school student. But amputation of her entire social network, for a highly social person, at a time
of crisis, while taking on absurd responsibility—that
could have ramifications way beyond Jackie's understanding at seventeen. I also wondered whether those
friendships were really over, or just badly stressed.
Inadvertently escalating to the media—beyond the
friends' reach—might be the real end.

Meanwhile, in the thick of it, Jackie saw it as an opportunity. She had a fresh perspective on the girl she

had been. "Honestly, Stoneman Douglas actually follows the stereotypical high school," she said. "And I would classify myself as used to be a part of the popular group, that's where I fell. I've always been kind of stuck in my area because it was just who I grew up with and I never was exposed to the other sectors. I'm really glad I am now because they're amazing people and I love them and I'm very intellectually stimulated around them. And I haven't really experienced that a lot. Like, I've always been this way, but I kind of had to hide the intellectual side of me."

3

Friend loss wasn't a big issue for most of her new group. Most of their friends had formed MFOL. Ryan, Alfonso, and Daniel hit on the more common problems in our group interview that week. They hated to see their town's name branded as the latest term for tragedy—but so much better than their school. MSD's seven-syllable name had probably saved them that indignation. But what did *they* call the shooting—obviously not "Parkland"? Columbine survivors had coalesced around "the tragedy," but other communities favor "the shooting" or "the attack." In New Orleans, it was commonly "pre-K" and "post-K" for Katrina. The boys pondered it a minute. They didn't seem to call it anything. "It!" Alfonso finally said. "Before it happened, I was blah blah blah blah blah, but after it happened—"

The others nodded. "Basically, whatever you say, you understand what we're talking about," Daniel said.

And how were they doing? They *seemed* to be OK, but . . . That was an extremely touchy subject for survivors. They tended to put on a brave face, but deeply resented people reading that as recovered.

"I've gotten this a lot," Alfonso said. "See, kids are like ogres, and ogres are like onions, because they've got layers. On the outside, the onion has the cover. We have the cover of being funny and saying dumb shit. But on the inside, it's completely different."

Daniel and Ryan rolled their eyes. His riff on *Shrek* had fallen flat. Alfonso was always trying out new material—most of it clicked, sometimes it bombed. He shrugged, smiled, and turned to Daniel.

Daniel mocked him gently, agreed, and elaborated. "It hits me in waves. Like right now I'm totally fine, but I have like two of my classes . . ." He described the empty chairs again. It was still bothering him. It was bothering a lot of kids. Couldn't they do something? Move that desk?

"The class that I had with Gina was in the freshman

building so it's technically not exactly the same scene," he said. "But the other, the class I had with Jaime, the teacher moved the desks around, but I can always picture where would she sit if she was still here." Daniel slumped in his chair. I asked them about triggers.

"Sirens, helicopters," Daniel said.

"Sounds," Ryan said.

Daniel whacked the table to demonstrate. It had a glass top balanced on a metal frame, and it made a hell of a sound. Despite watching the windup, Alfonso and Ryan practically jumped out of their chairs. They went white and silent for a moment, then everyone laughed hysterically. "That was a lot louder than I thought it would be," Daniel said.

That reminded Alfonso of a trip to the Capitol. He and Delaney Tarr were meeting with the Democratic House minority leader, Nancy Pelosi, when a buzzer sounded, alerting members to a floor vote. "It was just like a *beep beep beep beep,* and the second it started everyone was completely fine with it, but me and Delaney were, like, freaking out—our eyes the size of orange peels," Alfonso said. "And I mean, Nancy Pelosi was talking to us, so I didn't want to say, 'Hey! Shut up! I don't care what you're talking about, I'm really scared!' So I mean, we kept our cool but—" He shrugged.

I asked if she picked up on their freak-out.

"No."

Ryan laughed. It had unnerved him too. "It's so loud, and goes on way too long. No wonder they get nothing done in that building."

They discovered they were all sensitive to different sounds. Ryan went quiet. When they got on a roll, it was usually Alfonso riffing with Daniel, or Alfonso with Ryan, or Alfonso with Alfonso. Daniel and Alfonso went at it this time.

"Sirens don't like trigger me," Daniel said.

"Me either," Alfonso said. "But alarms—"

"When I hear a siren, I think of a shooting."

Alfonso nodded. "Oh yeah."

"Also."

"Guns."

"Obviously," Daniel said. "My friend told me he was gonna go to a gun range and shoot an AR-15. I don't know how that would ever help someone, but apparently that's a way of coping."

"I'm gonna be honest, I've shot a gun before," Alfonso said.

"I've never."

"I've shot several. It's fun to shoot guns. It is. I went to a range."

I asked about coping mechanisms:

"Joking," Daniel said.

Alfonso smiled. "This."

"Activism and jokes," Daniel said. "And, I mean, unfortunately they don't go well together, because when you are joking during an activist thing, then people—"

"Oh no, they love it!" Alfonso paused, reconsidered. "No they don't—"

"But the people that don't like you are like—"

"'Oh, you're so not funny! How dare you joke—'"

"'They're not real, because they're having fun—'"

"By the way, he asked about coping mechanisms," Alfonso said. "I think there's three very clear answers. One, Never Again activism, obviously. Two, absolute trash food. I seem to be incapable of eating healthy, which is a real pain. I just started going to the gym consistently and then all of this happened."

"That's terrible," Daniel said.

On his way to the third one, Alfonso got sidetracked on his girlfriend. They'd just broken up, that week, a few days shy of their six-month anniversary.

Was it related?

"Yeah, definitely. Beforehand we were having little problems, but after this we— My worldview changed. I'll be honest: one thing I'm noticing more is, I hate to admit it, but I'm pretty materialistic. There are those people in life, I am one of those people, I'm never gonna turn down a Gucci bag. You know like, how could I, right?"

"I could so easily turn down a Gucci bag."

"Me and Daniel are different."

Ryan chimed back in. "I'd be like, 'Ohhhhh, a pretty sack.'"

"Wow, a twenty-thousand-dollar sack," Alfonso said.

"With a shiny 'G' on it," Ryan said.

They kept rolling with it for a while, until Alfonso's smile suddenly sagged, followed by his shoulders, and his pitch. "People just mean a lot more to me. Because the reality of losing someone is a lot more real."

Everyone dropped the playful tone. "When I'm like texting people, I make sure to always say goodnight to them," Daniel said. "And I always hug like everybody now."

"I respond to everybody," Alfonso said. "I try to always be there for people that have been there for me—beforehand, not just now."

"I think I've become just altogether more social," Daniel said.

Ryan had gone silent again, so I asked him how it was affecting him. "Pretty much same thing. But I like didn't break up with my girlfriend."

"He's still with her," Alfonso said.

"It's been tense but like we just spoke at a church in New York last night."

I asked if both girlfriends were Douglas survivors. Yes, they said. Daniel seemed stunned about the breakup and asked if it was really over.

"We don't speak about that," Alfonso said.

I asked if he was comfortable sharing her name.

"No, you know, privacy. And I try to be respectful as much as possible. And by the way, please get this on the record: I'm an asshole, OK." He was smiling again.

"Good," I said. "I'm gonna put quotes around that."

There would be many more breakups ahead of them. When Columbine happened, the federal government rushed in a huge team of grief counselors. One of the leaders, who had just spent years with Oklahoma City survivors, outlined what lay ahead in the first week: Lots of long, healthy relationships would snap for no apparent reason—or sometimes for obvious reasons that had been brushed aside for months or years. Boys who had never kissed a girl would go on dating binges. Kids who had never sipped a beer would go on benders. They would take up smoking, or rock climbing, or weight training—or quit. Secretive kids would suddenly open up to their parents, talkative kids would stop. Drastic change was one of the most common coping mechanisms—to correct a problem, or for the sake of change. It was generally temporary. Most survivors settle back into old habits eventually, but for weeks or months or years, chaos can reign.

The activism seemed to be helping, but does it ever get to be a lot, I asked. Too much?

"It's a lot," Ryan said. "But—"

"It's manageable," Alfonso said.

"It's something we have to do," Ryan said. "We have to stand for the families of those who are grieving and not just in our community. I was in New York last night, at a church and these women from Harlem talked about losing their children years ago and they said that they've been fighting this fight for eleven years and nearly nothing has changed. And now like maybe change will happen here."

12

The Memes Men

1

Nine days until the march. They were all about the message now. A million little details to work out, but that was not the focus at MFOL headquarters. No one would remember if the buses got snarled getting folks there, or if some fine was levied for parking them wrong. If they failed to inspire young activists, they lost. If the march came off as too juvenile, too unfocused, too privileged, too white, or even too boring to keep millions tuned in to TV . . . loss. Every previous group of survivors had gotten a four-day window of relevance. The MFOL kids were the first to get a second shot, a shot they created, and they had to make the message sing.

They had mapped out message strategies for before, during, and after the march. During depended on the stage: the pacing, the visuals, the performers, and all the optics, because millions would be receiving their message through their eyes even more than their ears. The message was gun safety for *all* kids, so they all had better be visible. They had spent the spring meeting young urban activists, so they had a wide talent pool to draw from. Alex and D'Angelo from the Peace Warriors were no-brainers: passionate and articulate speakers—voices the world needed to hear. About half the performers and speakers would be people of color, representing hard-hit urban areas like Chicago, Brooklyn, and South Los Angeles.

Another major visual choice would be to exclusively feature kids at the podium. They wanted adults as allies—performers, for example—but their message would be delivered by kids. That was a powerful message itself. But they were wise enough to realize that kids were relatively new to this—and none of them had played a stage this big. They were not just handing them the mic cold. They had conducted a series of conference calls with speakers and organizers for DC and the sibling marches. "We want to make sure all of them have the same ideals that they're pushing," Jackie said. "Because people aren't very clear about that, even though we've made the message pretty clear. People still are a little cloudy." Repetition, repetition, repetition. They would keep scheduling conference calls until they heard everyone singing the same tune.

But even the world's best orators could never hold a worldwide TV audience for two hours. They calibrated their own short attention spans: Who would they watch? They needed lively performers and big names. 42 West had opened doors; it was up to the kids to woo the talent.

Jackie's top priority was recording personalized video for each performer they wanted—no frills, just straight to camera, expressing what it would mean to have them. They were casting a wide net, dreaming big and audacious, across hip-hop, pop, R&B, and country. Country was vital, Jackie said. Diversity didn't always mean color—this time it also meant conservatives, who had been tough to reach. Diversity meant gun enthusiasts, making sure the performers also included a streak of white.

Big names were already on board, but they were reaching for more. Jackie had just completed appeals with four other girls to Drake, Chance the Rapper, Kendrick Lamar, and Jason Aldean. They coaxed Dwayne Wade to appear with them in one. Jackie was especially hopeful about Aldean, who had been performing in Las Vegas during the Route 91 concert shooting. He felt like a kindred spirit, and could reach red America. "He's been involved in the issue, but he gets the different crowd," she said.

Jackie wasn't sure how the videos actually got to these people—not her problem. She just sent them to 42 West, she said, and whoosh, connected.

They reached out to a long list of performers, because many were previously committed. They didn't hear from Aldean. But Demi Lovato said yes, and so did Miley Cyrus, Ariana Grande, Lin-Manuel Miranda, Ben Platt, and several more.

They had expected to be pulling their hair out that week, but the office was eerily quiet. Things felt so in hand that most of the MFOL team left town. The drama club was off to Tampa for a statewide one-act competition, and the news team had a national competition in Nashville. At first, the whole team wondered if they should cancel, but what they needed right now was a break. "It wasn't a big deal," Jackie said. "It's kind of like a plateau week." She was not in news or drama, so she stayed back, stressing over her speech. She had never even attended a political rally before Valentine's Day. David, Emma, and Cameron also skipped the competitions. The teams could take a break, but not them.

Most of the details were delegated. Adults were employed to solve the vexing issues posed by all the in-kind generosity. Airlines and hotels had donated tickets and blocks of rooms, Lyft promised free rides, and so many kids were in need, but who was going to coordinate all that? Invitations were routed to Ryan Deitsch, who texted the information to Jeff Foster, the AP government teacher. Mr. Foster maintained a sign-up list, which ran about 750 students deep, and he built a detailed spreadsheet to capture all the details and match them up. Two other teachers were working different lists, and they corresponded with students to sort the details. Off-loading that clerical work was a no-brainer.

Jackie was drawn to logistics, and dove into the nitty-gritty, where it would make an impact. She decided they would sell blue hats and beanies at the march, but Douglas kids would be given maroon ones. "That was important," she said. Activists she was meeting around the country were eager to network together at the march, but they all wanted to meet the kids who'd lived through it.

After Tallahassee, Jackie described the experience as a dry run for DC, a small-scale proving ground to master the details. By early March, all that felt like the weeds. A few weeks later, I posed the same question of her biggest Tallahassee takeaway, and got a completely different answer. "I learned that even if I cry in front of a senator, they won't change their mind," she said.

"Did that happen?"

"Yeah, it happened. I cried twice in Tallahassee. Hearing them say that they're not changing their opinion even though we were there. And then the same thing happened in DC. I talked to Congressman Steve Scalise—he was shot during the baseball game—and hearing him say that guns aren't the problem, I started crying. I talked to Tim Scott of South Carolina—he is from Charleston; his church was the church! And to hear him say guns aren't the problem—I was crying, there were tears running down my face as I was saying this, and his eyes actually did swell up. I was like, 'We have a commonality between our hometowns. I don't understand why you can't see the one problem.' He's like, 'Mental health is the issue, blah blah blah.' I just can't fathom how people don't understand. They try to find a scapegoat and they think the scapegoat's the answer. Wake up!"

But that was February. Jackie would never be that naive again.

Jackie had shaken off the political naivete, but she still cried. "I'm honestly like, I'm a very sensitive person," she said. "Like if someone's going to be crying in the office, it's me."

The office. They were trying to keep a lid on its existence but the kids had started referring to "the office" instead of to "Cam's." They told me no press was allowed, but I asked Jackie again during an interview on March 15, at a Starbucks near the school.

"I'll ask," she said, and texted as she continued. "I'm asking them, but I don't really know. It's kind of Cameron's call."

I wasn't sure who "them" was—obviously a group thread, but who exactly? The entire group, I would soon learn. A massive thread that had expanded to nearly thirty people, hundreds of messages a day, running day and night. It was their primary form of communication, and they were keeping that quiet too. They were functioning as a democracy, everyone equal in theory, but some exerting a bit more weight. They often said they would have to check before sharing something, and when they named a particular person, it was usually Cameron.

Thirty minutes later, Jackie said I could come to the office. "David said not too long though. We can head over now if you want." David this time. It had been settled by group consensus, but David drew the boundaries in.

2

We drove to a nondescript strip mall on Sample Road, a busy commercial strip in Coral Springs, the next town over, six minutes from the school. It housed a wide assortment of small businesses behind putty-colored stucco walls with green metal awnings: a Weight Control Center, the Neck and Back Institute, and the No Hard Feelings Tattoo Gallery. We parked and I followed Jackie to an office tucked in the back, on the lower level, beside an office supply store and a martial arts studio. The blinds were closed, and the plate glass door was papered over on the inside. "It literally says 'Nurse Practitioner' on the window," she pointed out. "So no one really knows where it is." Death threats had continued, and some of the team was still jumpy.

She rapped five times loudly on the door.

"Who's there?"

"Jackie."

"Prove it."

We laughed, someone laughed inside, swung the door open, and Jackie nodded at me with a smirk as she walked in. "I'm with him."

Each time I arrived, it took a wisecrack or two to gain entry, followed by a flurry of silliness inside—mixed with a lot of hard work. The check-in station was empty, like most of the office. It was a tight space, even with most of the team gone. The main room was in the middle of the unit, presumably the nurse's exam room. Everyone was in there: eight people huddled around the oblong boardroom table that barely fit inside. More than twenty kids squeezed in for group meetings, leaning against the walls or sitting cross-legged on the floor.

The first thing I noticed was I'd never seen some of these people: in person, on TV, or on social media. It was hard to miss the guy in chunky black Rachel Maddow glasses, with flaming red hair radiating in all directions, like an Irish Albert Einstein. I caught them in the middle of a creative session, brainstorming ideas for some complicated Web content, and everyone seemed to be deferring to this guy, all the questions flying his way. But I had promised to be quick about this, so I moved on, and Jackie gave me a tour.

There was less space and less furniture than in Cameron's living room. "It feels cramped," someone I didn't recognize said. It was tight, but it was theirs. No parents, nobody's house, no community gatehouse.

I counted fewer than ten office chairs, which they wheeled from room to room for makeshift chats, and a cozy beanbag chair in what they called the writer's room. The space sported a toaster, a microwave with red Solo cups stacked on top, a full-size fridge stocked top to bottom with soft drinks, especially Living Juice bottles, and a minifridge, completely empty. There was a chest-high commercial photocopier with the box for a cheap all-in-one printer stacked on top: an HP Officejet Pro 8710.

"Somebody turn on the AC!" someone yelled. "It's brutally hot in here."

Background giggling was nearly constant.

The bathroom was spotless, which shocked me, and I commented on it.

"We treat it like a public bathroom," Jackie said. No public bathroom I'd ever seen was that clean.

They had made the place their own. There was a globe, an electric piano, and a faceless cloth doll near the toaster in a black and gray jumpsuit, with a clump of bright blue yarn for hair. Jackie reached for it. "This is the Dammit Doll. Slam it!" She battered the table in a burst of rage, as in a moment of possession, and then she was sweet, young Jackie again. It had made such a racket, Pippy rushed back to make sure we were OK.

"I slammed the Dammit Doll," Jackie said.

Pippy looked a little worried. I had never seen Jackie's menacing side, raging through her body for just a moment. Pippy apparently had.

I asked how often she whacked the doll.

Frequently.

"Are you still jumpy?"

"Uh-huh."

What were her triggers?

"When I pass a police car, I duck in the car," she said.

"Really?"

"I get scared."

There was a massive photo of Cameron's brother Holden in the hallway, nearly floor-to-ceiling, just his head with a huge grin. On a front wall they'd made a photo montage from some of the favorite cards they had received. A big close-up of Emma had been accessorized with a curly mustache. A huge US wall map was tacked with green pushpins, one for each sibling march, but just the early sign-ons, because they had come so fast and so furious, it was simpler to track them on their website. The map dominated an entire wall, with a piece of paper taped on either side. Each was creased twice, where it had been folded inside a business envelope. The notes were written with a thick Sharpie, in the same hand. The one on the left was addressed to Alfonso, who had shown it off eagerly on his phone earlier in the week:

DEAR ALFONSO—
SAW YOU ON CNN!
<u>PLEASE DO SOMETHING ABOUT YOUR ACNE</u>
—IT'S REPULSIVE!
YOU SHOULD NOT BE ON TELEVISION

Alfonso did have a harsh case of acne. And he was a very attractive young man. Delaney Tarr had no acne problem, and was outright beautiful, so her note was simpler:

DELANY—
SAW YOU ON CNN
SHUT THE FUCK UP <u>YOU</u> <u>STUPID</u>
<u>FUCKING CUNT!</u>
☺

They had been getting mean tweets daily, but this guy had taken the time to stamp and mail these to the school—with his return address. Alfonso said they didn't post the address, because why be mean? But there was no name on the notes, so it was safe to post. He and Delaney had each photographed and tweeted theirs and then donated them to the wall for the whole team to enjoy.

The prized possession in the office was a gold-colored bust of Robert F. Kennedy. The boys had raved about it during our group interview a few days earlier.

"Robert—such a great guy," Alfonso said.

"Was he?" I asked. "Cool? I never know."

"I'm fawning over him in my head." Alfonso said. The RFK Foundation had about four busts of his head, so they gave the group one, he said.

"Joe Kennedy the Third gave us a statue of Robert Kennedy," Ryan Deitsch said. "Looks like a macaroni art—"

Alfonso repeated the line to not quite finish his sentence, and they bounced back and forth: "It looked like macaroni art, but we were very—"

"Appreciative."

"Joe Kennedy escaped a snowstorm to give us the head of his grandfather," Alfonso continued.

"That's actually true."

"He brought it to a Democratic dinner we were also

invited to. He had a duffel bag with him. Everyone was just like—"

They all made horror-movie faces, including Daniel, who sat back, gleefully watching the older boys riff. "But it's amazing," Ryan said. "He was the keynote speaker and he controlled that room. Kennedy charisma."

They gushed about Joe for a while, but lamented that he slipped into politician bullshit at one point. "But you know, he gave us some pretty good answers," Alfonso said.

They were still getting used to the office—to any office, for many of them—and there were lots of functional items. A handwritten key roster, with seven color-coded keys, six of them signed out. A big whiteboard mostly dedicated to instructions on operating the printer. A corkboard with a BEFORE YOU LEAVE list printed in large type:

1. **Please make sure you turn off the air conditioner**

2. **Turn off all lights**

3. **Lock front and back doors.**

   Thanks!

Another version, taped to the front door, had a handwritten addition squeezed in:

4. Make sure trash/recycling go out.

A blue Post-it was stuck to the front door, with an arrow pointing to the latch that read THIS SHOCKS YOU EVERY TIME.

Some bullhorns were stacked up, still in the boxes. Someone had donated them after seeing the kids hop up on cars. Very nice intentions, a little too late, but maybe they would need them again.

3

I circled back to the main room to say goodbye, and meet the redhead—who still seemed to be directing. He introduced himself as Matthew Deitsch.

"Oh, Ryan's brother?"

"Yes."

"You've even got the same red hair."

"Nah, his is much more red than mine."

That didn't seem possible.

I asked if I could interview him before I left town, and he said, "How about now?" I explained my promise to leave quickly, and he waved that off. He had a brutal schedule and right here would be most efficient. And he could clear me to stay.

We headed toward the writer's room. The guy who had called the space cramped looked up from his laptop and called after Matt, "Do you have explosion on here?"

"No, but you could download a green-screen explosion pretty fast."

"Should it be an anime explosion?"

Matt didn't hear. He was already wheeling a chair into the writer's room. He motioned me toward it and flopped into a beanbag chair. When I asked if it was OK to record, he leaned forward and yelled toward the main room, "Guys! We're going to be recording, so just don't yell any racial slurs!" He watched for my reaction, and only then grinned.

Reporters were still wondering whether the kids could really pull this march off so quickly. I peppered Matt with logistical questions and he shrugged. No idea, why would he? "Just not where my focus is," he said. "I've had a month to be an expert in gun policy and write our five main points and platform." Matt turned out to be the recent grad who had led the research, selecting articles to route to the group. He enjoyed going bookworm. He loved deep dives to learn, and share, and debate. Nothing more gratifying than hearing your conclusions challenged and improving them.

Matt was obviously a force in this movement behind the scenes. But publicly, he and the other alumni were keeping a very low profile. He introduced himself as the MFOL community outreach director, which was true, but not the half of it. Later, they would name him chief strategist, the role he had been gravitating toward from the start. Matt was twenty, oldest of the group, and many of them had been looking up to him for years.

Matt saw MFOL changing the gun debate by adopting a new strategy. "The messaging of both political parties is awful. I think most people in this country have a distaste for politicians because most politicians are scared of actually making the right choice. The right thing to do would be to pass universal background checks; the right thing to do would be to lift the ban on CDC research; the right thing to do would require some form of tracking the guns that are being trafficked in this country. I think it's really important that we're all artists, we're all communicators, because we're able to communicate this hurt with the nation. We just really know how to be serious and focused and also entertaining."

Matt had graduated two years earlier but flew back from film school in California immediately when it happened, to be with Ryan, and his freshman sister, Samantha, and all his theater friends. He ended up at Cameron's house very quickly. Just mentioning Samantha made him emotional. She was celebrating her birthday on Valentine's Day, but mourned two friends instead.

Matt had moved back in with his family, but hardly saw Sam, because he was at the office so late, like an absentee dad. So he had signed her out of school for an alleged doctor's appointment that morning, and taken her instead for comfort food and family time at Chick-fil-A. Their mom and aunt and grandma were all there, and David's family, whom they met for the first time. Kevin Hogg was quiet but sweet, with a wry sense of humor—not at all what you would picture for an FBI agent, or a navy pilot, for that matter. Rebecca was a hoot. That big group—everyone had gone through it in different ways. Most of them had been miles from the school, but they were all hurting. Cutting up with them was as comforting as the crispy fried chicken. Therapists could get annoying, forcing you back to the tragedy with their probing questions, but it came up naturally with that crowd, and everybody spilled. The empty desks seemed to haunt everyone. "[Samantha] was like, 'We don't know what to do with those desks,'" Matt said. "'Other periods, people probably sit there and they have no idea this desk is the one we all look at in our class.'"

And the bathrooms. So many kids were afraid to use the bathrooms. They kept triggering Samantha. "She says, 'Now when I go to the bathroom I think if I take a little longer to wash my hands maybe I'll survive if it happens again,'" Matt said. "Or, 'If I take the long way from lunch instead of the short way from lunch, will that make me stay alive or will I die because of those choices?'"

Then he shrugged it off and got silly again. Matt cracks himself up constantly—along with most everyone in his vicinity—but he got particularly giggly describing how he first met Cameron. Matt was a senior in drama club when Cameron first showed up as a freshman. It was the first meeting of the Improv Club, started by Matt's brother Ryan Deitsch, then a sophomore. "He did not know what he was going to do with the club," Matt said. "Should we do improv games or blah blah blah? And the TV teacher was the sponsor, and he said, 'You can run with it. You can do whatever.' He was literally improv-ing the entire experience."

Ryan held the intro meeting in the TV production

room, and all the kids who came were from drama club. Matt was kind of the elder statesman: president of TV production, vice president of the senior class, and founder and editor of the school's anonymous satire blog, *The Cold Beak*. Cameron was some scrawny freshman he'd never seen or heard of. "So we're in a skit and we're improv-ing and for some reason it's a date scene or something, and me and Cameron are on a date and the whole time—I had no idea who this kid is, this little shit—and he just keeps trying to kiss me!" Ballsy move for a straight freshman guy. Matt had thought he was the adventurous one. And this little upstart was playing in a different league. Matt loved it. He recruited Cam to write for *The Cold Beak*. "We've been friends ever since," Matt said.

Nine days until the march, Matt was looking way past it. He was not here to put on a show—though a powerful show of force would etch itself into the minds of every candidate, which was the horizon Matt had his eyes on: the midterms, midterms, midterms. And he was also looking beyond them. He knew they weren't going to win South Carolina or Texas or Tennessee. Not this year, or probably this decade. But Matt's children might have very different ideas about whom to elect there. Most of the MFOL kids would likely have kids of their own, and Matt hoped their children would thank them.

Their short-term strategy for earning that thanks was fueling this movement with some victories in the midterms. The long-term strategy was taking this issue out of the red-blue brawl.

Matt also understood already that the main impact his small band could have on the midterms was leveraging the thousands of young activists in the hundreds of new groups mushrooming across the country.

All the media could see right now was Washington, but Matt saw the future in those sibling marches. Each one was a trial by fire for a young group of activists. Most were neophytes beginning with nothing, trying to build an organization and stage an event in five weeks or much less. (Groups were still signing up.) What a surge of confidence when they pulled it off. MFOL had hoped to inspire dozens of these sibling marches. The count was over eight hundred, in every state and around the world. (The final domestic count would be 762.) "We just got our first African march, in one of the East African islands, starts with an 'M,'" Matt said.

"Mauritius?" I asked.

"Mauritius, yeah. Africa was the last one, because we had scientists in Antarctica saying they were going to officially put one together. So we're on every continent."

Matt was about to conduct another mandatory conference call with the 800-plus organizers. That was far too many to speak, so most were in listen-only mode. "We have to create a unified front," he said. "The people in power would like nothing more than for us to be diverted. And we cannot be diverted."

Matt corrected me when I called them the sister marches. "Sibling marches. Sister marches were the Women's March thing. We're not trying to completely rip off their branding." They were actually navigating their own branding issue. MFOL had been quietly inching away from the Never Again label, and Matt explained why. "We can't actually use that, because it's owned by the Anti-Defamation League. But we did get permission to use it through the march. We can use it for messaging, but we can't use it for our name." They chartered as March for Our Lives, and slowly worked it into their messaging. That was temporary, they confided. The march was a one-day event, so once it was over, they would permanently rebrand as Fight for Our Lives.

That never happened. They would tease the name on march day, by sprinkling it throughout their speeches.

But they were already reconsidering by then. Three names in two months was too many. And "march" had many connotations, so they kept it.

Two big movements had been percolating for years: the struggle to address urban gun violence, and the struggle to address mass shooters. MFOL's vision was to merge them. Matt thought that seemed obvious, but the media seemed oblivious to it. The whole team was talking about it relentlessly, in posts and in person—Berkeley, Baltimore, Chicago, Liberty City—but the media was obsessed with suburban white kids. That was Matt's biggest frustration with the entire experience thus far.

As he spoke about the messaging, he mentioned the writer's room again. I stopped him this time. "Writer's room?"

He chuckled. Did I think all this material was writing itself?

4

MFOL had broken all the rules of sustaining the national spotlight. For now. The media was notorious for having attention deficit disorder. It would go gaga for the march and then forget these kids the next day. What was their strategy for life after media?

You mean old media, Matt said. "We've already established our platform. We're on social media, we have these speaking engagements. I taught Emma how to use Twitter. She still gets things wrong. She's using the wrong terminology and she gets more impressions per hour than the president now." The network cameras had helped them amass their following, but their own cameras had greater pull now, he said. Ten million would watch the kids on *60 Minutes* that Sunday, but the group believed they beat that online every week. Emma was up to 1.2 million Twitter followers. David, Cameron, and Sarah Chadwick had another 1.1 million collectively, and the count was expanding fast. With the multiplier of retweets, a single hot meme could draw millions of impressions. Twitter had been their biggest platform, but they were pumping out clever, shareable content that could be customized to Twitter, Instagram, or Snapchat, and they were prepping a YouTube launch. "That's where our generation lives," Dylan Baierlein said the next day. Dylan had been the kid asking about the anime explosion. Dylan was MFOL's secret weapon online.

"What a lot of my generation does is basically come home from school, eat a snack, and watch whatever's in their subscription box from YouTube," David said. "That's how they get a lot of their information and build this into their daily routine."

A powerful platform requires two big elements: attract an audience, and satisfy them. Attracting was complete. Sustaining massive numbers meant great content. This group was born to meme. Every teen in America is now a content creator, churning out posts on Instagram and Snapchat—without a second thought, they would tell you, but actually employing tremendous thought. They have grown so skilled at it that it can seem effortless. The Columbine kids could have never done something like this. Several Columbine survivors went to Hollywood, and at least two of them created stellar films. But that was a decade or more down the road. The Parkland generation was prepared on day one. Some more than others. Most kids can amuse their friends online, but only a few are truly gifted. For most of the MFOL kids, content creation was a way of life.

"We're the communicators," David said. And they were communicating on two wavelengths—emotional and intellectual—which was the key to their appeal. "They're actors, they know like how to communicate human emotion," David said. "I'm news director, and I'm educated in this area from speech and debate." He excelled on the rational side.

MFOL had a deep bench. Cameron could also pull the heartstrings, Sarah Chadwick, Delaney Tarr, and later Matt on the head—but the power of Emma

González was her gift to pierce both organs simultaneously.

Everyone was worried about the cult of personality around Emma, though, especially Emma. And they rolled their eyes at the central tenets of the cult. "We have this celebrity culture that would love to say Emma is this trailblazing feminist hero," Matt said. "I've known her for a long time, and I'd say she's one of the more down-to-earth people I know. She does have this way of evoking emotion from just being an artist and being in spoken word." We discussed the power of her authenticity, and he asked, "Why is that rare?"

Reason and emotion were crucial. So was a third element: humor.

From first sight of him, I had a sense Dylan Baierlein played a big part in that. On my way out, I asked about that anime explosion. What was that about? He gleefully showed off the GIF he had found, and the meme he had assembled while I was talking to Matt. He stopped midsentence, with a concerned look. "Do you know what a meme is?"

I did.

OK. He plunged ahead—couldn't wait to show me what he was working on next.

I didn't want to risk the wrath of David, so we agreed

to meet there the next afternoon. He had class in the morning, then several MFOL meetings, but he could squeeze me in for an hour. It was late, and I picked up Indian takeout across the street.

5

I texted Dylan for the address the next morning, and he said he couldn't give it out. He knew I had just been there, but still. Thank God for the Indian food. Google Maps got me back that way.

Dylan was friendly and self-effacing. He had graduated Douglas the year prior, and described himself as "a five-foot-six scrawny white boy." He wore Ray-Ban prescription glasses, dyed his blond hair with Revlon brown-black, and spiked it with Axe Messy Look Flexible Paste. He was still squeezing in psychology classes at Florida Atlantic University, but treating MFOL as his full-time job, cranking out memes. Dylan called himself the memes man periodically over the next several months, and snickered every time.

Dylan didn't have a title, but he was the backbone of the content creation team. It came naturally. "I started memein' when I came out the womb," he said. At eighteen, Dylan had written short films, plays, monologues, comedy sketches, news packages, and was at work on a musical when the shooting put a stop to all that. He had collaborated with the other MFOL kids on most of it. Everything Dylan was doing now was collaborative. Even with most of the team gone, the conference room buzzed with an *SNL* writers' room vibe.

One of Dylan's favorite pre-Valentine's projects had been *The Cold Beak*, an anonymous, satirical version of MSD's school paper, *The Eagle Eye*. Matt Deitsch created and edited it, and Cameron, who was then a freshman, was his chief writing partner. Dylan, Ryan Deitsch, and Alex Wind were regular contributors. It started on Instagram but migrated across platforms, and Matt estimated it peaked at around three thousand readers a day. The school administration was not amused. "We actually had encrypted email and hidden identities, because we were threatened to be kicked out of our clubs if they found out who was writing it," Matt said. "I was the vice president of the honor society for journalism and they had me read a memo saying that anyone who was in *The Cold Beak* would get kicked out of the honor society. And it was me reading the memo, and I was like, I'm the founder of it." It started getting scary, but all the more fun. Best parody of the whole endeavor, and they could never use it.

Matt said *The Cold Beak* really taught a lot of them how to reach an audience. And how to collaborate. "A lot of what people liked about us was we never spoke down to our audience," he said. "We never made fun of their intelligence. And that's the same with what we're doing now." They were gobsmacked by much of the NRA's message machine, and satire was still their instinctive response.

Dylan took over as *Beak* editor the next year, but the heat was getting fierce. The administration was going hard-core trying to identify them, and they had mined the parody vein pretty well already. The *Beak* also taught them that even great material was finite. More fun to reinvent anyway. They shut it down.

MFOL's mission now was to keep their audience captivated. Constant reinvention on the content side was key. "We will soon be starting to create YouTube content," Dylan said. "We're working on the logistics. I'm writing scripts and whatnot already." They were planning short videos, two to five minutes max—what kids would actually watch and enjoy. He had a range of topics in mind, political and educational, like the history of gun violence, and how to register to vote. Always, always lighthearted, though. "We don't want to lose sight of our actual selves and our youth." People were always clamoring for peeks backstage, so he was constantly filming, creating, meeting, everything. He would definitely have his camera rolling backstage at the march.

At first blush, they felt like a group that would really push the boundaries on outrageous posts. Quite the opposite—that was my biggest surprise. They were brash and bold in the brainstorming phase, cautious in the editing room. They had to be. One big error could set them back. They were in this for the long haul.

Every member had veto power, and they wielded it liberally. Veto power? They were reviewing each other's tweets? Not every tweet, Dylan said, but the big stuff: their popular memes, the ones getting hundreds of thousands of retweets, everything coming out of the writer's room. For such a playful group, they were very stern about the rules. Dylan had made four memes that could have been viral but released only two, because the other two were harshly satirical. "And the media yells at us when we're laughing."

"Everything we do, everything we put out there, is vetted through all of us," he said. "Somebody has an idea for a tweet, they type it out, they send it to everybody else and we say, 'That's good!' or 'Change this thing.'"

There was a lot of spitballing. "Somebody will say something, and if even one person on the other side of the room says, 'I like that!' Boom!" Dylan said. Connection. "If you were watching that, you'd think, 'OK, they liked that, but nobody jumped on that idea.' No, those two people have now had a silent agreement where they are going to work together on that, and make it real. And then it happens." Most of them had been collaborating that way for years, so the unspoken language was already set. The new kids brought fresh talent. David was wonkish and acerbic, so when they needed a pit bull, they had their man. Sarah Chadwick was great that way, too. "Emma is wonderful at writing emotional speeches and getting the crowd on her side and cheered and pumped," Dylan said. Some of them were talented conceptually, others from TV and film production could turn ideas into quality video fast. And someone on the team always had access to the equipment they needed, and the apps. "Everyone has a different niche and the entire movement needs all of them," Dylan said. "So we're all working in tandem to make sure that the tones that are needed are used."

Their basic rules were simple: no profanity, no violence—actual, symbolic, or implied—and no ad hominem attacks. MLK's six principles had been helpful. Personal digs are cheap, dirty, and counterproductive. Chiding politicians was the trickiest to navigate: they wanted to call out bad behavior quick and hard, but without getting personal or too derisive, especially with Republicans. They were battling adversaries, not enemies. Matt Deitsch stressed that point repeatedly that week. He took ahold of his dog tags at one point to demonstrate how dear the ideas were—he kept them literally dangling over his heart. He was wearing number 6 that day, but number 3 kept coming up in our conversations: "Nonviolence seeks to defeat injustice, not people."

They pulled the plug on one meme showing a prominent politician flailing in a defense of gun laws on national TV. Then they edited a short montage of his awkward moments, and overlaid the theme music from *Curb Your Enthusiasm*. Very funny, but too mean. He let me watch the video after I agreed not to divulge the politician—that would just be a passive-aggressive way of still ridiculing him. It was very funny, but surprisingly mild. I'd seen much worse on the Web that afternoon. Yeah, he said: that's a low bar.

Even rejected memes could be useful: giggling at them on the group thread was great for morale. "These guys are some of my closest friends and they're going through a lot," Dylan said. "That's why I came here. Of course the movement is incredibly important to me, and the change in the nation is the overarching goal. But personally, I just want to make sure my friends are all right. Make sure my friends are smiling."

Dylan picked out two of their most successful memes, and walked me through how they developed, from conception to viral explosion. Their biggest to that point, their hourglass parody of the NRA, started as a joke. "We saw the hourglass video that Dana Loesch made, and we thought it was hilarious," Dylan said. "The next day, we were joking about it"—meaning by group text, of course. "It was just me jokingly being like, 'So we're writing like a spoof of it, right?' And everybody was like, 'Yeah that's hilarious.' And I was like, 'OK, I'm writing it!' And then Emma González was like, 'No, that's a bad idea.'"

All night he kept thinking, *I've got to write that parody! That would make such a great parody!* So he wrote it anyway. He thought the script might win her over. Worst case, he'd make them laugh.

"And then Emma read the script and was like, 'Wait, I love it! We're going to make it!'" he said. "So jokes happen, people realize that within that joke there is an actual great idea, and then it comes to fruition. We say what comes to mind, and some things are shot down and some things are picked up. And when it happens, it's just lightning fast."

The hourglass meme was really fast. Dylan recruited Ryan to film it and Sarah Chadwick as the talent, because it fit her fiery personality. She also had a big Twitter following, nearly 300,000, who relished her caustic tweets. Ryan was a TV production student, so he had great cameras, a boom mic, lights, and reflectors. They collected all the equipment from his house and filmed the clip in the office. Emma manned the boom. They edited it on Ryan's laptop and Sarah tweeted it. From script approval to posting took only a couple of hours. The clip quickly racked up 1.2 million views.

Their "Enough Is Enough" meme came together even more easily. Just that week, the NRA tweeted a close-up picture of a gleaming AR-15 with the text "I'll control my own guns, thank you." It was the one-month anniversary of the shooting, and the kids were livid. "Why do you think that's a good idea?" Dylan said. "We have to do a rebuttal. Something, anything. So I said to the group chat, 'Can you guys send me emotional, powerful pictures?'" He got a boatload of images, and picked one showing a protester holding up a sign reading ENOUGH IS ENOUGH. Dylan sent that back to the group and said he was working on a parody of the gun tweet. "Nobody said, 'No, that's a bad idea,'" he said. "Nobody necessarily said, 'That's a great idea!' but if you don't get a no, you take it as a yes."

Dylan described the rest of his process as "so not professionally done." He uploaded the picture to Snapchat on his phone and typed in his reply caption: "We'll control our own lives, thank you." He saved the Snapchat, dumped it into the Photoshop Express app on his phone, and then added the March for Our Lives logo. That failed to save, since it's a premium option and he was using the free version of Photoshop Express. So he took a screenshot, cropped his phone's border clutter, and discovered that the image now looked too blurry. So he uploaded *that* one into Instagram, sharpened it, took a screenshot of that, cropped it again, and texted the improved shot to the group chat. They loved it.

"Who wants to post it?" he asked.

Sarah and Cameron. Sarah drew 722 retweets and 4,878 likes. Cameron got 1,238 retweets and 6,565 likes.

From first spotting the offensive tweet to posting the rebuttal and multiple team members tweeting it took about an hour, Dylan said. Quick and dirty, and it looked fine. They needed to stay nimble to match the NRA beat for beat, without getting diverted from their own message. And without forgetting to have fun.

"It's funny," Dylan said. "If you came to one of our meetings and watched us and listened to us, you would think, 'Nothing is getting done!' But amidst this chaos and nonsense, somehow we are getting it done in our own way. I don't know why it works, I don't know how it works—but it does. And it's incredible."

6

The MFOL office had a brief life. The group had let a few other media outlets in, and that didn't work out well. *Time* ran a cover story that omitted the location but included several revealing clues. And a TV crew used an outside shot that David believes was the final straw. "I saw them taking the shot and I told them not to use it and to delete it and they were like, 'OK, we will,'" he said. "The one shot they used was that. Within twelve hours of the documentary airing, the Nazis, because I won't call them the alt-Right, basically found where our office is, based off a door handle, had a hundred pizzas sent in my name, had death threats sent there. We all had to leave."

They worked from their homes again for quite a while, without a good meeting spot. Months later, they got a new office. No press this time.

13

Harvard

1

Four days to go, they took a detour to Harvard for two of them. It was an inconvenient time, but a hell of an opportunity: a crash course on their primary objective, not just from Harvard, but the guy who specialized in their target cohort. The diversion seemed crazy to me, because I still didn't understand. If it had come the first week of November, they would have taken a rain check. The midterms were the mission, not the march.

They came for a two-day seminar on young Americans' attitudes toward politics, led by an authority on that topic: John Della Volpe, director of polling at Harvard's Kennedy School Institute of Politics. The seminar was packed with concepts, strategies, and data, but one paramount idea: "Young Americans vote when they believe their efforts have tangible results."

That was the headline of the most important slide in a presentation titled "7 Things Everyone Should Know About Young Americans in 2018." That's the whole ball game with young voters, Della Volpe said—with *potential* young voters, because so few of them vote. And that's why they don't vote. The data demonstrates that overwhelmingly, he said. Because they don't see tangible results from politics. They roll their eyes at adult fascination with a process totally unrelated to their lives. You can drive canvassers weary trying to register them; you can cajole them on Snapchat and Instagram; you can rock the vote until their ears bleed—and all that is necessary but woefully insufficient, Della Volpe said. You're never going to get them to vote until you make that direct connection to their lives.

And that usually fails, Della Volpe told the MFOL kids. Most of the things most politicians run on are just not this demographic's prime concerns. That was the bad news. The good news was that every now and then, perhaps once in a generation, that changed. And it was changing now, he said. A companion slide laid it out in huge block letters filling the entire screen:

**Once-in-a-generation
attitudinal shifts about [the]
efficacy of political
engagement [are] now underway**

For two decades, the Harvard institute had been polling young voters (under thirty) on the key question: Does political involvement have any tangible results? The results were generally miserable—with two exceptions: immediately after 9/11, and immediately after the inauguration of President Trump. The Trump administration woke the Parkland generation up. Young people saw exactly what elections could do to them, and they were overwhelmingly displeased. Pollsters tend to focus on the displeasure—a president's approval rating. That's the lesser indicator, Della Volpe said. It was the recognition that politics affects them, directly—that was the radical change.

After 9/11, when young voters saw the connection, they voted more—particularly when someone reached out to them directly, Della Volpe said. It was that one-two combination that's required: demonstrating that voting matters, and then a candidate emerging who can win them over. And then that candidate has to do the groundwork: create a powerhouse operation to reach this group and turn voting into a habit. So all that canvassing the MFOL kids were revving up, that mattered, too. You still have to find the kids, sign them up, and cajole them—*after* you demonstrate why they should.

That latter point was a huge and overlooked lesson of the Obama campaign, Della Volpe said. Young voter turnout increased in 2008 and 2012 because Obama was on the ticket, and because his team went out and found them. Many political scientists have written off the Obama increases as fairly modest, but they are missing a huge point, Della Volpe said. Young turnout increased dramatically in the so-called battleground states, where the election was contested, and where the Obama campaigns concentrated most of their organizing to reach young people. Because that was fewer than a dozen states, the impact is diluted if you just look at national numbers, he said. It's actually a one-two-three punch that's required: convince young voters politics matters, field candidates who address their concerns, and then do the grunt work to get to them.

Della Volpe shared an anecdote that surprised me—and explained an unusual argument I heard from the kids repeatedly in the three months after they met with him. Della Volpe had been talking to a teenager, asking whether gun control would be a major factor in his first vote. "And he said to me, 'Well, I don't think guns are on the ballot,'" Della Volpe said. "I said I could make the case that they are on the ballot in every city and town across America, because every member of Congress is up for reelection." To take full advantage of the Parkland kids, Della Volpe pointed out, voters should make it their business to know where every member of Congress stands on the Parkland agenda. "It took me a couple of minutes to kind of make that case to a first-time voter," he said. "That's the kind of effort it's going to take in order to really take full advantage of the Parkland kids."

I had heard the Parkland kids hammer that point repeatedly and I had found it a little odd. Didn't it go without saying? No. For a lot of new voters and nonvoters it did not. Young voters have long been a sleeping giant of American politics, because most of them stay home. If they ever turned out in percentages to match their older counterparts, they could swing many elections. And over the past year, young people had been turning out to vote in special elections. Della Volpe said there were signs that year really could be different. The MFOL movement came at exactly the right political moment. "The attitudinal shift has already happened," Della Volpe said. MFOL was tapping into an energy that was already boiling on Valentine's Day. It was waiting to be activated. MFOL stepped up.

Della Volpe said Harvard's research indicates that young voters were 50 percent more likely to say politics matters than they were pre-Trump. Democrats were particularly charged up. In the spring of 2018, Della Volpe found that the number of registered Democrats between the ages of eighteen and twenty-nine who said they intended to vote surged to 51 percent, from just 28 percent in 2014. On the Republican side, the number rose from 31 to 36 percent.

The Parkland kids were having a major impact—building on the energy already in play.

Della Volpe was impressed that these kids understood they had launched a generational campaign. Even if they devoted their lives to the fight, ultimately they would hand the baton to kids who had not yet been born. They also understood that they had to motivate people, especially young people, to vote.

The public has bought into the NRA's air of invincibility and won't rally behind gun safety candidates because it doesn't believe they can win. Most of the public refuses to push their candidates too far into the gun debate. Most Democrats, and lots of moderate and even conservative legislators, back the MFOL agenda.

But they won't go near gun legislation. They don't want to vote on it, and you'll rarely hear it in a stump speech, almost never in a campaign ad.

"You have to begin to slowly build momentum because most voters don't have a lot of faith in anyone outmaneuvering the NRA," Della Volpe said. "You need to believe there's an opportunity that you can win. It gives voters, especially young voters, faith. And the Parkland students, they've had more success already than many others have in many years. And I believe that has to be part of their narrative. 'We've done this, we've done that: help us take it to the next level.'" Jackie Corin had come to the same conclusion by day two.

2

An entourage of journalists, academics, activists, and fans followed this story with fascination. Most experienced the kids electronically first. And the burning questions once they finally got to spend a day or two with them in person were always: Are these kids real? Are they the same in person as they are online? Or is that all rehearsed or manufactured? Can they spout all those statistics or sling those clever zingers on the fly? Yes, yes, no, yes. Most came away stunned that the kids were even more poised, informed, and charismatic in person. Their TV/Twitter personalities were authentic, but wildly incomplete.

Of all the people I discussed them with, the one who captured them best was Della Volpe. He encountered groups of the MFOL kids at several conferences throughout the year, as well as the Harvard seminar. That began with a breakfast at Harvard's central dining hall. "One minute they're like any other fifteen-, sixteen-, seventeen-year-olds—being goofy, playing with their food," he said. "And then, they step outside and we have a conversation and they turned into some of the most inspirational leaders in the world today."

Della Volpe found Emma entrancing, but not at first. He sat beside her at breakfast, and his first big impression was "What was she doing with her eggs? She put two packs of mayonnaise on her eggs, which I found really odd." She told him how excited she was to be heading to New College of Florida in Sarasota in the fall. He said she described it as small and kind of hippie-like and inexpensive enough for her to afford. "She looked forward to sitting under a tree and reading and hanging out and being a kid," he said. Ordinary. And then she turned to business, and she seized the room. And held it.

As one of the movement's brightest stars, Emma projects determination, authenticity, and candor through any screen—just as she would when she'd stare silently into the lens for four and a half minutes and bring the house down at the DC march. But it's such a different vibe in person, where she exudes a sense of tranquility. Others see her as absorbing anxiety so that all the tension in the room fades. "A sense of calmness," Volpe said.

The one-two combination of the head and the heart was especially powerful in person. Della Volpe marveled at their symbiotic relationship at the National Conference of Mayors a few months later. Alfonso went first. That was vital. He painted a portrait of ordinary life for a fifteen-year-old in America: homework, silly fights, and friendships—and a gunman down the hallway. "I came home, I told my friends," Della Volpe said. "About sixty kids in a ten-foot closet with a seven-foot wall, cuddling with them, and crying, and then the look on his friend's face, she knew she was going to die. I get chills just thinking about it. I had never had anyone describe what it was like to have a gunman run around the hallway, what it's like to see one of your best friends die. Cool, composed, caring." The room was captivated, he said. "And then David takes it bigger: 'OK now, America. This is what we need to do about it.'"

Della Volpe observes politicians for a living. He sees hundreds of speeches a year and couldn't recall a more powerful combination of speakers in the past several decades. He'd wondered if they had choreographed it that way, so I asked them later, and they had a good laugh. They were just thrown together that day, but they realized Alfonso had to lead off: heart first, then head. Reignite the imperative to act, and then map out how we get there.

14
March for Their Lives

1

Daniel Duff said it was going to be huge. Huge? What did that mean? He had no idea, really, but expected it to feel huge. A lot had been made about all the celebrities coming, but Daniel had no interest in that. I asked him about it anyway, when he got to DC the night before—anyone he wanted to meet?

Nah. So not what this was about. But then he thought it over and changed his mind. George Clooney would be cool. Daniel liked his directing and acting, and what an impact he'd had on their movement, opening his wallet so publicly, so fast. A talented artist who also had their back. Yeah, Clooney would be pretty cool. George. Ha-ha. If he came. Maybe Amal too.

The team stayed together at the same hotel. Wake-up time was reasonable, around seven. Most were milling about the lobby sleepily at eight. Big-name allies were also there, and Gabby Giffords and Mark Kelly looked wide awake. Cameron was all smiles as always, and came over to hug Daniel and his brother Brendan and crack jokes. Emma glided by with David, looking reserved and meek, as though she were physically retreating into her baggy white March for Our Lives long-sleeved T-shirt. Her jeans were ripped aggressively, and she slung a heavy black backpack over both shoulders with PEACE WARRIORS emblazoned on the straps. Her trademark scalp was hidden under a slouchy gray beanie, with a Twitter logo apparently, or something close.

Daniel was giddier than I've ever seen him. This might literally be the biggest day of his life, he said. Seemed kind of early. But who knows? Most of the MFOL team were juniors or seniors. Some would surely keep up the fight from college, some might move on. Eventually, the torch would pass. To whom, to do what—who knows?

Daniel had come with his family, who said they were bagels people, so we hit the Bagels Etc. across the street. Daniel's dad and brothers relived the horror of

Valentine's Day, frantically texting each other about the ominous signs. Brendan looked right at Daniel. "I was so terrified," he said.

After breakfast, Daniel was supposed to rendezvous with his friend Ryan Servaites, another Douglas freshman. They were supposed to be filmed by a documentary crew, but the streets were swelling fast, and it was getting hard to move. They were also running out of time. Daniel and Brendan had an MFOL team meeting at a steakhouse until the march. They would try to film sometime that afternoon.

2

Two hours to showtime, and Pennsylvania Avenue was already jammed. The stage straddled the entire avenue, about fifty feet wide and forty feet high, flanked by massive Jumbotrons. It was lit by eight 4,000-watt lighting towers, and built by over a dozen mast-and-boom forklifts, scissor lifts, and manlift jibs, rising up to fifty-five feet high. Five strategically placed banners with the massive MARCH FOR OUR LIVES logo ensured it would appear in every shot: directly beneath each Jumbotron, angled on both sides of the performance area, and a modified version above the width of the stage, with extra stick figures over the Jumbotrons, so the full name would appear above a tight shot of the performance. They had thought about this.

Metal barricades walled off a few levels of VIP access near the stage. Celebrities mixed among them, but it was mostly students, hundreds of them, from local schools and bused in from around the country. They carried hand-painted signs like WE WILL VOTE, WE WILL RISE; THE SMALLEST COFFINS ARE THE HEAVIEST; and BAN ASSAULT WEAPONS OR WE WILL BAN YOU; and many wore big orange *Price Is Right*–style price tags reading $1.05. Organizers were distributing them, and the MFOL website had a feature to print one out, and invited kids to create their own.

Early revelers were bopping to tunes thumping out of two 7,000-pound sound towers, powered by two massive generators cranking out 220,000 watts. The audio carried clearly for the three-quarters of a mile to Twelfth Street, thanks to eighteen more Jumbotrons along the route, plus seven additional sound delay towers, each one powered by a 70,000 watt generator. Free water bottles were everywhere, a hundred and twenty pallets of them, stacked six cases high. About 1,900 hundred Porta Potties were arranged in clusters stretching along Jefferson Drive to Seventh Street, and Madison Drive to Twelfth.

As I walked Pennsylvania Avenue, the early arriv-

als were enthusiastic but jittery. They were all true believers at that hour, and fear was rampant that the kids
had made a strategic blunder. One person after another
told me their friends had stayed home to attend local
marches. Would that drain their force? All the coverage would hinge on the number of people who turned
out in Washington. No one would remember how many
people showed up in Denver or Boise or Birmingham.

A large press area was set up stage right to maximize
coverage. In addition to two special access areas—the
interview tent and a riser for cameras—there was a
large roaming area with an assortment of views, extra
monitors, and speakers, and a filing tent set up like
a makeshift office, with monitors so you could watch
the event and file a story without ever peeking outside.
They had high-speed Wi-Fi, but forgot to post the
password, and it remained a mystery for much of the
morning.

My biggest surprise in the press area was a nervous
young girl with braces, oversize glasses, and a long
brown ponytail. She was one of us, though. A reporter's notebook protruded from her puffy black winter
jacket, and the 35 millimeter Cannon camera around
her neck looked heavy enough to topple her over. It
had telephoto lenses two to three times the length of

her slim fingers. Half the pink polish was worn from her nails.

I introduced myself. My hand swallowed hers, but her shake was firm, voice confident. She was Julia Walker, reporting for the *Viking Saga* at East Lyme High School in Connecticut. Credentialing had been crazy, I said. How did she manage, when did she start?

"Well, today I was in the crowd and I looked in my camera bag and I found a press pass," Julia said. She dug it out: just a beat-up laminated green card stamped PRESS PASS. It said "Go Vikes!" beneath a Norse logo, and it named the school and the paper, but not her. But she was getting ahead of herself. When she first saw the media area, she had tried to coax the guard with moxie alone. "They said, 'No, you're not allowed to come in.'" she said. "But I looked and I found this and I thought, 'This might work.' And then they let me in."

I was amazed. Julia was a sophomore, but could easily pass for middle school. It was her first year writing for the *Viking Saga*, and she had never operated a camera like that before, but her teacher offered to lend it, and when would she get a chance like this?

"I came here with my mom because we wanted to march, but also because as a journalist I feel like it's important to spread awareness about everything happening," she said. "I mean, no one should be scared to go to school every day. And it's very inspiring. I feel like this will be in history."

She was missing her mom right now, thinking about going back to find her. I offered to sneak her into the interview tent instead. Her eyes widened. Could I do that? I explained the goofy system they had rigged, pasting a tiny red dot to my badge for interview access, red for the riser, but they were barely noticeable, and the guard was mainly going by face. Just stick close, avoid eye contact, and move with a purpose, I said. If anyone asks, you're with me.

She looked terrified but exhilarated. I said we should head over early and brainstorm some questions, did she want help? Of course, she said. But as I nodded toward the tent, I noticed activity. "They're early," I said. "Let's go!"

She froze there, on the verge of tears. "I don't have any questions!"

"That's OK," I said. I didn't have mine ready either. "Come on!"

I nodded at the guard, he opened the gate, and she whisked in behind me without eye contact or incident. She was an unexpected asset, because I'm terrible with names and hadn't met some of the MFOL kids, and she seemed to know them all by sight. She gasped as each one entered, and whispered their names. Sometimes she was overcome, and shouted: "That's Delaney Tarr!"

The kids came through fast, and the goofy system the PR team had organized disintegrated immediately. They had taped a piece of letter paper with each media outlet's name on the concrete floor, which grew invisible beneath us once the tent filled. They made two rows, with cameras in front to get the shots and reporters behind to ask questions. But many of the kids had not been briefed, and answered the camera operators' questions along the front line and moved on. We started jostling up to the front to get to them, and I lost Julia briefly in the chaos. I spotted her panicking, waved her over, and nudged her to jump in with a question.

"How are you coming up with them?" she whispered.

"Just wing it. What have you been wondering?"

Julia was starting to scribble some ideas when Emma González bounced in. She chatted effortlessly with reporters while mouthing the lyrics to the song pulsing in. A distraught PR person felt the surge around Emma, and the gravitational thrust of everybody in that direction, and suddenly took control. "Organize yourself into small groups!" she ordered, which was a welcome idea, and we quickly grouped up. I landed with three other reporters—lost Julia again—and the PR person allotted us three minutes. As we squeezed in, Emma was finishing up with the last group, answering whether politicians had seemed receptive to them the past month.

"Not really. Some really, really small baby steps. Someone said it was like they tried to take a giant leap forward and then tripped and fell really bad. This was stuff that should've just been there already."

I asked her about Jackie's assessment, that it would take years, like the civil rights movement.

"Probably. Probably going to be years. And like at this point, I don't know if I mind, because like nothing that's worth it is easy. So why would this be easy? We're going against the largest gun lobby in America. We could very well die trying to do this, but we could very well die not trying to do this, so why not die for something rather than for nothing?"

Die trying? That unnerved me, and I asked what she meant.

"We could get shot by someone who's like, 'Don't take away my guns!' Which is not what we're trying to do. We're not trying to take away anybody's guns, but they misconstrue our message because they're afraid of this becoming a slippery slope. They're afraid of us because we have a voice now."

A reporter asked about Emma's expectations, and the PR person got angry that we were over quota and shouted as she tried to move Emma along: "Everyone back up!" But Emma was suddenly distracted, gliding over the concrete, sliding her hips to a Latin rhythm starting up on the massive sound system. She giggled that she and Sarah Chadwick had added Celia Cruz to the playlist, and what a bolt of joy for it to fill the air. She was eighteen—the right song could change everything. She danced back to the reporter who had asked about expectations, looked her right in the eye, and said, "My expectations just shot up!"

She apologized to another reporter who had tried to ask something while she'd gotten lost in the song. He repeated it: What was it like to be an inspiration?

"Why not inspire each other?" Emma asked.

After the last MFOL kid came and went, I reunited with Julia, who was glowing. "You're a real journalist now," I said. Most high school reporters were watching the stage show back home on TV. She had interviewed Sofie Whitney, Delaney Tarr, and Emma González—because she got her butt down there and had the courage to bluff her way in. "You've got to just keep trying," I said. "Anytime somebody says no, treat no as a maybe."

"I feel like that's exactly what the kids from Parkland are doing right now," Julia said. "They're being told no by the most powerful people, the president of the United States, but they keep pushing to get here."

Wow. Best insight of the day. These kids were all seeing things with different eyes.

3

Andra Day kicked off the show with a stirring performance of "Rise Up"—already powerful, but took on a whole new meaning. David Hogg broke with the norm to dress formally, with one of the $1.05 price tags clipped to his suit lapel. He gleefully explained the mystery to the crowd. They'd calculated the NRA's donations to Marco Rubio, and divided it by the number of students in Florida. That's how much each kid was worth to their senator, David said. $1.05.

The speeches were generally impressive, though most of the kids seemed to have written a tagline, and repeated it several times, à la "We call BS." None would catch on. The speakers were all kids, and some of the scene-stealers were exceptionally young. Jackie Corin gave an uplifting speech, then said she had someone special to introduce, and returned with Martin Luther King Jr.'s ten-year-old granddaughter, Yolanda Renee

King. Not all King's progeny inherited his oratorical skills, but afterward, Daniel Duff and Ryan Servaites agreed she was easily the second-most-powerful speaker. "She really is carrying on the voice and the legacy," Ryan said. And for that family to lend that name to their movement—they were both kind of awed.

"I know for a fact that if Martin Luther King were still alive, he would be here right now," Daniel said. "And very proud of her."

Daniel wasn't there for the celebrities, but had to admit it was fun meeting some. And they were everywhere backstage and in the VIP lounge. Some older lady in a tweed coat and knit cap was getting a ton of attention, so Daniel took a selfie with her, and then my photographer asked if he knew who she was.

Not really. Actually, not a clue.

"That's Cher."

"Oh my god, Cher!" Daniel yelled. He had just met Cher! Cher was in his phone.

He knew *of* Cher, he told me later, as an entity, not as a person.

Ryan Servaites wasn't on the MFOL team, so he didn't get Daniel's all-access pass. So Daniel mostly gave up that access. He made quick trips backstage to check in with his MFOL friends, but for the most part returned to hang with Ryan. George and Amal Clooney wound up next to them. Daniel and Ryan were intimidated, but the Clooneys kept making small talk, and the boys came around. The four spent most of the show together.

The Peace Warriors Alex and D'Angelo made a big impression. They took the stage together in blue MFOL hoodies, their mouths sealed in neon duct tape. D'Angelo stripped his off. "We are survivors of a cruel and silent nation," he said. "For we are survivors not only of gun violence, but of silence. For we are survivors of the erratic productions of poverty. We are the survivors of unjust policies and practices upheld by our Senate. We are survivors of lack of resources within our schools. We are survivors of social, emotional, and physical harm."

Delaney Tarr demonstrated how comfortable she had grown as a public figure when her speech flew off the podium. She calmly walked over, picked it up, and resumed her speech with a smile. She had nothing on her classmate Sam Fuentes, who threw up in the middle of her impassioned speech. Two minutes in, near the climax of her poem "Enough," she shouted, "It's as if we need permission to ask our friends not to die!" But she began to falter on the next line: "Lawmakers and politicians will scream guns are not the issue, but can't look me in the eye." She tried to choke it back, but realized it was hopeless, turned her back, and let it rip. There were gasps, brief confusion, then a big round of supportive cheers that quickly died down. CNN cut away to crowd shots—distressed moms, shaking their heads, unsure whether to clap or cheer. It took nearly a minute for Sam to recover. Kids started chanting "Enough is enough!" Sam returned to the podium with a hearty laugh, and shouted, "I just threw up on international television, and it feels great!" Tyra Hemans rubbed her back tenderly at first, and then pumped her fist at the end of that line. Sam continued full bore: "We're not asking for a ban, we're asking for compromise. Forget your size and colors, let's save one another."

Some of the older Sandy Hook survivors, now in high school, recounted their horror in 2012. At the worst of it, they'd drawn tremendous solace from a simple act of solidarity, when Columbine survivors sent a banner encouraging them. Then they unfurled their own banner with their school logo, reading "Newtown High School stands with Stoneman Douglas" over a huge red ribbon. Messages had been handwritten in a rainbow of colors.

Eleven-year-old Naomi Wadler had beaten back a month of obstacles to reach that stage. In February, she began organizing the walkout at George Mason Elementary School in Alexandria, Virginia, where she was in fifth grade. Her principal's staff were opposing it, out of safety concerns on the school lawn. *Were they safe inside?* Naomi asked. She fought for her proposal at a town hall organized by her congressman. "How will we be safe in our own classrooms in the world we live in now when it's OK for someone to walk into a store with an expired ID and buy an assault rifle?" she asked. She won that day, and sixty students participated. Naomi also insisted they honor the Parkland kids, and urban kids dying as well. Seventeen minutes was extended to eighteen, to recognize an African American girl gunned down in Alabama that week.

Naomi brought the same passion and confidence to the MFOL stage. She electrified the crowd. She also distilled a theme repeated throughout the rally. "I am here today to acknowledge and represent the African American girls whose stories don't make the front page of every national newspaper. I represent the African American women who are victims of gun violence, who are simply statistics instead of vibrant, beautiful girls full of potential."

Shortly before three, Emma González took the stage and stole the show. She had put on the self-embroidered bomber jacket, and had shed the slouchy beanie to bare her signature scalp. She gave a short, fiery speech, recited the seventeen names, and then went silent. She looked straight ahead, began to grimace, fought back tears, lost that battle, and let them stream. She didn't even wipe them off this time. The camera zoomed in and projected her face on the Jumbotrons—fifteen feet high, so the hundreds of thousands there, and millions tuned to laptops, phones, and TVs, could watch every quiver. It was spellbinding. She continued to hold it, and the crowd stood silent, awed. But as the minutes passed, people grew nervous: *Was this intentional? Was she fighting to speak? Having a breakdown?* Some kids in the crowd decided to "help," and started a chant: "Never again! Never again!" The bulk of the crowd knew better, and it died down. A sea of moms—so many moms that day—stood transfixed. Emma suspended that crowd for four and a half minutes that way, then leaned back into the microphone to explain: "Since the time that I came out here, it has been six minutes and twenty seconds. Fight for your lives before it's someone else's job."

4

Two questions had murmured through the crowd, and the media tent, all morning: Would a massive crowd materialize, and could Emma possibly live up to her own hype? That "We Call BS" speech seemed sui generis. How could she compete with that? Had she found an even better line, could she wow the crowd without one? Or would she prove a one-hit wonder—the perfect alchemy of the moment, never to be repeated in her lifetime? (Yes, of course reporters are that catty. But civilians were wondering aloud too.)

She had not just matched We Call BS, she had blown it out of the water. I watched the speech with my colleague and mentor Joan Walsh, now a CNN analyst and a writer for *The Nation*, whose story that night ran under the headline, "6 Minutes and 20 Seconds That Could Change the World." Would it? I wondered. I was pretty sure of one thing, though. For the hopeful gathered in Washington that day, this was the Emma we would carry for the rest of our lives.

But not everybody saw it that way. Joan and I had moved down to the railing along the edge of the press area, to watch Emma with the rest of the crowd. Debbi Schapiro, a Parkland resident and substitute teacher, stood beside us, and deep into the silence, she shook her head and murmured, "This is too much responsibility for these kids."

I was aghast. Emma had decided it was exactly enough. Why deprive her of the agency to make her own brutal choices? My cheeks were soaked, it was hard to watch, but I saw a young woman radiating power. Emma was galvanizing a country like no man or woman, pope or president. And this well-wisher was just snatching it away. Adult reaction—maybe adults were the problem. I pictured Emma's friends overhearing that. They were so sick of hearing that stuff. David Hogg said it day one: If adults had stepped up, they wouldn't have to. And their friends would still be alive.

But I was torn. Schapiro saw a teenage girl breaking down in public. I saw that as the point, and felt pride and awe for Emma, not fear. She seemed so fearless whenever she spoke to me. Just a few hours earlier, she had told us she was prepared to die. That rattled me. This, she seemed capable of handling. But was she? Why was I so sure?

I remembered a story Linda Mauser had told me ten years after losing her son, Daniel, at Columbine. She was having her teeth cleaned and began sobbing uncontrollably in her dental hygienist's chair. The woman pulled back her instrument, and Linda apologized for disrupting the cleaning and failing to floss. "My child died! I'm sorry, I just didn't feel like flossing." The hygienist apologized, asked if it was recent, and didn't hide her incredulity at the ten years. "When your child dies, it's always recent!" Linda snapped.

I think about that story often. It was eye opening but humbling. I would have hidden it better than the dental hygienist, but after ten years, I still didn't grasp the immediacy of her pain. I have no kids. I'll never see this through Dad's eyes, or Mom's. So I watched the end of Emma's silent speech trying to envision Patricia Oliver taking it in, or Andrew Pollack, Jennifer Guttenberg, Ryan Petty, all the moms and dads of the victims and the survivors. When Natalie Weiss had described Cameron calling to say "active shooter," I'd gasped and said that must be the worst thing a mom could hear. Natalie cast her eyes down and said very quietly, "Second worst."

So I carried Schapiro's warning with me through the spring, summer, and fall. I heard it so many times, as I saw the kids teeter on the edge, or what I feared might be the edge—because that's the tricky part. Trauma is unpredictable. It lurks for months or years, and can take you down in an instant. Debilitating depression can follow, or worse. Sometimes the cliff comes with warning signs. Other times, other kids dance along the edge oblivious, until the moment they career off.

In Joan Walsh's story, she also described Schapiro's gush of relief when Emma broke her silence. "It was phenomenal; it went straight to the heart," Schapiro said. "We are a broken community. One that is going to band together. But we are truly broken."

5

Emma closed out the rally. Daniel and Ryan bounded out gleefully, running toward the Capitol to meet up with the documentary film crew. Traffic was snarled by the crowd letting out, and police officers had stepped in to direct it. A burst of sirens, lights, and bullhorn orders stopped the boys cold. They actually froze there briefly in the middle of traffic, in the busy intersection. Still getting triggered. It sullied the mood for a minute or two, then they shook it off. They were raving about Emma's speech. Ryan admitted that with so many speakers, his mind had wandered. "You're not always paying the most attention," he said. "But the moment everyone shuts up, it's the moment you're like, 'OK, what's happening?' People started crying. Silence is really powerful."

A cluster of Capitol Police called out, "Where are y'all from?"

"Parkland."

The cops were amazed, and a little starstruck. They chatted up the boys and then thanked them for protecting their kids. They were scared for their kids. Then they sheepishly asked for a selfie. Daniel and Ryan posed for several, then ran on. They were too excited to walk.

One of the cops called after them to hashtag it on Facebook: #USCP.

Daniel looked back to make sure the cops were out of earshot, then chuckled to Ryan. "He thinks we still use Facebook." But he was excited to be asked. And they could hardly believe this doc crew wanted to feature them. The working title was "We Are Kids." They had been on the fringe of the spotlight for five weeks now, but it had never settled on them. Two hours later, they were still giggling over George and Amal. Not just hanging out together—they got separated toward the end, and the Clooneys made a point to come find them to say goodbye.

6

Lefties fear the worst. The turnout was huge. The academic team behind the Crowd Counting Consortium put their best guess at 470,000 attending the march in Washington, and 1.4 to 2.1 million people at 763 locations nationwide, plus 84 uncounted marches abroad. That made it the third-largest protest day since Trump's inauguration, behind the two women's marches. "That is in comparison with some of the largest marches ever seen in the United States, an extraordinary period of national political mobilization," it said. For comparison, the historic 1963 civil rights March on Washington drew about a quarter million. Prior to the Trump era, the *Washington Post* identified the largest demonstrations in US history as the protest to the US invasion of Iraq, and the Vietnam War Moratoriums in 1969 and 1970. They drew about one million and two million nationwide, respectively. That would put MFOL as the third- or more likely fourth-largest demonstration in national history. And it was the first big one organized by high school kids.

The kids were targeting the youth vote but connecting with a much broader demographic. A university team conducted detailed crowd composition surveys of all the major Trump-era protests. They published their MFOL findings in the *Washington Post*. Only 10 percent of attendees were under eighteen, and the average age of the remainder was about forty-nine—older than at recent rallies. They were highly educated and highly female: 72 percent college graduates and 70 percent women. (Women composed 85 percent of the Women's March.) The kids seemed to reach their other main target audience: unengaged voters on the sidelines. Over a quarter of the marchers were attending the first protest of their lives.

And *The Trace*'s data had previously shown the kids kept gun safety alive with 2 percent of all news stories for a solid month, spiking to 5 percent for the first walkout. It hit 9 percent the day of the march. No other tragedy, not even Newtown, not even Columbine, had accomplished anything near that.

7

They had set an audacious goal, and surpassed it in five weeks. Now what? The horizon always looks different at the summit. No predicting how it would feel.

The mood all morning was electric—with an undercurrent of reverie. Even the kids exuded it. Hour by hour, you could see their bodies relax, feel them exhaling the calm. Of course. They had to catch their breath. They envisioned this march as the birth of their movement, not the climax, but it was sure feeling like a curtain call. The press tents, that's where you could really feel that. Row after row of frenetic fingers clacking along the keyboards, shaping the movement's swan song.

The kids were dreaming even bigger now, but would they be rallying in obscurity? Reporters were using the last of their Wi-Fi to put a big bow on this story. Would anything bring the press back?

15

PTSD

1

S ome of the kids were suffering from post-traumatic stress disorder. Technically, they didn't qualify for the diagnosis until a month after the shooting. For the first thirty days, a severe trauma reaction is classified as acute stress disorder (ASD), not PTSD. The condition is marked by symptoms like prolonged distress; problems with sleep, concentration, or memory; an inability to experience positive emotions; hypervigilance; a dissociation from reality; and recurrent dreams or memories. ASD is diagnosed in trauma survivors experiencing distressing symptoms and a marked impairment in the ability to function. PTSD is essentially the persistence of ASD beyond one month.

About 6 to 12 percent of survivors suffer ASD after an industrial accident, 10 percent from a severe burn, and 13 to 21 percent from a car accident. The risk surges if the survivor has been attacked by another person: the numbers go up to 20 to 50 percent after an assault, rape, or mass murder. These are wide ranges, due to differences in the nature and severity of the trauma, each person's coping skills, and other risk factors. Prior trauma, or existing struggles with depression or drug abuse, drastically increase the risk. And much of our response is determined by how we perceive the event. "The way two people experience and perceive the exact same trauma can be totally different," said Dr. Alyse Ley. "Even if they saw the same thing, they can have a very different experience of that event." Dr. Ley specializes in child and adolescent trauma, and is the director of the child and adolescent psychiatry fellowship program at Michigan State University.

About half the people treated for ASD are eventually diagnosed with PTSD, and the other half improve enough in that first month to avoid it. While it's optimal to get treatment as early as possible, the one-month milestone is a good marker for parents or friends to observe. At that point, the afflicted survivor with full-blown PTSD needs more sophisticated help than loved ones can generally provide.

And there are additional conditions to watch for. "Individuals who have experienced a trauma injury may also develop panic disorders, major depressive disorder, substance abuse, and anxiety disorders," Dr. Ley said. "Often if you have one, you have the other—sometimes the disorders have overlapping symptoms and are difficult to tease apart." Major depressive disorder is serious, and extremely common in trauma survivors. "So what a parent is really going to want to watch for is a change in the child, in their behavior and their functioning," Dr. Ley said. "And major depression is not just a sad mood—it affects your entire body. It affects your sleep, your appetite, your feelings about yourself, feelings of guilt and worthlessness. Their energy level is affected. Suicidal ideation is also extraordinarily common in a person who has major depression." Weight change is also a major marker of depression, but it can look different in adolescents who are still growing. A loss of appetite might lead to failure to make expected weight gains, or to dropping off the growth curve. "Children and adolescents who have been traumatized need to be monitored for depression and anxiety, as well as PTSD," Dr. Ley said.

The long-term consequences can be heightened for adolescents, because these symptoms can alter their cognitive development. "There's a negative filter across everything you do and see and how you view people and yourself in relationships," Dr. Ley said. "Untreated PTSD can change the developmental trajectory. The goal of the therapist is to get the young person back on track with developmental milestones and coping skills."

2

I met Dr. Ley at the three-day Academy of Critical Incident Analysis (ACIA) conference on the Las Vegas shooting in early May, along with two survivors, Chris and Jenny Babij. We discussed the MFOL kids at length. Chris and Jenny had experienced their attack side by side, but completely differently. They had been standing right in front of the Route 91 music festival stage, so hundreds of people were taken down by gunfire all around them. Chris was badly wounded in the shoulder, and he'd tripped as they fled the grounds. Jenny was running just ahead and did not discover until too late that he was gone. They were separated until the morning, and Jenny was wracked by guilt for "abandoning" him, despite her relentless attempts to reach him. Chis lay on a gurney within the chaos of an overwhelmed ER awaiting treatment for several hours. Over and over, a custodian rolled a bucket by to mop up all the fresh blood. So much blood. A triage nurse came by with three color-coded tags: Chris was tagged as non-life-threatening, which meant he had to wait. He said he didn't mind. He had seen so many people in a horrible state. It was actually a great comfort to get tagged, he said. It meant he was in the system, would not be forgotten, and would be treated after the people in danger of dying.

Four months into their recovery, Parkland rattled Chris and Jenny Babij—enough to impede their progress temporarily. They were awed by the MFOL kids but concerned. Recovery had been their primary pursuit, advancing at a pace that worked for them. Chris was just then preparing to return to work. Were the kids taking on too much?

"We have to trust them," Dr. Ley said. Adults can be too eager to step in and "help" people like Emma. "People just assumed, 'Oh, she's having a breakdown,'" Dr. Ley said of Emma's tearful speech. "So what? Shouldn't she? My first thought was, 'Yeah, it's about time. Look at what this kid has been through.'" If she were breaking down hourly, riddled by intrusive thoughts, and couldn't sleep or function, that would be entirely different. But crying can be cathartic, even onstage.

"Adults will always think of ten thousand reasons

why you can't do something," Dr. Ley said. "Kids won't do that. That's what's glorious about young people: the still-developing impulse control. They see something, they see a cause, and they say, 'I'm going to do what's right. You're not going to stop me.'"

Still, the responsibility the kids had hoisted onto their shoulders posed risks, Dr. Ley said. So did the painful glare of the spotlight and the abject cruelty of their adversaries. Nobody can anticipate how badly that spotlight can twist you, she said, and trusting the survivors doesn't mean trusting them blindly. "We need to have parents who are very aware," she said. "A parent has to be able to sort of look at their own child and say, 'Yeah, they've got the coping skills to handle some of this'—but be watchful and know when to say, 'Wait a second, you're beyond your limits. This is not going well.' Then they have to take steps back. What's really important in trauma work is finding out what the individual needs."

She talked about siblings on different trajectories, and she could have been describing David and Lauren Hogg. David was relentless, and he seemed not just capable of the responsibility, but buoyed by it. His parents, Rebecca and Kevin, gave him wide latitude—insisting that one of them chaperone him out of town, but generally letting him chart his own course. Lauren was in no position to take that on, and her parents were far more protective of her. Lauren saw her own limits and eased into the MFOL group gradually.

Dr. Frank Ochberg, who was part of the committee that first created the diagnosis of PTSD, concurred. "There are going to be adults who criticize the kids and the supporters of the kids, saying, 'Hey, you're abusing them, they're abusing themselves, they're missing out on teenage life,'" he said. "Yes, there's a certain risk, but let's not patronize them or overly parent them. Let's celebrate their wisdom and dedication and leadership."

There's a profound therapeutic benefit of their activism, he said, and Dr. Ley elaborated. What most people failed to see in Emma's tears—and in the march, in the movement—was the power of reasserting control. Control. Such an elusive element. Control is crucial to recovery—recovering the feeling that was ripped away in the moment of violation. It's especially profound in violent crimes: gunshots, rape, assault, and mass murder. "At that moment you're being terrorized, there is chaos," Dr. Ley said. "You feel like you have no control of your body, your destiny, your future. And that fear of the unknown, of whether you're going to live or die, sticks with you. So one of the main things in treatment is allowing a person to reassume the control of their own life, their body, their destiny." That can mean a long, arduous recovery. It's rarely possible to reassert control over the brutalizer, or effectively counteract the damage. Therapists help their patients simulate control, or visualize, but that can feel contrived to some, and painfully slow to others.

"That's why what these Parkland kids are doing is so powerful," Dr. Ley said. "They're saying, 'Hang on. Stop. I'm going to regain control. We're going to do something about these weapons that we had no control over.'" To hell with simulations—they made it real. They could not rewrite Valentine's Day, but they could reframe it. They had looked beyond that powerless afternoon, determined they had been made powerless their entire childhoods by gunmen who could strike at any moment. They set their sights on that larger problem, and reclaimed their power by working to protect seventy-four million American kids. To hell with simulations—reality felt more powerful. They didn't start this as a form of therapy, but Dr. Ley said they could hardly have designed a better treatment plan.

PART III

The Long Road

Nonviolence believes that the universe
is on the side of justice.

—MARTIN LUTHER KING JR.'S
SIXTH PRINCIPLE OF NONVIOLENCE

16

Denver Noticed

1

Boise noticed and Birmingham noticed. Each drew 5,000 marchers, and 15,000 to 25,000 turned out in Phoenix. They turned out in large, small, and medium towns all across America. In Denver, tens of thousands showed, nearly 100,000 according to one local news outlet. The Denver organizers were stunned. "On Facebook it was about thirty thousand who said they were coming, and it jumped so fast!" said Jessica Maher, one of the Denver organizers. Jessica was a college senior who had never done anything political in her life. Now she was director of political affairs for Never Again Colorado. The waves of supporters pouring into Civic Center Park and marching past the Colorado capitol dome on March 24 changed everything. This was real, she realized. This was powerful.

MFOL had mobilized on two fronts: inspiring millions of kids, and then recruiting them into a vast grassroots network. It was all about the network now: 762 potential affiliates had come of age that day. National media tacked on the sibling march story as an afterthought. The intersectional message got even less ink or air. *The New Yorker*, *The Nation*, and a few others noticed MFOL's signal that they were fusing with the urban gun safety movement, but it was mostly mentioned in passing. But urban activists heard it loud and clear.

For sibling organizers, the march was already their second local event. Most had been involved with a walkout, and some had organized a die-in or other protest as well. They used each undertaking as a building block to grow their network, to learn from mistakes, and to gather momentum for the next one. The feverish pace had been a blessing and a curse. Now they had time—which could easily translate to boredom and fading interest. Time to map out eight months of initiatives to maintain excitement, register millions of young voters, and turn them out on Election Day.

In Denver, it began with Madison Rose. Madison was a college student who watched the Douglas students erupt on social media day one. That was all it took. Anger had been simmering for years. Why were adults just letting them die? That first night, Madison decided she wanted to organize a Denver march. Then Never Again announced its plan. Perfect, Madison said. She signed Denver up as a sibling.

Logistics were overwhelming—no one to delegate the permitting or grunt work. That forced Madison to reach out aggressively and cobble together a metro-wide team. That proved surprisingly easy. New groups were mushrooming across the city and suburbs. She would eventually hook up with Emmy Adams and Kaylee Tyner, who were part of a fledgling network in the Jefferson County School District. Kaylee was a junior at Columbine High, and Emmy was a senior at Golden High. All of Jefferson County (Jeffco) still felt the Columbine scars, and Parkland had hit hard. "I just couldn't take seeing the community have their hearts broken again," Emmy said. "So I started by reaching out to people at my school, saying, 'Hey, does anyone want to help me create some solutions?' I thought like five people would show up to this meeting, and it ended up being over seventy kids. I was like, 'OK, if we can get this many at Golden, we can spread this across the district.'" That turned into Jeffco Students Demand Action. It included students from every high school in the county.

Emmy became copresident, and the group organized the first school walkout across the county. They paired that with a rally after school that day, to bring all the young activists together. A big contingent from the group marched in Washington and networked with other cities. Most of the cities in America had a story like that.

When the marches ended, all those groups came together to brainstorm the road ahead. They settled on one big venture to throw their collective weight behind: a rally just outside Columbine, on April 19, the eve of the anniversary, the day before the second national walkout. Columbine kids couldn't walk out on April 20, because that is a solemn day in the area, and classes have never been conducted on that day since. But there was another reason.

2

Grieving Douglas students did not all respond with activism. Most supported gun reform, came out to the occasional walkout or rally, but their priority was healing. The Columbine event helped some Douglas students do both.

It began with an invitation to the MFOL kids. Emmy, Madison, and the other organizers worked with the former Columbine principal Frank DeAngelis to honor them with a leadership award. The MFOL leaders had made a prior commitment, so the organizers invited a handful of other Douglas students they met at the DC march. Abiding Hope, a local church supporting the event, agreed to pay their way out. The Douglas kids would headline the rally, but that was not the primary objective. They would come for two to three days and just relax and breathe in the mountain air.

Word of the trip spread, and more students wanted to come—mostly low-income kids who could never afford a trip like this. The congregation had been through Columbine, and was happy to support them. More signed on, and eventually about fifty came.

The Douglas and Columbine students would perform a service day together on the anniversary: making a stone garden path at a local memory care facility, and upgrading the landscaping at Dave Sanders Memorial Softball Field just outside the school. It was named for the Columbine teacher who died saving students. The weather was gorgeous, the trees just leafing out for spring. Columbine students took them up to Lookout Mountain, and scrambled around Red Rocks Amphitheater. They were having a ball.

They were still playful when they got to the Columbine Memorial. They grew somber fast. The memorial is carved out of the shallow slope of Rebel Hill, which rises in Clement Park just past Dave Sanders Field. Beyond it, the sun was sinking, drifting toward the Rocky peaks. The Wall of Healing curves around the memorial's border to enclose the quiet space. It is built of craggy russet bricks, matching the cobblestone path and the red clay earth all around. A central ring of memorial tablets commemorates the thirteen murdered nearby. The kids wandered among the young trees, running their fingers over the wall and tablets, feeling the inscriptions as they read. Many said it felt like chilling contact with the first generation to endure this—their first connection to kindred spirits. They marveled how tranquil they had grown. Everything felt different there. They wondered aloud: Was this a glimpse of their future? Serenity? Would it take nineteen years?

Gerardo Cadagan, a Douglas senior, said the memorial had taken him by surprise. He had not expected it to affect him so deeply. He had expected that to come later in the afternoon, when they were set to meet survivors who had lived through the ordeal there. He wasn't sure how that would affect him either, but he was so desperate to meet someone who would understand. And to get away from that campus—it just reeked of death. He had a class in building 12 before Valentine's Day. Now it was surrounded by an ominous fence, with cops moving in and out. "The scene of the crime, being around the building every day—just kind of brings the bad memories back," he said. He couldn't get enough of the crisp mountain air. Such a different feel from South Florida. Aspen trees, red clay earth, air so dry and thin and cool. The Rockies still had snow on their peaks. "I've never seen anything like this," he said. "Florida's flat. All of this to me is amazing."

3

Some Douglas kids had soured on activism—or forgone it entirely, working with apolitical groups like Shine MSD, or hurling themselves into sports or arts or performing to distract from the darkness, and add joy and meaning to their lives. During a rehearsal break for *Legally Blonde*, four Douglas students stepped out to the boardwalk outside the studio to discuss their experience. They had all gone through lockdown in the drama room with the MFOL kids.

"I wanted to be very involved in the politics just because I'm so passionate about what I believe," junior Melanie Weber said. She had made the Tallahassee trip, and two of the others had gone to the march. "But then I realized like how draining it was. I would rather put my time into doing something like Shine that would have raised money for a good cause and made people happy, instead of just yelling and screaming and politics and 'You're wrong!' and stuff like that. I felt like it helped me more."

Their grief had been erratic. "It comes out of nowhere," freshman June Felman said.

"This is weird, but like the further away we get from it, the more real it seems," Melanie said. "Now the shock is wearing off. It's sinking in that it actually happened."

June had gotten an emotional support dog, a Boston terrier, and that made a huge difference. "He's four months old and he's adorable," she said. "Just having him around makes me happy."

June described being irritated by random people asking prying questions: Where were they during the shooting, what did they go through, what was it like? "It's a little invasive sometimes," she said. It had happened earlier that day at the hair salon. It was close to the school, that was a clue, but the support dog was a total giveaway.

Most of them said they had not been to therapy.

"I went like, once," June said.

"I'm too stubborn to go but my mom thinks I should start going," Melanie said.

Junior Alex Athanasiou said he had conversations in his head about it. "I'm taking psychology classes. I'm trying to be my own therapist." He was also trying to help his sister, who had been on the second floor of the freshman building, where it happened. "After a month of her being like really quiet, I kind of went to her room and I was like, 'Hey,' and we had this really long conversation." After that, she began to open up about it more.

They were mostly depending on each other. "We've all gone through the same thing," June said. "That will always link us forever."

Some of them had soured on their peers. Melanie said she used to be friends with Jackie. And they were very touchy about the attention MFOL was getting. National media had been in and out of that studio for weeks, a film crew was shooting an entire documentary on *Spring Awakening*, Broadway stars had come down to coach that cast and then hang out with them, and no one bothered to speak to them. They had lived through the same tragedy. There were actually more survivors in their production of *Legally Blonde* than *Spring Awakening*, but their cast didn't include Cameron.

"The twelve kids in Never Again are not the entire student body," June said. "They weren't even near the freshman building. Not to call them out, but like—"

"Call them out!" Melanie said, and June continued:

"None of them were in the freshman building, none of them lost anyone close to them, yet they're oh, like, survivors."

This was making the boys uncomfortable. She was going too far, Alex said. The MFOL kids had lost friends too.

"It just bothers me how they're getting all the attention in the world, yet there are kids who were in the freshman building that like, their voices aren't being heard," June said.

Junior Brian Martinez defended them too. "I know a lot of people from the freshman building that prefer not to talk about it, so they prefer having others talk for them."

"But there also are a lot of people who do want to talk about it, but they can't because like all the media is obsessed with these twelve kids," June said.

The MFOL kids were well aware of this criticism. They heard it every day, and caught the silences and scowls. Cam and Alex Wind were steps away inside the studio at that moment. Much of the team had drama class with these kids every day.

4

The Douglas group traveling to Columbine was supportive of the MFOL kids. Some came from undocumented families, so they were keeping a low media profile. Others just didn't feel comfortable in the role. But they wanted gunmen to stop shooting them. Many echoed Brian's sentiment appreciating the MFOL kids speaking up for them. They all appeared onstage at the Columbine rally that night, and a few gave rousing speeches.

The highlight of the trip was a meeting with Columbine survivors. About a dozen, plus a handful from other mass shootings, met them in a private session in the Columbine auditorium. Frank DeAngelis told them how pissed off he got at all the people telling him what he should feel. They were constantly trying to "help" by telling him that it was OK, pushing misguided "suggestions," and generally telling him what to do. You're probably feeling that right now, he said. That got a hearty laugh. They had all experienced it, endlessly. So DeAngelis said he wouldn't push therapy on them, but he'd share what a Vietnam War vet told him: You're a big mess, and if you don't get help, you can't help anyone else. DeAngelis loved the airplane oxygen mask analogy, and shared it with these kids: They always instruct you to put your own on before helping others. You're useless if you don't help yourself first.

It took a little while for the Parkland students to warm up. Finally one of them broached a touchy subject they had all been thinking about: prom and graduation were coming, and . . . The words caught in his throat, and he barely got them out through his sobs. What he was asking—and he thought it sounded terrible—but would it be horrible to have fun?

"Grief is not a competition," Kiki Leyba said. He had been a new teacher when the shooting started, and he still taught English down the hall. But it took them far too long to accept that, he said. Some of the survivors admitted they had gotten mad at peers who seemed to recover "too fast," and enjoyed life too much. They regretted that. It's hard enough. When a good day comes, take it. When prom comes, give yourself a break. Enjoy it as much as you can.

Leyba had traveled to Sandy Hook with his fellow teacher Paula Reed to help the staff there. He recounted an exchange in which one of the teachers said she just wanted to know when she would get her life back. Leyba didn't know how to respond, but Reed did. Never, she said. That woman is gone. You are never getting her back. You will get past this, and you will do amazing things in your life, but it will be a different you from who you once were. And you will never begin that path out of the pain until you let go of that woman and say goodbye.

Kiki Leyba told some of the most poignant stories that session, but he omitted one. He had crashed his new car a few nights earlier, just as the Parkland kids were arriving.

"I'm worried about him," his wife confided. "He's in an April fog." This happened every year. It took different forms, not usually a crash, but never good. His buddy Frank DeAngelis had crashed several cars in April, she said. Nineteen years later, the trauma was still reexerting itself. Your mind might claim it's forgotten, but your body refuses. So Columbine survivors have told me a similar story, year after year: something feels odd, they can't put their finger on it, then they realize it's April. Cues are everywhere: spring thaw, green returning, senioritis, prom and graduation plans. Your body remembers.

The crash was on Leyba's mind when he saw the kids. He had to drive another car to get there. The crumpled car was still in his driveway. He was too upset to call the insurance company—how could this still be happening? Maybe it was unrelated, but . . . he didn't really believe that. He would never be over it, but he was OK. He was healthy and happy, and successful enough to replace that car.

Leyba chose to withhold that warning from the Parkland kids. Telling them this early would just be cruel. Two months out, they needed hope.

5

President Trump had proposed arming teachers. That was his big proposal to combat school shootings. The NRA loved it. Teachers were generally appalled. Paula Reed ridiculed the idea at the Columbine rally that evening. She was speaking on behalf of Columbine's faculty survivors. Reed said a big change since 1999 was that she no longer feels completely safe at work. "Now, there are some people who think I'd feel a whole lot safer and so would my students if I were armed. Take a look at me. And imagine that I have a gun in a holster. And an angry young man, six feet tall or so, decides to wrestle that gun away from me. It's not that hard to do. And people say to me, 'Well, Paula, no one would require you to carry a gun.' Well, what if I decide I want to? Does that change my stature? Does it change the ultimate outcome? Or does that just make me a five-foot-two middle-aged woman with questionable judgment and a sidearm?"

Reed recounted incidents in which armed teachers had injured students. In one case, a teacher had left the weapon in a school bathroom, where it was found by several elementary school kids. Several more troubling incidents had occurred just the prior month. A Georgia teacher was arrested after barricading himself in a classroom and firing a handgun out the window. A teacher in Seaside, California, had mistakenly fired his pistol during a gun safety class and injured a student. He was also a reserve police officer and Seaside's mayor pro tem. And a resource officer in Alexandria, Virginia, had accidentally discharged his weapon in a middle school. Luckily, no one was hit. "As far as I can tell, more guns in school have not amounted to greater safety," Reed said. "Quite the opposite."

Reed described a former student lovingly, and read a letter she had written before she died. Rachel Scott was the first person murdered at Columbine. Following her tribute, Reed broke a Columbine taboo: discussing victim and attacker in the same speech. Survivors still found it offensive for their memories to cross. But Reed had taught both Rachel and Dylan Klebold, she said. "I cared about both of them, because I care about all of my students. I know that many people have terrifying memories of Dylan, and I am genuinely sorry for what they went through. But the only Dylan I ever knew was a sweet, shy sophomore. I think it's important to understand that when we talk about arming teachers you're not just asking me to protect the Rachels of this world. You're asking me to kill the Dylans. Maybe that sounds easy to you, and I'm not saying I wouldn't have protected Rachel if I could have, but I really can't imagine shooting Dylan either. Not the Dylan I knew, anyway. I suppose I would have if I could have, and if I had to, but do you understand what you're asking of me? You're asking me to kill one of my students. It's too much to ask. And so instead, I'm asking my elected leaders to make sure that no teacher ever has to lose a student to a school shooting again. Not any student at anyone's hands, each other's or mine. I'm asking our elected leaders to pass meaningful legislation to keep guns out of the hands of children and teenagers, and I hope that everyone here will do the same."

17

Setbacks

1

The most exciting phase of this movement was watching seven hundred semiautonomous groups take off. Self-propulsion, amazing to behold. The downside was lack of control. The second National School Walkout caused some blowback. It was timed to commemorate the nineteenth anniversary of the Columbine massacre, and Columbine refused to participate. The victims it sought to revere were furious. The national media never got wind of the controversy, but it happened at the scene of the original crime. Columbine is part of the Jefferson County School District, with 86,000 students in 155 schools. All boycotted the walkout.

The problem was the date. The failure to grasp

the solemnity of the Combine anniversary was generational. The Parkland generation had no idea that the lockdown drills, now ubiquitous, barely predated them. They were sick of hiding as a strategy, and tragedy meant response, anniversaries demanded action.

The Columbine survivors had never been trained in lockdown drills. They had never heard the term. They didn't rise up against the epidemic of school shooters, because they had no idea it had begun. The surviving students were in their late thirties now. The faculty were retired or approaching it. A great number of them supported the Parkland uprising. But their emotional response to April 20 was conditioned by a different experience, and that would never change.

"April twentieth is a sacred day," Emmy Adams said. "It is the most horrible day of the year." She was a senior at Golden High, and now the copresident of two of the groups organizing the Columbine rally for April 19. Adams got wind of the walkout in mid-February, and sensed it would horrify the Columbine community. So she checked in with prominent survivors, including Frank DeAngelis. Pick any other date, they said—the eve of the anniversary was fine. "When the people who were in that building nineteen years ago say 'Please don't do this,' you should listen to them," Adams said. Many of the survivors battle PTSD symptoms that day. The community has turned it into a day of service and kindness, and reserve politics to the other 364 days of the year.

DeAngelis and the current Columbine principal, Scott Christy, quietly lobbied for the Connecticut organizers to change the date. About a week before the event, the principals released a gently worded statement to the media. It did not name the organizers or denounce the walkout, but explained why they would not participate, and it extended an invitation to join them in service projects. All the schools in Jefferson County revamped or rescheduled their events.

Adams herself met the organizers at the march in DC and pleaded with them. She sent a letter from the Columbine principals. Columbine's lead student organizer, Kaylee Tyner, reached out repeatedly.

No one wanted the dispute to erupt in public. Adams, Tyner, and DeAngelis were all energetic MFOL supporters. They didn't want to undermine the walkout, just shift it a day. The MFOL kids learned of the controversy late in the game. They were aghast, but caught in the middle. "When we first heard about the National School Walkout, and we knew it was the day of Columbine, we figured that they had talked—that Columbine was all for it," the memes man Dylan Baierlein said. "And then we found out Columbine wasn't for it, and we were like, 'What do we do?'"

The train had left the station. So much was riding on it. So MFOL tried to rally groups toward acts of service as well. They promoted the idea online. "But we didn't want to shut down this incredible project that the National School Walkout kids tried to organize," Dylan said.

David Hogg in particular struggled. When DeAngelis and Christy released their statement, David retweeted it in support. He was up to 800,000 Twitter followers, and few of them had an inkling what the discreet statement was driving at. But enclaves in Colorado and Connecticut understood, and David had just publicly taken a side. He ultimately deleted the tweet, returning to neutral.

"When he tweeted that, we all were so thankful and excited," Adams said. "And then it was honestly really insulting when he deleted it. You know I'm not attacking him or anyone at MSD or Connecticut—they're all trying to do the right thing. I'm just saying. It's frustrating. It's really frustrating."

2

The second walkout also raised some cautionary flags. Thousands of schools had sanctioned the first protest, but many were taking a hard line against the prospect of making this a habit. Local organizers from around the country said punishment had risen from nothing following the first walkout to detention or suspension following the second.

Diego Garcia and a friend organized both walkouts at Mansueto High School, in Chicago's Brighton Park neighborhood. He was a senior there, one of the Latino kids working with MFOL since early March. "My school's like super strict, so the first walkout they said, 'Fine you guys can walk out but you can only stay behind the school, you can't chat or anything,'" he said. "About a hundred and twenty kids walked out." That was a quarter of the student body, and he was thrilled with that number, considering the cultural resistance. A lot of people were undocumented. That meant staying out of trouble. Preferably invisible. "They like to stay quiet, because they feel like they're going to put their lives in danger," he said. And anyone around them causing a ruckus could bring trouble too. "In the beginning, people would tell me to be careful," Diego said. His co-organizer actually chose to remain anonymous. "Sometimes it's better to work from the shadows," he said.

But Diego was tired of watching his community hush itself. The Parkland kids had taken threats and abuse, but they weren't letting it silence them. "You've seen it with Emma, you've seen it with Cam, they become a target," Diego said. "David especially. He's just like a big lightning rod for hate mail. People bash David Hogg specifically." Diego was ready to take that chance. Meeting them in person made a huge difference. He chuckled trying to describe David. "He's a great guy who's just got ideas coming out like a conveyer belt out of his head."

Diego kept pushing. He convinced his pastor to fund a group of fifteen students to attend the march in Washington. But he hit a roadblock from the school administration on organizing the second walkout. "They said, 'You know what, you guys are getting too out of hand; if you walk out you're going to get suspended,'" he said. "So I still tried to plan it and I got three other kids to walk out." It was demoralizing, but he earned a lot of respect for resisting.

Coverage of the second walkout was also slightly ominous. *The Trace*'s analysis indicated it bumped gun topics back up to 2 percent of all news stories for a few days. That was great by the standards of previous shootings, but far below the 5.4 percent of the first walkout. It was the first big event to *lose* coverage. You couldn't ring that bell twice.

Was it the lack of originality, or was this shooting doomed to be like all the others? Was the country losing interest after all?

3

Occasionally, blowback hit MFOL directly. That same day in Arizona, things were going a bit awry. Bad time and place for a hiccup, because all eyes were on the Phoenix suburbs.

The president's daily antics and "the Resistance" were the full-time obsession of the American media. MFOL had erupted at exactly the right moment to ride that fury. And Arizona was their first chance to harness it. It was just one US House seat, but the implications were enormous. The midterms were seven months away, an eternity in politics, but talk was already bubbling about a possible "blue wave" developing that might sweep the Democrats to victory, overturning the House of Representatives. No one would know until November, but two special elections offered an early glimpse. The first had been a shocker, just five weeks earlier. Conor Lamb, a Democrat, had flipped the US House seat in Pennsylvania's eighteenth district, which had been so reliably Republican that the Democrats had not even fielded a candidate in 2016. However, Lamb had refused to make gun safety an issue in the race. The second special election was coming to a climax now.

Arizona's eighth US House district was a bigger reach. The Republican margin in 2016 had been 37 points. With no local scandal or outbreak of war, that was generally an impossible margin to reverse. Polls showed the Democratic challenger, Hiral Tipirneni, trailing but within striking distance. Winning would be a political earthquake. Even coming in close could be a powerful harbinger for the fall. Politics can be a momentum battle, so both parties had invested vast sums, and the media was all in.

It was also the first big contest since Parkland on guns. And it had landed on the NRA's turf, in the heart of gun country. The Republican candidate, Debbie Lesko, proudly cited her NRA endorsement, and ridiculed gun reform advocates. She promised to protect the Second Amendment from "reckless and irresponsible legislation that attempts to undermine this precious civil right." Tipirneni came out publicly for most of the MFOL agenda. She also voiced support for the Second Amendment, as did they. MFOL was hungry for candidates like that: out and proud on gun reform. Just the sort of race they wanted to energize young voters—or anyone angry about lax gun laws. A strong showing might embolden cowardly Democrats to quit hiding from the gun issue. It might even coax a few swing-district Republicans to embrace their side. So Alfonso and Charlie Mirsky, another MFOL activist, headed to Phoenix for the walkout, and much more. There was also lots of spadework to be done for the fall. Arizona had been a solid red state for decades. It had gone Democratic in only one presidential election since 1952. Chunks of the Southwest had been drifting into the purple range, and Arizona's demographics suggested it was headed that way, though perhaps a full shift was several elections away. There was an open US Senate seat, which seemed like another long shot for Democrats, but they were going for it. Their leading candidate was a bisexual woman unabashedly supporting gun reform. A multitude of local races were also at play. Every voter Alfonso and Charlie registered could help turn that tide in November. They had to win the registration battle first.

They landed in Phoenix a bit before midnight Thursday, and went straight to a late-night strategy session with the coalition of different groups they were partnering with. It was very late when Geraldine Hills, president of Arizonans for Gun Safety, affectionately known as Momma Bear, said enough: the kids are going to bed now.

They had an early wake-up, and organizers had packed their schedule. At ten a.m., Alfonso and Charlie walked out with students at Metro Tech High, and marched the two and a half miles with them to the state capitol. They staged a rally and gave speeches there, and that got dicey. Arizona is an open-carry state, and there were a lot of counterprotesters berating the kids, toting AK-47s, and waving bright yellow Gadsden flags. There were state troopers, armored Humvees, and a SWAT team. It was tense. Hundreds of students staged die-ins on the floors of the House and Senate lobbies, and outside the governor's office for several hours. Officials warned them that arrests were imminent, so Alfonso and Charlie took the advice to leave. Alfonso later said he could afford to get arrested at home, where he had friends to bail him out, but they felt exposed in Arizona.

More disturbing for Alfonso and Charlie were the headlines. The *Arizona Republic*, the state's largest newspaper, ran a big story titled "Parkland Student to Campaign for Hiral Tipirneni in Arizona Special Election." Huge problem. Endorsing a candidate was verboten. Campaigning for them was worse. Of course MFOL hoped that candidates backing their issue would win. But they could campaign only on the issue, not the person. It was a subtle distinction, but that made it more important, not less. And the inherent confusion made it all the more vital to keep the distinction clear. They could write off future Republican partners if they were seen as Democratic flacks. They might begin attracting Republican candidates if they could demonstrate power to move a race on issue advocacy, and coax them with that voting block.

Before flying in, Alfonso had released a statement to the press to make MFOL's intentions clear: "Our only goals are to register, educate and inspire people to vote on the issues of gun control." The *Arizona Republic* quoted that in its story, but contradicted it in both the headline and the lede, which were quickly retweeted and re-reported everywhere. The story also quoted a named Tipirneni spokesman saying the campaign was "honored by the student's offer to help." This apparent endorsement was huge news in Phoenix, and it drew major national attention as well.

For Alfonso and Charlie, this was a disaster. "The boys got very upset: 'We can't be here; we can't do this,'" said a member of the coalition that brought them to Arizona. "They were being misrepresented," she said. "That's not what they came here for."

That source spoke on condition of anonymity, because it was such a touchy issue among her team. When I first asked Alfonso about it a month later, he was reluctant to cast it in a bad light. He'd had a great experience with most of the activists there, and he didn't want to burn any bridges. But months later, he confirmed that her account was accurate, and that they had been deeply upset.

More events were booked for Saturday. Alfonso and Charlie "were tired, they were really overwhelmed, overloaded, and people are pushing them to do things outside their comfort zone," the local activist said. She said at least one of the handlers tried to strong-arm them, pointing out that his group had paid for their plane tickets home. They felt a little like hostages. Others in the coalition were appalled, and felt the boys needed to be rescued. So someone called Gabby Giffords's office and she got them out of there and bought them plane tickets home.

Tuesday, Tipirneni lost, but her 47.4 percent of the vote was seen as a rosy indicator for the fall. Arizona hadn't elected a Democratic senator in thirty years. Could this be the year?

Arizona was a rough trip for Alfonso and Charlie, but also a symptom of a much bigger problem with the group: a growing *appearance* of alignment with the Democratic Party. That was a violation of their prime directive: to be a force for change outside the tribalism that had separated the country into sniping factions. That was a losing game. They had to stay nonpartisan—in appearance as well as fact.

That was the only hope, but was it feasible in the political climate that birthed them? They were right about all the Republicans supporting them, but naive about how toxic they were to that tribe. The crux of the red/blue divide, which the country had ossified into in the 1990s, was that most voters had picked a team, and the teams picked their issues, and then fought to the political death for each one, whether they agreed with their team or not. Some touchy issues, like guns, had been chosen by only one side. Republicans had embraced the NRA agenda and run with it, despite the opposition of most of their constituents. When Al Gore lost West Virginia and hence the presidency in 2000, guns were blamed for it. An absurd proposition for his loss, but for Dems already skittish on the issue, it had been a full retreat ever since. Hence two decades of unabated losses on gun legislation. MFOL had reinvigorated three constituencies on gun reform: Democratic officials, Democratic voters, and Republican voters. Polls showed majorities of Republican voters backing their demands—plus huge majorities of the crucial independents. In theory, that fourth quadrant should follow. More important, in swing districts and battleground states, gun reform drew huge majorities of Republican voters. Theoretically, that should have drawn a huge swath of Republican senators and congresspersons over to their side, for pure political expediency.

But that was the old system. In the red/blue world, representatives no longer responded to their con- stituents, they responded to their team. The red team backed guns, and the NRA dictated its terms. Its terms were absolutist: no reforms, no matter how sensible, or how many kids would die. Hold the line. Any red team member who peeled off to support his or her constitu- ency risked being branded a traitor and primaried out.

None of that shocked the MFOL kids. They hoped to chip away at the stalemate by appealing to voters to demonstrate the political peril of opposing the vast majority so aggressively for so long. What did surprise them somewhat was that the red team wouldn't even talk to them. They were toxic just by association—at least that was still the calculation in Washington. That might change if they could turn an election, but cer- tainly not in round one.

But here's where it got really tricky, and they hadn't counted on this: Democrats embraced them, eagerly inviting the kids to their big events, and posing for every possible selfie with them, plastering their im- ages together over social media. So as Republican officials rebuffed them, by allowing their images to be co-opted, the perception became that they had sided with the Democratic Party. That alienated Republican voters, endangering the crucial third quadrant that was central to their strategy. Lose the Republican electorate, and they would lose the war.

"We are doing everything we can to remain nonpartisan and anything that screams Democratic we're trying to stay away from," Dylan Baierlein said. "We can't continue to show up to Democratic events, because the Democrats are inviting us and the Republicans are not." They made a bigger point of saying in public statements that they welcomed talking to Republicans but what they really wanted to do was talk openly with politicians from both parties who disagreed with them, and try to find common ground. But as Dylan explained, "People who are against us generally are afraid to talk to us. That's just the world that we live in—people don't like listening to each other. But that's what we're trying to change."

It felt like a no-win situation, a political system that had boxed them out. What it did was strengthen their resolve on a few key fronts. The midterms were growing ever more vital: the only hope for breaking this gridlock was a powerful electoral victory to jump-start a very long process. They had to convince swing Re-

publicans to release guns from the all-or-nothing lit-
mus test list. Health care, abortion, and immigration
were all currently nonnegotiable on both sides, but the
two parties were still working across the aisle on some
issues, like the need for a sweeping infrastructure plan,
digital privacy, and terrorism. Long term, the MFOL
kids wanted guns on that cross-party list.

In the short term, the Arizona debacle proved incon-
trovertibly that they had to turn their attention to gun
country. They had always intended to go straight to
voters there, to bubble up momentum on guns from the
red grassroots. But as their perception problem rose,
gun country was an obvious antidote: forget Nancy
Pelosi and Clooney and Obama too. Start showing up
all over Instagram in South Carolina, Texas, and Utah.
But the third reason was perhaps biggest of all. Listen
to these people in the red states. Why did most of the
population of Texas support their agenda but reject
the idea of their cause? Texans were their best hope of
understanding Texas. Time to get their butts there.

4

Their media coverage had taken a disconcerting turn.
Early on, it was mostly about the movement: their demands, their insurgency, and especially the march. The

news value of all that had been mined, and the media had moved on to profile pieces. That made the group uneasy. "We don't want to be celebrities," Dylan said. "We were kind of riding that line, affiliated with all these celebrities who were at the march. We're not celebrities. We're activists just trying to make a change."

They didn't like the personality pieces at all, but there was a much bigger problem. Nearly all the profiles were about David or Emma, especially Emma. It was a touchy subject, and most of the kids shied away from going on the record about it, but they were discussing it. No one wanted to reverse that more than Emma. "She is our face," Dylan said. "She doesn't really want to be. She doesn't want to take the credit for all of the work that we're all doing. She doesn't want it to become the Emma Show. So she's backed away. She's having the time of her life, and she's still doing amazing things, just at a lower profile."

5

Internet trolls kept at them, viciously, though that didn't really bother them. (Threats did, and those continued, but that was another matter.) It was the sniping within their own school that hurt the most. Much of that was about them squeezing out their 3,200 classmates from media coverage. That was true, and unique among mass shootings. The media always did its best to create celebrity victims and survivors. Columbine had produced the mistaken Christian martyr Cassie Bernall; "The Boy in the Window," Patrick Ireland; and the heroic teacher Dave Sanders. There were usually several, but even taken together, specific individuals formed a tiny fraction of the coverage. With Parkland, the national media honed in on these twenty-plus kids the vast majority of the time. The MFOL kids acknowledged that, but made no apologies. They were on a mission, and exposure was the fuel.

But there was another accusation against them, growing in pitch, and they realized their accusers had a point. It went back to how MFOL had come together—so organically and so perfectly, it had seemed to them at the time. They had decided early to govern by consensus: meeting together, talking together, deciding together. That required the group to stay small. And every passing day, the bonds grew stronger, the trust greater, which was perfect, except . . . they were still a bunch of white and brown kids.

Nobody was quite hashtagging them #MOFLso White, not yet, but the pushback was gathering force. David Hogg actually helped bring it to a head with a few interviews leading up to the Washington march.

In a livestream interview, *Axios*'s Mike Allen asked what the media's biggest mistake was in covering the shooting. "Not giving black students a voice," David said. "My school is about 25 percent black, but the way we're covered doesn't reflect that."

Several news outlets ran stories leading with that quote, including *Teen Vogue* and *Newsweek*. That evening, Douglas junior Tyah-Amoy Roberts tweeted David with a link to one of them. "Don't get me wrong @davidhogg111," she tweeted. "I appreciate your gesture of calling out the media for the lack of black faces in the aftermath of the incident at our school, but I don't recall (nor do any of our black peers at Douglas) getting any invites from you to . . ." She maxed out her character count there, and continued in a long thread: "join the #NeverAgain 'figureheads' at any of your meetings or interviews. This is not the first time you have called out racial disparity, but you have yet to take tangible action to help change it with your classmates. So here's my challenge to you: allow me to be the first Volunteer to take a seat at the table with you guys to advocate for a cause that has affected everyone at MSD regardless of race. After all, as has been previously stated in the media, 'these parkland kids are eloquent and outspoken,' and just like you, I fall into that category." She tagged various cable news anchors,

Bernie Sanders, and several of the MSD kids. It drew a lot of responses and nearly four hundred retweets.

Five days later, Tyah-Amoy joined a group of eight African American Douglas students conducting a press conference outside the school to chastise both MFOL and the media for ignoring them. "I am here today with my classmates because we have been sorely underrepresented and in some cases misrepresented," Tyah-Amoy said. "The Black Lives Matter movement has been addressing the topic since the murder of Trayvon Martin in 2012 and we have never seen this kind of support for our cause. We surely do not feel that the lives or voices of minorities are valued as much as those of our white counterparts. The media have neglected us, our peers have neglected us, though they are doing great work. And we have neglected ourselves until this very moment, by not using our voice to demand to be seen and acknowledged. Well, here we are. Do you see us?"

That evening, Nadege Green, an African American reporter for South Florida's public radio station, tweeted out a series of photos and video from the press conference, beginning: "A group of Black students from Marjorie Stoneman Douglas High called a press conference today to say they have concerns that may not mirror those of their white peers. And that the media should listen. #MSDStrong." She was retweeted over thirty thousand times.

Green pointed out that the national media had mostly missed the press conference as well. She wrote that about eight news organizations had shown up, most of them local. The national media was noticing now. And Green tweeted a powerful clip of Tyah-Amoy's speech, which gave them the video so crucial to turning it viral. A bevy of national coverage followed.

Tyah-Amoy was right. Over the next few months, MFOL added nearly ten members, all Douglas students, mostly African American. When it launched the next big phase of the movement in June, Tyah-Amoy was a proud member of the group.

18
Graduation

1

Cameron was a ball of stress. The musicals were supposed to be a relief from the activism, and they were, but he had loaded up a full plate before his school was attacked. "Obviously, I could barely get him to rehearsal," Christine Barclay said. "He really did try to abide by the rehearsal schedule, but there were times it was impossible."

"And try directing him," Barclay said. She would say, "OK, Cameron, can you please put your phone down?" and he'd say, "I'm texting George Clooney," or the kids from Sandy Hook. "How do you direct the King of the World? He's literally become basically famous for talking down to grown-ups, and putting them in their place." She reconsidered. That was strong, but that's how it felt. He was a handful. And her hands were literally full with her newborn—the kids got used to her nursing in the rehearsal, calling out directions while Caroline quietly ate. All of them were in over their heads.

It got worse when Cam was under attack. "It kind of got to a point where I kept yelling at everybody online who would harass them," Barclay said. "I mean, these are kids. Yeah, maybe they're saying something too aggressively or they're being a little brazen or being emotional. But these are seventeen-year-old kids. They're not supposed to know how to handle this. They're already having enough trouble navigating who they're taking to prom and what to do with their acne; how are they supposed to know how to handle a media onslaught and people throwing mud at them? It's like *Lord of the Flies*."

Opening night for *Spring Awakening* was May 2. As showtime hurtled toward them, everyone was feeling the heat. "And the other kids were kind of sitting on pins and needles, because they had been holding down the fort," Barclay said. "It was like, 'Dudes, please pull this off, because we've been here.'"

But then Obama wrote an article about them, *Time* named them to its 100 Most Influential list, they were

invited to the White House Correspondents' Din-
ner . . . it just didn't stop. "He tried, he really tried, but
Cam would come to rehearsals, Alfonso would come
to rehearsals, all these kids would come to rehearsals
from red-eye flights," Barclay said. "They'd come in
looking bleary eyed, and it's like, 'OK guys, now you
have a seven-hour rehearsal where you have to sing and
cry'—and then they'd get on a plane and go back to
wherever."

They had the lines, and the moves, but they were
holding back. Barclay was frustrated. "I finally said,
'You guys are known for your big voices. I can't hear
you!'" Those big media voices, that was the trouble.
The stage demands a certain bravado: faking it when
you don't feel it, projecting to the back row. Activism
can too, sometimes: tussling with a US senator when
you haven't even begun AP gov class, and you're certain of the objective but fuzzy on the details, and can
never let a whiff of uncertainty show. Broadway actors
do it two hours a night, eight shows a week, and they're
exhausted. These kids were spent.

There was another issue. There was a gunshot. It felt
unthinkable to fire a gun in that community that spring,
but it was a crucial plot point, the suicide. Moritz shot
himself, and his ghost returned to argue with Cameron

in the climactic graveyard scene. Barclay consulted with a lot of people. The conversation veered between "You have to leave it in because it'll be too much of a statement not to" and "It would be giving in too much if you don't. You have to rip off the Band-Aid."

Barclay didn't bring the gun prop to the set. "We didn't even want to go there. Astin, who played Moritz, kept using his fingers." Two days before the opening, Barclay finally brought in a plastic gun. "Everyone took a moment. It's plastic. I showed it to them when it was still orange, before we sprayed it black. They just kind of stared at it."

Meanwhile, her assistant director watched a lot of other performances on YouTube and discovered that many omitted the blast. OK, Barclay decided. He would raise it to his mouth, lights out, and the audience would figure it out. "It's not going to look like we're afraid," she said. "I didn't want it to be overdramatic—just dramatic enough."

The roller coaster to opening night was a lot of fun. A group of Broadway and television entertainers staged several Broadway benefits for Parkland, and gave the kids advice over the phone. The show's creators, Steven Sater and Duncan Sheik, flew down for opening night and did a talk-back with the kids after the show.

"We came to honor you guys," Sater told them. "Because for us, you guys are like a beacon of hope."

The kids had done their homework. Cameron asked about the Masked Man in the nineteenth-century text. In that incarnation, Moritz goads Cameron's character, Melchior, to join him in suicide, and the Masked Man appears to coax him to go on. Both are projections of Melchior's own psyche, Sater said. "That's the birth of expressionism in the Western theater. A character walks onstage, as present as everyone else, and yet he's embodying what's going on in the mind of another character. Some force, subjective and arbitrary, has entered into scene with a character who is in fact projecting him." There has been a century of debate about the Masked Man. "To me, he's the principle of life, of going on, of going forward," Sater said. He and Sheik spent eight years wrestling the material to the Broadway stage, and that Masked Man was a conundrum for much of the ride. They actually included him at the Lincoln Center staging six years in. And then they cut him loose. "What we recognized was that in our production, the music played that role," Sater said. "It provided the propulsion of the story. The impulse which drove us forward. So we no longer needed the Masked Man himself. He had become kind of an irrelevance, or a redundancy."

They also jettisoned a key plot point from the final scene: Moritz coaxing his best friend to join him in the grave. What worked in the abstract, in nineteenth-century Germany, felt monstrous in the wake of Columbine. "We didn't want to see the Moritz we had been rooting for all night come back and betray his friend by urging him to kill himself," Sater said. "It just didn't make sense to us."

Confronted with an actual atrocity, they contemplated what the victims might wish for their peers, the distraught survivors, fumbling for a way to walk on. "We pondered that for a really long time," Sater said. He kept writing different lyrics until he found a theme that felt right. "You go on," he said. "You carry the loss of those you've known with you, and you go forward on their behalf as well as your own. That's our message: 'Those you've known and lost still walk beside you.'" That's the final note that closes the show. "I don't think our show would have the resonance it has had without that song, without that message," Sater said. "I don't know that so many people would be performing the show today."

It's a theme so many stricken communities have chosen, depicting their lost children as angels, silently walking beside them, encouraging the survivors on. It took the Columbine survivors eight years to break ground on their permanent memorial, and Dawn Anna Beck, who lost her daughter, Lauren Townsend, in the library, spoke on behalf of the dead. "They're here," she said. "Can you feel them? Our angels?" Six months later, *Spring Awakening* opened on Broadway with Melchior's fallen comrades encouraging him on. And by the second sunset after the Parkland shooting, seventeen giant angels were illuminating Pine Trails Park.

As Sater returned to New York, he found he had not left Parkland behind him. Haunted by thoughts of his visit to Douglas, and the memories of vacations in Florida he'd enjoyed in high school, he found himself writing a sonnet:

> *with the students of Stoneman Douglas*
>
> In my dream I knew the sorrow had no end,
> and I would fall upon this in regret,
> for my unremembered Florida—the bald flamingos
>   on the table lamps,
> the days of suntanned childhood here I spent . . .
>
> Today I went (remember this, as Florida), to school
>   I went,
> and I the public, I the scarecrow man,

to study, with the schoolchildren, how not a word
   they wept;
their bleeding throats perhaps too numb
to sing some song of student death,
another, call it, battle hymn,
an outlet song for our America;

Walt Whitman's psalm within the night, by now
   so far recessed,
the earth itself absorbed their cries, the guns
   renew their threats.

And in mid-April, most of the original Broadway cast of *Spring Awakening* came down to Boca to meet with them for a master class. Lea Michele, Jonathan Groff, Gideon Glick, and half a dozen more flew in. Lilli Cooper was starring in *SpongeBob SquarePants* on Broadway, so she FaceTimed. Lots of press appeared to capture it, and the *New York Times* led its arts section with a feature. The kids idolized these people, and Barclay was eager to bring not only joy to their lives, but wisdom as well. These actors had navigated the peril of dark material: how to take the character to the dark place, without getting lost there yourself.

Both generations warmed up together. Then the pros took seats near the stage to watch them rehearse.

They left a few rows open to give them a little breathing room. Phoebe Strole, who played Anna on Broadway, sobbed. She praised their vulnerability during the feedback period. "I can see in your faces and on your bodies what we felt as well when we were first doing the show," she said. "It's like taking your heart out of your chest and shoving it at us."

Volume was still an issue, though. Gideon Glick, who played Ernst on Broadway, told them they had to be louder. "I don't want to be a Jewish mother," he added apologetically.

"Please Jewish-mother them," Barclay said.

They wanted help with the vulnerability without discussing the source directly. Cameron was his usual silly self through most of the rehearsal, but tensed up when someone asked a question headed that way. "We want to talk less about the shooting," he said.

The kids were generally delirious. Alfonso called the actors "his celebrity crushes and dreams." But awe came at a price. He had to simulate masturbation a few rows away from them, big and bold, projecting way beyond them to the empty back rows. The *Times* described him as "ashen" when he was done.

That was nothing, Barclay said. Wait till opening night: "Simulating sex in front of their moms and dads.

It's different than getting up there for a March for Your Life speech talking about gun control."

"It was so uncomfortable," Cameron's mom said. "I kept my eyes directly on the ground. I didn't want them seeing me with my head turned. My husband had purchased the seats and in his mind front row was a great idea, but in this context, Cameron does not want to see his mother in the front row. He didn't say that, but it was pretty obvious. I was five shades of purple, super proud."

The show sold out both nights, so they added two more. They went on without Alfonso. The previous weekend, he had had a tough choice to make. The White House Correspondents' Dinner—when would they get an invite like that again? Seemed like an opportunity for the movement—and a desperately needed break. But it meant missing tech rehearsals. Cameron stayed, Alfonso went, and lost his place in the show. Alex Wind, an understudy and one of the MFOL leaders, took his place.

Opening night, most of the MFOL kids came to support Cameron, Sawyer, Alex, and all the other Douglas kids taking this on. And they were having a blast. They were scattered about the audience in little clusters, searching each other out at intermission, snickering over "The Bitch of Living," and "My Junk," and their friends miming masturbation. They were making plans for the prom, three nights away. During intermission, there was a mild commotion midway back in the audience. Dozens of kids were leaning in toward one magnetic figure, hidden inside a hoodie pulled up over her head, arms flailing, miming some frenetic scenario. David was beside her, giggling uncontrollably. Finally, the hood dropped back just enough to reveal a wispy little butterfly of a young woman. Emma, of course.

But not everyone was responding the same. Dylan Baierlein, perpetually silly and able to find a laugh in anything, looked stricken in the men's room line. "It's a lot," he said gravely. They hadn't even gotten to the death of his best friend yet, or the graveyard scene, but Dylan knew it was coming. He was very close to Cameron. It was hard.

It was a rollicking performance, and the crowd was cheering throughout. When the last scene arrived, and Cameron entered the graveyard, the room fell silent. He discovered Wendla's gravestone, grasped what had happened, and collapsed onto the stage floor sobbing so convincingly through dialogue that it was hard not to picture him holding on to Holden in lockdown. The ghost of his dead friend Moritz then appeared; Cameron told him he'd had the right idea and drew the razor to his neck. But then Wendla rose and both ghosts gently coaxed him back in song:

> *Those you've known,*
> *And lost, still walk behind you.*
> *All alone,*
> *Their song still seems to find you. . . .*

He put away the blade and joined them:

> *All alone,*
> *But still I hear their yearning;*
> *Through the dark, the moon, alone there, burning.*

He gathered his resolve, to live on, to walk on, to call out their names, and belted out:

> *You watch me*
> *Just watch me. . . .*
> *And one day all will know.*

It was eerie. As if the part had been written for these kids. It practically had been. Sater and Sheik had embarked on the project to honor the children of Columbine.

The full cast returned, for a final coda number, which began:

> *Listen to what's in the heart of a child,*
> *A song so big in one so small. . . .*

And when they finished, the applause was uproarious, and for several minutes, the audience remained on its feet. Twelve hundred miles away, an hour or so later, about three dozen shows would take curtain calls on Broadway, and many of their casts would bow to thunderous applause. It might sound the same, but nothing on Broadway could match the feeling in that room in Boca. This audience was applauding not just the performances, but their willingness to go there. To take us there.

Cameron, in particular. I couldn't help but hear the voice of that Parkland teacher at the march two months earlier: "Too much responsibility for these kids." When he wasn't onstage that weekend, Cameron seemed light as a feather. The second show was a Sunday matinee, and three hours earlier, he was clowning around in the studio next door, trying to break a castmate out of his meditation with silly jokes. He was wearing his dog tag from the Peace Warriors. The blue one, to match his outfit.

Not too much responsibility, I thought. Just enough. But maybe I was wrong.

2

Everyone saw a change in David Hogg. Twitter David would escalate, but in real life, the more vicious the attack, the more likely he flipped to anti-David, calmest person in the room. "He's the one who brought the love and compassion to even some of the most fringe groups," Ryan Deitsch said. "David would say, 'Hey, do you want other people to live?' 'Yeah.' And he says, 'Well, let's talk.' And then within fifteen, ten minutes, they're hugging it out. The white supremacists, the neo-Nazis—we disagree on a great variety of things, but some of them have been willing to support some of the things we've been working with."

David had spent a lot of time around Emma, and some of the kids thought she was centering him. "That's true," Pippy said. "He's very much like a kid when Emma's around."

Twitter David's mellowing was more gradual. By May, several of the kids said they had discovered he got less bombastic if they let him vent a little.

"He's calmer a lot more recently, but when something ticks him off, like on Twitter, you can't get him out of it, it's done," Pippy said. She said he would obsess and intensify until one of them told him just tweet it already. "And he's like, 'OK it's done.' It doesn't last long."

Cameron and David had grown accustomed to the media glare, but it was striking how they dealt with it so differently. Cameron needed his audience to love him. His yearning for validation seemed boundless and dramatic. David didn't give a shit. In fact, he kind of enjoyed being attacked. Sure, it pissed him off, but he relished the counterpunch. Few things made him happier than eviscerating an Internet troll.

I bounced that analysis of the two of them off David. He chuckled and agreed. "Yeah, I would say he kind of needs people's validation. Just being an actor and all." He smirked. "Not a crisis actor. I like using acting and theater as a symbolism for politics, because it's spectacle." He admitted that you need people to like you to be effective, though. "That's what politicians need, too. It's just politicians acting in the real world, and never taking down their facade. For me, I don't have that facade." He said his brutal candor was "the best and worst part about me. People know how I feel, and if you're an asshole, I'm going to say it."

He smiled when he said that. He was smiling a lot now. His parents marveled at the return to serenity—bouts of it, at least. "I just think over time it kind of settled out," he said. "The anger in this marathon, it's like a drug. It's good at getting things done quickly, but not in the longer term. Love and compassion and patience is the stamina you need to make long, substantial change. This is a slow burn. We started out as one spark in a field of tinder, and now we've really, really started to burn into the hundred-year-old oaks. That's what we have to do. If we have to burn down the entire forest to grow a new one, without the sprouting of corruption, through voting, we'll do it."

Calmer, but still David. In the middle of his reflection on love and tranquility, the metaphor grabbed hold of him and burned the forest down.

He kept catching himself swearing that visit. He was trying to kick that, at least in interviews. But he still said "fuck" twenty-eight times in two hours. They were softer curses, though, without the vitriol.

The NRA was still most likely to draw a "fuck" out of David. Their five-million-members claim annoyed him. "I highly doubt that. They say they speak for the majority of gun owners. Only one in ten gun owners is actually a member. They're a loud minority."

MFOL was speaking for the majority, he said—though he wished his cohort would speak up on Election Days. "Whenever I talk to groups and they ask me why young people vote so little, I look at them blankly and I say it's because they don't give a fuck." David said. "It's not that hard to get out and vote."

But he echoed Harvard's Della Volpe on how to change that. "People need to see impact," David said. "For somebody to cross the bridge of fear, they need to see materialization." The real test wasn't electing the legislators or passing the legislation, or quibbling about what constitutes "meaningful" change. Those were all means, and only the end mattered: driving down the rate of gun deaths. That was a long way off, and until they reached that threshold, it would be "like trying to prove that bigfoot doesn't exist."

3

Prom was the same weekend as *Spring Awakening*. Best chance all spring to put guns aside for one night. "Prom is really important to keep morale high," Dylan said. "That's a night of happiness and fun. You can't lose sight of those things. Somebody brought up this idea of having something about the shooting at prom, and we were like, 'That's the worst idea you've ever come up with!' Prom should be a night where they can be normal. Nobody should feel guilty about being happy. It's something we all deserve."

But Dylan had never been sucked into a mass shooting vortex before. They were rife with competing agendas, and the most sensitive was honoring the dead. Columbine remained closed for four months after its tragedy, until the first day of fall semester. Students felt so robbed of their school's identity that they staged an elaborate Take Back the School rally, including a human shield of parents to block the press from witnessing it. The school consulted closely with grief counselors, who recommended that for that one day, the focus be entirely on the kids and moving forward, with just a brief gesture toward the deaths. Minutes after the kids cut the ribbon and joyously retook their school, parents of the fallen staged an impromptu press conference to berate the school for failing to properly acknowledge their loss.

Douglas High was not going to repeat that mistake. The dead were honored several ways at the prom. There was a montage of photos submitted by students, and a memorial mall just outside the main ballroom honoring the four seniors killed on Valentine's Day—Meadow Pollack, Nicholas Dworet, Joaquin Oliver, and Carmen Schentrup—plus two members of the class of 2018 who had died in 2016. They observed seventeen seconds of silence between dinner and dancing.

But mostly it was fun. The Westin Fort Lauderdale Beach Resort was transformed into an enchanted forest, with a thicket of imitation trees, roamed by actors in elaborate costumes playing wood nymphs, forest creatures, and deer. Real butterflies fluttered down from the roof. Most of the services were donated, so kids had to pay only a fraction of the cost. Many had their hair and makeup done at a free makeover event.

Joaquin Oliver's girlfriend, Victoria González, went with his best friend, Dillon McCooty. Only seniors and their dates can attend prom at Douglas, so several of the MFOL kids paired off so juniors could go as well. Neither David nor Emma was dating anyone, so they both went with the person they felt closest to: each other. It wasn't a political statement or any kind of statement. But it sure as hell would be taken that way. The rumor mill would go nuts.

David's mom, Rebecca, wanted Emma to feel special. David was supposed to get her a wrist corsage, and of course he had no idea what to choose, but Rebecca did. She wanted something unique and exotic. She found a braided silver bracelet, capped by a succulent bloom, tiny green and white bulbs, with rosy pink tips.

It was stunning and different, a gorgeous flower but stronger and prickly. It was Emma.

Rebecca wanted three things from that wrist corsage, for three different people. She wanted Emma to light up when she saw it. She wanted David to swell with pride for bringing her that joy. And she wanted to savor that moment and share it with all her friends—on Facebook. She wanted her life back too. Just for one night. She had just one son, and he would never have another prom. Let her be a mom again for one night.

The price was too high, David said. He would love to make her happy, but did she understand what they were up against? This whole movement seemed to be turning into a cult of personalities. The stories were not about the group anymore, or the movement; they had turned into profile pieces now, nearly always about him and Emma. He spent every day fighting that, trying to train the media onto the message, and the two of them dating? The Internet would go nuts. So would a lot of mainstream press. They weren't dating, but that would hardly matter. It would set them back months.

They had a wonderful time at the prom. Social media was awash in photos. Alfonso posted pictures with Delaney. Emma and David appeared in lots of group photos, but none made it out with them as a couple.

Months later, *New York* magazine ran a profile of David, and he let them mention the prom pairing in passing. It was old news by then, and The Internet likes its rumors fresh. It didn't cause a ripple.

4

I met Lauren Hogg once or twice a month throughout much of the year, and over that time, her recovery played out visibly on her face. A month out she looked ashen, with a borderline blank affect. At the first school walkout, she held up a hand-painted sign with David at the rally, and spoke enthusiastically about the surprise breakout from school, but she still looked stricken. Defiant, but stricken. Six weeks later, on David's prom night, she was a completely different person. She looked joyful, like an ordinary teen.

"I guess I've kind of gotten better, but I don't really know how you get better from stuff like this," she said. "For me, it really just goes in waves." She had come on board as a full-fledged MFOL member, and that was making a huge difference. "Activism and hanging out with my March for Our Lives friends and my friends from school has really helped. Definitely therapeutic for me."

Actual therapy was helping too. "My mom makes me

go to therapy every week—like if not once, twice," she said.

Many in the group described a sort of group self-therapy they were conducting during their meetings, which they still held at least once a week. Dylan described a typical recent session: "We all went around to every single person and we talked about how we were doing emotionally and mentally, so it's all out there in the open. We help each other with it, because we trust each other more than we trust any therapist or shrink. There's that stubbornness that kids have, that 'I don't want to talk to an adult—I'd rather talk to my friends.' So we are each other's best help."

"We would call that a process group," Dr. Ley said. "Processing the trauma together, with people who've been through a similar experience, and who are really a close-knit group, can be helpful, can be lifesaving." The kids had incredible instincts to create what they needed and ensure everyone participated, she said. But there are limits. "If they reach the level of having psychiatric symptoms, post-traumatic stress disorder, or depression, anxiety, I don't think that process group is going to rise to the level of what they need."

Many of the kids expressed mixed feelings about professional therapy. Lauren figured it was probably good for her, but she hated talking about the horror, bringing it back over and over. They were great at the beginning, she said—being available in the moment, when the wave struck, instead of dredging it up on a schedule. "When we first went back to school there were therapists literally everywhere. There were therapists in the media center." Now, if she needed one, if a friend was having a crisis . . . "I don't know. I couldn't tell you where to go."

That had been a big problem when *The Eagle Eye* produced a special glossy edition on the seventeen victims in April. There was a two-page spread on each of them, with lots of photos and magazine-quality production values. It's a gut punch for even a stranger to read. It was distributed in fourth period, to coincide with the shooting, and Lauren was OK at first, but began to break down as the portraits drew her in. Some girls in the class responded with gallows humor. Lauren mustered all her politeness to say that she was having a really hard time and asked them to stop. "This one girl turned around—I don't know how she could do this, she was there that day," Lauren said. "She was like, 'No.' They started laughing. And I kind of lost it. I broke down, I started crying—I don't usually cry at school. But I started crying so hard and these kids were laughing." She said other kids told them to stop, but she had to get out of there. "I literally got up, I grabbed tissues and I went and stood in the hallway by myself. Because I didn't know where to go."

She told the story on prom day, and found the magazine nearby in the living room to show me. She flipped through it again and it brought her right back—to the episode receiving it, and to Valentine's Day. It was a trigger, but it was also beautiful, and she kept it nearby. "I feel like I'm having an identity crisis," she said. "I went into that building and I came out a different person. I don't know who I am anymore. Sometimes I feel like I'm an adult trapped in a fourteen-year-old's body."

The MFOL kids were the only ones who understood, Lauren said. "We go from joking around and laughing and being like five-year-olds to being like a thirty-year-old. I feel like I have this capability to talk to adults and politicians in a mature way, but then I kind of sit there and I'm like, 'Wait, I'm fourteen! Like what am I doing here?'"

David thought Lauren was doing better. Probably. "I think so," he said. "It's hard to tell." It was frustrating. He didn't know how to help her. So many people he couldn't help. "I'll be with friends and sometimes they'll just break down," he said. "It's really fucking

shitty to be there for them and not be able to do anything. You can't bring somebody back from the dead."

Their mom, Rebecca, gasped at the idea that Lauren
was appreciably better. "I think she's having a really
hard time," she said. "She's having nightmares about
her friends bleeding. Last week she climbed into our
bed. Last night she fell asleep at three in the morning, but when she got home from school yesterday, we
didn't see her for four hours because she was sleeping.
So her whole sleep schedule's off. We've gone to the
pediatrician and I was hoping for something more
powerful but they recommended lemon balm. 'Fuck' is
what I have to say. I was thinking Xanax and sleeping
pills. But they're going the natural route."

5

Mother's Day had been looming. Seventeen parents
had lost their son or daughter. Some of the victims were
adults, but they were all someone's child. The pain was
compounded by the three-month anniversary, landing
just a day afterward.

Tío Manny and Patricia were bracing for it. They
had a plan. "Mother's Day is going to be an intimate
moment at home," Manny said. "We can get away by
putting some food together, and not have anybody at

home. Because the whole approach of people giving condolences at this point, it's not helping, it's only making things worse."

It was horrible, but they got through it. The occasion that really scared them was graduation. "We don't control what they're planning to do," Tío Manny said. "I assume they're going to have emotional moments, because they always do that. They want to be good. It's not that they do this to hurt us, but at the end of the day it does hurt us. I would rather have a graduation day where you go there and then be home in a minute." He considered for a moment, and began to waver. "I need to be there. So I don't know."

6

Graduation, for so many school-shooting survivors, is the most conflicted day of their recovery. From that first day of life after "it," graduation rises dimly on some distant horizon, painfully far and unattainable. Few kids think about it in the early days, as they console each other to "just get through it," whatever that means. But as graduation approaches, more than any other milestone, the emotional finish line hardens into The Day: graduation from the first horrible phase. So June 3 brought a huge rush of accomplishment, a weight lifted, and for many a big FU moment to the perp. *We got this!*

But the pain. Meadow Pollack, Nicholas Dworet, Joaquin Oliver, and Carmen Schentrup were missing from their graduating class. That was news to no one, yet the act of eight hundred peers donning caps and gowns to celebrate, moving on to college, to life, to adulthood, without them felt almost cruel.

Graduation day was as bad as Tío Manny envisioned, but he would unleash his rage on a mural in Chicago twelve days later. At the graduation ceremony, he contained it. Tío Manny attended with his wife and daughter. When Joaquin's name was called out, his parents came forward, and Patricia accepted his diploma. She wore a lemon yellow T-shirt emblazoned top to bottom:

THIS
SHOULD BE
MY
SON

The crowd roared, Patricia smiled, blew a kiss, and raised her open arms. Manny raised his fist.

"Some people thought that we weren't going to show at graduation, because it was too sad," Tío Manny said. "Yes, it is sad, but that's not as important as sending a message. You need to take these opportunities and just change it. Flip them."

19

Road to Change

1

Now what? The march was over, summer demanded something big. They could never top DC for national exposure, but they were focused on local networks now—expanding and energizing all the fledgling groups. It was all about direct contact: where they were needed was on the road. They had been traveling in twos and threes—what if they multiplied that? Create some sort of event status, sustained over a season. They kept brainstorming, and a two-month bus tour took shape. The entire summer vacation, essentially, from a week after graduation through the last free weekend before returning to school. They hashtagged it #RoadToChange.

So where to go? There were lots of competing ideas: swing districts, swing states, sites of previous tragedies, centers of urban violence, big population centers, cities with vibrant groups, groups crying out for help.

So they researched it heavily, and mapped out a route to hit all of them. But they all agreed that one element was critical: they had to return to gun country. Their focus was the midterms, but this was only year one; they had to look beyond November as well. They routed most of the summer's bus tour through deep red states: Texas, Kansas, Nebraska, and South Carolina. "Most of the tour stops are the places where it's most likely people disagree with us," Jackie said. The Farm Belt, the Mountain West, and the Deep South. "We want them to show up and listen to what we have to say. They'll bring back that conversation to other people that disagree."

Matt Deitsch, now the group's chief strategist, referred to those stops as "the places where the hate comes from." He meant the hate against them. But when I called it enemy territory, he cringed. Those stops were all about *talking* with antagonists—not *fighting*. Even hard-core Second Amendment warriors often agreed with them on background checks, and sometimes with their whole list of demands. But the myths had spread so quickly about those demands. Matt recounted an angry man berating him for trying to repeal the Second Amendment. "We have never advocated that," Matt assured him. "Yes you did, it was on your website," the man said. No, that was probably John Paul Stevens, Matt said. The retired Supreme Court justice had published a *New York Times* op-ed advising repeal three days after the march. "Oh no, that's not good," Matt had thought immediately. "People will associate that with us." And they had. The gun debate was fueled by anger, with very little listening.

And no one was really listening on social media. "We knew from the start that tweeting just wasn't going to do it," Jackie said. "When we try to have conversations with people online that disagree with us, it's really unsuccessful. When we actually sit down, there's something about human connection that's just different."

They spent much of the spring working out the details, right up to departure. But by April, they had made the single biggest decision of the tour: where to begin. They knew the media; everything had to be fresh, first, early. It was all about anticipation. The national media would show up exactly one time—on day one—then disappear. They might get more coverage announcing the tour than actually doing it, if they kept it under wraps and unveiled it as a big surprise. They had one big chance, to choose one big symbol. They chose the Peace March.

For ten years, Father Pfleger and Saint Sabina church had organized fed-up citizens to march through their South Side neighborhood weekly to reclaim it. Every Friday night of summer, they put the gangs and drug lords and anyone else with a gun on notice: *Meet the resistance—we do not accept the madness.* MFOL chose Chicago as a signal too. They chose to march through that neighborhood with the national press corps marching at their sides, to send a message to every Peace Warrior and BRAVE kid on the front lines, and every ally in their communities: *We are with you.*

Choosing the Peace March dovetailed with another prime objective: helping local activists strengthen their own initiatives. This community had been working on this project for a decade. They built it from scratch, when people thought they were crazy. They persevered, and they were really having an impact, bigger every year. MFOL could bring tremendous exposure, which would likely translate into fund-raising dollars as well. Why create a one-off event, when they could have such a powerful impact for one of their partners? "The Peace March has been proven to save lives," Matt said. "Why not support something actually saving lives?"

———————

They embargoed coverage until a big announcement on June 4. That would give the group a tight ten-day window to kickoff: long enough for media to schedule coverage, but short enough to forestall its ADHD.

They settled on two buses on simultaneous tours: one across America, and the other across Florida, hitting every congressional district in their home state. But who would travel on each bus? It's a question that ultimately answered itself. The national tour would be far more grueling, covering several hundred miles over many days. Some of the kids were eager to take that on; others wanted to stay close to home. Everybody on the bus would get plenty of opportunities to speak. They would use a panel format at the town halls, and rotate the speakers every night. Emma and David needed to be on the national bus, because kids really wanted to meet them, but they didn't need to be onstage—and they generally weren't.

The group did its usual due diligence and anticipated all the ways their plan could go wrong. Then they got realistic. Sixty straight days was way too much. Showing up in each city beat-up mentally, physically, and emotionally would be worse than not showing up at all.

They broke the national tour into three legs, around two weeks each, with short breaks in between. They would cover a city a day, and a new hotel every night. It became clear that there were not enough hours to sleep, so they hired a jumbo bus with a bunk section.

It was very much like a rock band tour, and that was the model. They hired a tour manager and a staff of about half a dozen. Much of that was security, which their parents demanded. The bus would be unmarked. There was no way to go stealth in a vehicle that size, but they didn't have to announce themselves with blaring logos. A separate van would follow with security, in case the bus was attacked. They hired a PR firm, and its leader would travel on the whole tour. All that staff also solved the chaperone dilemma. And the parents demanded one more thing: a mental health worker.

Scheduling and organizing the events would be a massive undertaking. It would require them to establish a remote network in every city, and then to work with that network from afar. That seemed like way too much for one person, yet it would be most efficient if someone could pull it off. Jackie stepped up.

Combined, the two buses would cover more than ten thousand miles, fifty cities, and twenty-eight states. Each event would light up local media coverage of the issue. The primary goal, however, was juicing 762 fledgling networks: connecting young local leaders, energizing them, guiding them, validating their achievements, and putting them onstage so they could be featured on the TV news.

2

June 14, the #RoadToChange tour kicked off in Chicago. The Peace March was heavily promoted on-line, with Jennifer Hudson and Chance the Rapper performing. But Emma González got top billing. One of the posters was dominated by a photo of her, with the others mentioned only by name, below hers.

All the kids from both bus tours came. The press came too. Saint Sabina built a media riser, and filled it with reporters from several networks and national magazines. That was great, but two months of local media was the real prize. Local media has an inor-dinately large influence on voters, so that's where legislators and candidates direct their attention. The Parkland kids wanted to inject guns back into the con-versation at each stop, influence candidates to make it a campaign issue, energize local activists to keep the issue alive, and do the relentless spadework needed to register waves of young voters and entice them to vote for the first time.

The June Peace March drew a crowd of thousands, its largest ever by far. No one had bothered to size them before, but Trevon Bosley estimated it was 50 percent bigger than the previous high. He had been working with BRAVE for years, and had attended most of the marches. "There's always a lot of people, but this march . . ." He shook his head in disbelief. "And the vibe is different. Usually it's a serious, calm vibe. This year it was a lot of energy. Happy energy. Being spread through the community, as well as through the group."

"This is my first one," Alex King said. "It was lit. It was a whole lot of positive vibes. It was our time to show we can have all these people together and have a good time. It doesn't have to end in violence or lead to that."

Everyone marveled at all the white people. The locals said they were thrilled to have them. They needed those white people, and if it took the Parkland kids to bring them, bless those kids.

Emma did not speak at the rally, which caused a bit of consternation in the press. The whole group of Parkland kids came onstage together for a show of support, and that was it. They were highly visible throughout the parade, though, and spirits were soaring. Residents came down their front porch steps and spilled out of shops to join the march or to dance along with the music on the sidewalk. Daniel Duff, the freshman who discovered Cher on march day, lost his friends in the melee, but found new ones, several girls from Michigan giddy about marching with one of the Parkland kids. "I haven't felt anything like this since DC," Daniel said. Jennifer Hudson walked the two miles in floppy bedroom slippers with bows. Despite the unsensible footgear, she was all hugs and smiles at the finish line.

The Peace March was for the public; the private meeting the next morning was for the kids. It was the same nucleus that had been conferring since the March meeting at Emma's house, but expanded on both sides. The whole MFOL team was there now—the Peace Warriors, BRAVE students, and more kids from Mansueto High. They had breakfast together, talked, and played games for four hours.

There was a press avail afterward, with a stipulation: Parkland kids would speak only when paired with a local kid—and the interview had better focus on the locals, or they would walk away. That infuriated some of the reporters, but it was an astute tactic. The kids tended to be one step ahead of us. They couldn't force us to write Chicago stories, but they could force us to hear a few. And they got how we operated. We tend to move in packs, and come in with our stories mentally prewritten. The only way to alter that is to give us a better story. And the Chicago kids had amazing stories.

Trevon Bosley told one of them. His brother Terrell was shot and killed stepping out of church on Chicago's Far South Side in 2006. "He was getting ready for band rehearsal," Trevon said. "He was loading drums out of his friend's car outside of church." Terrell was eighteen, just starting college, making his way out of the neighborhood. Trevon was seven.

"The killer of my brother is still free because, many people don't know this, but only seventeen percent get convicted," Trevon said. These kids knew their statistics, cited them constantly, and they checked out. "It's the code in Chicago that if you talk, something might happen to you," he said. "If everybody talks, they might come after everybody." The police tended to drop the ball too, Trevon said. His family had gotten an anonymous tip and passed it to the detectives, but they never followed up. "But when it was an ATF agent that was shot here in Chicago, they got that case solved in like the same week."

Trevon joined BRAVE when he was ten or eleven, and he was still active as a junior at Southern Illinois University. BRAVE was doing amazing work, he said, but what a struggle for resources. Media attention was crucial to building a donor base, but that was a struggle too.

"We did a press conference probably like three years ago, and there was no press at all," he said. They had organized a big collection of advocacy groups to maximize impact at a critical moment, but the media passed. "A month of shootings had happened where it was probably fifty-plus shootings. The youth were tired of it, the kids were tired of it. We had some little kids; they spoke. No media came. We still had our press conference, because we still wanted everybody to understand, at least the people that did show up. That was tough. They say, 'We care youth are dying, oh we care about it.' But when we call you to show up for us, where are you?"

He said that had begun to change since February. Media interest in their efforts had picked up—not enough, but a start. And that weekend was a huge infusion. If they came back.

Was it a little insulting that it took the Parkland kids to bring in the press?

"It was a little upsetting at first, but then you have to realize at least it's here," Trevon said. "You can't just dwell on the past."

They talked about the future, what they hoped to see five years down the road. "I'd love to see a lot of the youth activists, whether it's Peace Warriors, BRAVE, any of those different groups, I'd love to see some of us in office by that time," Trevon said. "I'd love to see us holding down political spots. As well as I would love to see divisions start to disappear. Chicago's a tale of two cities. Whether you're downtown or you're on the South Side, it's going to be completely different. I'd love to see more equality throughout the city. I want to see gun violence just go down immensely. I want to see the education system change. I know that's a lot to ask for."

"Don't say it's a lot to ask for," Aalayah Eastmond said. "We deserve it." Aalayah was a Parkland student, African American, and one of the recent additions to the team.

"I want to see happiness in my community," Alex King said. "I want to see the next generation, I want to see them being able to play outside. Being able to sit on the porch and nothing happen to them. Being able to go to their neighborhood park, being able to go to a friend's house. Being able to go to church. Being able to go to school and be safe. I want to see that joy. I want to see the sense of people wanting to be alive, and not fearing for their lives."

The tour was all about connecting with young locals, who had typically gotten their activist feet wet organizing a sibling march or a school walkout. They had tasted success, proved their ability to peers and themselves, and flung themselves into the fight for the midterms. The Parkland kids had provided a model, validation, and hope.

Diego Garcia was there, the Latino kid who had struggled for adult respect in his community. The Parkland kids' approval had been key to earning it, but it came at a price. He had just organized a die-in at Chicago's Trump International Hotel and Tower, and the Parkland kids helped spur attendance by retweeting it. But Twitter trolls descended and terrified him with some of their threats. The MFOL kids were used to that, but he wasn't. Yet.

A big element of the tour that was not announced to the media in advance was connecting with some of the promising activists by bringing them on board—literally. If it worked out, the group would look for candidates in other cities. "Once we hung out with them, they were like, 'We want to come!'" Jackie said. "So we added a lot more people." They left Saint Sabina with seven Chicago recruits, including Alex and D'Angelo from the Peace Warriors, Diego Garcia, and Trevon. They filled out release forms with family contact information at the barbeque. "It's quite literally like the Freedom Riders, where people hop on and hop off," Jackie said.

3

Town halls were the tour staple: the Parkland kids in conversation with young local activists, and sometimes a third contingent. Night two of the bus tour was only thirty miles from Saint Sabina, but culturally worlds away. The town hall was held at a Unitarian Universalist church in suburban Naperville, mostly white, and also Asian—not just affluent, genteel. The crowd was wildly enthusiastic. They leapt to their feet for the Parkland kids' arrival. When it ended, much of the crowd rushed the stage: not just to chat up the Parkland kids and grab a selfie, but to talk to the local teens as well. They were ecstatic. To appear on that stage as peers, beside these national sensations, completely changed their sense of this mission. Changed the way they were seen by their parents, teachers, and school administrators—some of whom had chastised them as being immature for participating in the walkouts. Changed their image of themselves. Possibly forever.

The event definitely fired up the young activists, but it was hard to imagine changing any minds that night. The free tickets had been snapped up in a few hours online, and the room seemed packed with true believers. But believers in what? Gun legislation, definitely, but how many members of that genteel suburban community were engaged in the deadly struggle underway on the South Side or West Side of Chicago, thirty miles away? Probably very few. But many were making that connection for the first time and thinking about "the gun problem" in a new light.

The new freedom riders from Chicago provided some of the most poignant moments at the Naperville event, and provoked most of the standing ovations. These minority activists were bright and charismatic. They might have rivaled Emma and David in an alternate universe that cared about black kids.

A telling thing happened at the end of the Naperville event. Jackie was moderating, and after the last question, she asked if any of the panelists had a final thought. One of the Chicago kids made a plea for donations for the Peace Warriors, "Even if it's five dollars." And then it was over, and the local host activists on the panel, mostly from Downers Grove North High School, rose to present a check to the Parkland kids. They had been working their butts off on fundraisers to support the bus tour, selling wristbands and buttons, and holding a car wash that very afternoon, and had raised $1,118, a few dollars at a time. They had printed up one of those huge cardboard blow-up checks to present together, and were all smiles. Cameron Kasky was one of the MFOL kids on the panel, and before the Downers Grove kids even reached him with the check, he said, "As our first gesture to work with Chicago students, we are pledging all of that money to ChicagoStrong.org." ChicagoStrong is an umbrella organization created in the wake of Parkland to connect and support like-minded groups across the city, including Peace Warriors and BRAVE. Jackie was across the stage from Cameron, and seconds later she added, "We're also going to double it."

Had they planned this? Staged it? Jackie and Cameron had no time to confer with the group—had they acted on their own? A few days later, Jackie said she had seen the check during the event, but the rest of the MFOL panel was taken aback. "We all came to the same conclusion, I think. We all looked at each other, and we were like, 'No, we can't take that! Are you kidding?' We've had tons of great foundation [support] for March for Our Lives, and these kids literally were begging for money onstage."

What happened later, behind the scenes, embodied what the Parkland kids are trying to do. "I talked to the Naperville girl after she gave the check and she was

like, 'Wow, I didn't even think about giving it to ChicagoStrong, but that is such a good idea!'" Jackie said.
So she tried to steer the conversation toward "How are
we going to continue the relationship between Naperville and the surrounding suburbs, and the Chicago
students?" she said. "Because I don't think that they
realize they should create that connection and continue
it after."

That's really the whole ball game. Thirty Parkland
kids cannot turn 435 House races around—or influence thousands of races on local ballots. One night
in Naperville, Bismarck, or San Antonio won't even
jump-start a struggling campaign. But it can fire up a
movement.

"Teenagers are sometimes nervous to make friends
and stuff," Jackie said. "So creating a network of kids
and organizations that can help each other without us
being the mediators is so important. Because we're not
superheroes. This Road to Change is connecting people along the way—so they can work together in the
future."

The Parkland, Chicago, and Naperville kids all
talked about that afterward, Jackie said. "And they
were like, 'We definitely want to work with them in the
future.' And we all went to dinner afterwards together,
so we definitely connected."

4

The Parkland kids had either helped amp up interest in the midterms, or picked the right year to engage with voters. A Pew Research Center survey that summer found 51 percent of voters—and 55 percent of voters supporting Democrats—enthusiastic about the midterms. Those are the highest numbers ever recorded since it began asking twenty-one years ago, and double digits above five of the last six midterms at the same point.

By summer, signs had been accumulating that gun control was finally becoming a viable issue on the Left. The established wisdom has always been that Democrats don't vote on guns. Neither do most Republicans. But a small subset does—sometimes enough to sway a primary. This asymmetry allows a tiny minority to consistently defeat huge majorities, or to convince politicians they will.

In late spring and early summer, national polls identified gun legislation as the third or fourth priority for voters heading into the midterms—after the economy and health care, but ahead of immigration and taxes. That's up from rarely making the list in recent years. CNN's polling unit regularly asked voters to rate issues in importance on their next vote for Congress. Gun policy had soared to 49 percent "extremely important" and

30 percent "very important" a week after Parkland—
numbers some predicted would fall just as fast as they
had risen. But their next poll in May had "extremely"
important ticking down just four points—still more
than double the figure from 2002—and "very important" rising one.

But would these trends translate to votes? In late July,
TargetSmart released an analysis of Parkland's impact
on voter registration. Six battleground states showed an
increase of 8 to 16 percent among voters aged eighteen
to twenty-nine. The numbers are actually better than
they look at first blush. The *Miami Herald* did a great
analysis of the Florida numbers, in much more detail.
In Florida, young voters added 7 percent new registra-
tions in 2.5 months. This may sound modest, but that's
7 percent of people choosing to register for the first time
in their lives. A better comparison is looking at compa-
rable time frames. For all Florida voters, fewer people
registered in the 2.5 months immediately after Parkland
than before. But in the under-twenty-nine group, registration surged by an unprecedented 41 percent.

5

Cameron had a personal message for the group's skep-
tics out in gun country. "I have guns in my home," he

told one audience. "My friend David does as well." Both their dads work in law enforcement, and the guns are stored responsibly in their homes, he said. "I don't know where the key is. I don't want to know where the key is. Our house practices responsible gun ownership. I was at a gun range when I was eight. We are trying to promote laws and changes that make gun ownership in this country more responsible."

On the bus tour, they typically wrapped up around nine p.m., followed by selfies, one-on-one connections with audience members, and dinners with local organizers. By the time the kids staggered back to their hotel rooms it was usually midnight. Then they'd wake up around dawn, drive four to eight hours, and repeat.

It was a massive logistical undertaking. And a tough slog. Halfway through, in Denver, the Parkland kids were still in good spirits, but the grueling schedule was wearing them down. "You eat unhealthy food and you don't sleep properly and your body's just always confused," Jackie said.

"Your body, it's not made to sleep on a bus," Alfonso said. "So like I'll go to sleep, I'll wake up in two hours, my body will be completely destroyed, right? I'll drink some water, chew some gum, and it's just the same thing for so, so long." He described bus life as a big crew crammed into a small apartment. "We're twenty-two people in total on the bus and we have about like twenty square feet of up and down and it's basically split up. There's a little section where most of the adults stay to do their work, and then there's just the strip with like beds, the front where the tables are." Some of the kids would always be working at the tables, Jackie for sure.

Jackie said she was unable to sleep on the bus, so she tried to get work cranked out. Her big challenge was the logistics. She had taken the lead on organizing all the events. Whatever cornfields or mountains were rolling by her bus window, Jackie's head and phone were several days and thousands of miles ahead, arranging venues, permits, publicity, and speakers. She coordinated with local chapters to handle a thousand tiny details, like T-shirt sales and check-in wristbands, and of course all those kids with clipboards registering young new voters.

"Every morning I wake up to anywhere between twenty and one hundred texts," Jackie said in late July, as she geared up for the tour's final leg. She typically worked with three to four lead organizers in each city, and juggled several states at a time.

Many of the connections are with adults as well, and meeting the diminutive seventeen-year-old behind the tour sometimes took them by surprise. Paula Reed, the

Columbine teacher who'd met with the other Parkland group in April, was again asked to speak when the bus tour came to Denver. Later, Reed posted this on Facebook: "When I got out of my car and met Jaclyn, I thought she had to be a different Jaclyn than the one I'd been in contact with about the event. I just didn't picture someone so young."

The MFOL team scoured each city for promising young leaders. Every few stops, they coax one or more on board. They arrived in Denver with four kids they had picked up in Houston, one from Milwaukee, and three from Chicago, plus one from Harlem they had connected with earlier. They are cultivating a cadre of young leaders and giving them crash courses in public speaking and other skills. For the first time, MFOL expanded beyond Douglas students and recent graduates on the bus tour, widening out to a national network, with many of these new recruits full members of the national team.

MFOL prides itself on being nimble, and by midsummer the Florida tour was rechristened the "Southern Tour" and expanded to include Alabama, Mississippi, and Louisiana. Based on RSVPs over the course of the summer, the group would estimate it met fifty thousand people. The events tended to be well organized, if not always well promoted. They relied on their local contacts to reach local media and local networks. Some kids were great at that, with big networks to plug into. Others clearly had no idea. Most events were sell-outs, often standing-room only, but some houses were half-full. Media and promotion was clearly the organization's weak link.

<h1 style="text-align:center">6</h1>

A gun group decided to follow them for four days across Texas. It staged small counterprotests at every stop "with guns bigger than they were," as one of the kids mentioned. When they pulled into Denver a few days later, some of the kids were shaken up. "People had like two ARs, two pistols, two handguns strapped on their belt, and a knife," Jackie said. "Are you trying to prove a point? Because you look dumb." She was a bit rattled, but not deterred.

And as they were leaving Texas, another group in Utah announced it would follow the kids' bus there with a military-style vehicle, topped with a replica machine gun. The Salt Lake City movie theater scheduled to host their event promptly disinvited them, citing fear of violence. Jackie had three days to salvage the event as they pulled into Denver, a challenging stop. In addition to the town hall and a barbeque there, she had organized a meeting between her group and two dozen survivors of Columbine, Aurora, and a host of other mass shootings. "We are getting a new venue! No worries!" Jackie tweeted the same day the theater canceled. "A lot of venues reached out to us in the area because they felt bad," she said. "The other venue just canceled because they were scared for security reasons. We're targets."

It was generally Matt and David who peeled off from the group to engage with the counterprotestors. David may have seemed like the most inflammatory choice, but he was really good at deescalating when he wanted to, and in person, he generally wanted to. Cameron told a town hall about David getting accosted at a Publix supermarket, someone "spewing hate into his face," and David calmly talked him down.

The gun-toters' effect on the kids varied. Some said it didn't bother them at all—and it didn't seem to. Just more people trying to intimidate them. No real danger. But others, grappling with trauma issues that weren't going away, were having a rough time in these situations. Symptoms of trauma and depression are not always overt. No one knows when you're fighting to get out of bed every day, or quietly breaking down in your room. Parents, siblings, and close friends are often taken by surprise.

The kids also made a conscious decision to route their tour through the sites of several tragic shootings—including Newtown, Aurora, Ferguson, and Columbine. The survivors taught them a great deal about recovery, coping with the spotlight, and the stages of trauma ahead. And they got a crash course on an entire generation of survivors struggling to find a way out of this blight: tactics that have succeeded, as well as others that had seemed promising but fell flat.

Tom Mauser, perhaps the godfather of their movement, appeared with them at the Denver town hall. Tom was the only parent or spouse of the thirteen murdered at Columbine to take on gun safety aggressively in 1999. He soldiered on alone, later joined by hundreds affected by subsequent tragedies—and in nineteen years, he's learned a thing or two. Though most of the crowd came out to see the Parkland kids, it was Tom Mauser's name on so many lips as the audience drifted out.

Mauser had lamented that Eric Harris and Dylan Klebold had gotten three of their four guns through the so-called gun show loophole. For a year, legislators failed to close that loophole, even in Colorado in the wake of the tragedy. Finally Mauser helped lead an effort to put it on the state ballot. It passed by 40 points. "If you put something reasonable in front of people, they will support it," he said.

He also cautioned that the NRA had been winning with a narrative suggesting that cities like Chicago with the most restrictive gun laws suffer the worst gun violence. But most of Chicago's guns came from Indiana. "It's a lie!" he shouted. "But the NRA narrative is believed by a lot of people. You have to change that."

The most powerful moments on the tour were often unforeseen. One night in Denver, Paula Reed, who had also taught Tom Mauser's son, Daniel, appeared with him, and she repeated her story about the horror of being asked to shoot Dylan. What she didn't realize was that Dylan's mother, Sue Klebold, was seated in the front row, facing her, barely ten feet away. Sue stopped taking notes and set her notepad down. She appears so rarely in public that even in that crowd, she had gone unnoticed. Sue had come to support the MFOL kids, who had asked to meet her for dinner afterward. She and the Parkland kids chose to keep the conversation private, but each raved about the other. "I'm smitten by those kids," Sue emailed me the next morning.

20

Homeward Bound

1

The bus tour was a time of reckoning. Exhausting, monotonous, and mind-numbingly repetitive. It mirrored the strains that tear apart so many touring bands: same faces, in the same small space, repeating the same greatest hits every night. They had been honing their best lines and best anecdotes for six months. So sick of their own words. The cities, the stages, and the faces staring back changed, but blurred together too quickly to make an impression.

But for some, it was also invigorating. Like troubadours, they were drawn to it. "You just picked up a hitcher / A prisoner of the white lines on the freeway," Joni Mitchell once sang.

The timing was also consequential: six months into this new relationship with their new selves. If the first four seemed breakneck, it was nothing compared with this. And as they gazed ahead to the last stops, a new version of their old lives awaited them. The younger contingent would arrive back in Parkland on Monday, have a single day off; then on Wednesday morning, they'd start their senior, junior, or sophomore years. And for others like Emma, it was a bigger change. First day of college, first day of adulthood—which they had been thrust into prematurely on Valentine's Day.

And so, as the tour wound down, everyone was reevaluating. Some would be moving on with their lives. Others would be collecting themselves for even bigger roles.

2

Jackie landed in the reinvigorated camp. On February 13, the day before her world changed, her plan had been to graduate in the top 1 percent of her class and then pursue a nursing career. "I was on the road to getting straight A's this year, and I was going to, but I was on a trip for the *Time* One Hundred gala, and I couldn't take my math final," she said. For the first time, Jackie had to choose between academics and activism.

Even after she skipped the final, her precalc scores were high enough to give her a B plus, her second ever. "I was top one percent of my class, but now I'll be like top fifteen percent. That's fine," she said. "It messed up everyone. Everyone in the group is smart, and all of our GPAs dropped, because we just didn't have time."

Her fall schedule was dramatically different too. They turned in course cards the week before Valentine's Day, and Jackie had four AP classes scheduled for senior year. She ultimately pared it back to just one. "Honestly, the end of this year was so hard for me—not only because of the emotions, but also because I always had work to do," she said. "And I didn't feel the need or want to force interest in precalculus. I'll look at the board in my English classroom and be like, 'This isn't helping me.'" She kept one AP course, government, "because it's probably what's going to intrigue me," she said.

A week after Tallahassee, she was starting to consider a career in politics—a prospect she found startling but also electrifying. Then she spent months mucking around with politicians. She was not impressed. "I don't really know what I want to do, but I feel like I don't want to be a politician when I'm older," she had concluded by June. "Politics is always going to be dirty. And I don't want to be around that environment."

She envisioned a nonprofit role helping improve kids'

lives. She planned to keep up the gun fight for a while, but not forever. "I feel like I work well with kids," she said. "I quit my camp-counselor job this summer to do Road to Change, but it breaks my heart because I'm not with my girls."

One thing is certain: uncertainty. "Before all this, I was always the person who had my future set and planned. And now there's nothing about my life that's set and planned. So it's a very different way of living, but the discomfort is kind of . . ." She trailed off. "I don't know the word for it. I've been getting adjusted to the discomfort, actually—that's a better way to put it. Because before I was always comfortable, and this discomfort is new, yet welcome."

David had gone in the opposite direction. He had a seven-year plan laid out, culminating in 2025, when he turns twenty-five, and will be eligible to serve in the House of Representatives. Yes, politics would be dirty—so who better to wield the spade? David was leaning into his gap year, to hurl all his energy into the midterms, an arrangement he hoped to repeat in 2020, helping to elect a worthy new president. Before and after, he would go to college, starting in the fall of 2019, and "read a shitload of books." That would give him plenty of time to prep for that first congressional run.

———

Ryan Deitsch and Delaney Tarr also ended up deferring college for at least a semester to throw everything they had into the midterms.

Matt Deitsch continued to defer his college career to keep working at MFOL full-time.

Lauren Hogg and Daniel Duff were sophomores now, eager to stick with MFOL and excited to start taking on more responsibility. After six months interacting with the media, Daniel was thinking about joining us. He had a few years to pick a college major, but was starting to lean toward journalism. "I'm spending a lot of my time with like film and TV production and all that," he said. "But I'm also very interested in creative writing and journalism, and they kind of go hand in hand."

A temporary casualty of the MFOL success was the Douglas drama program. "It decimated the drama program," Alfonso said. He chose not to go out for the fall play; so did Cameron and most of the others from MFOL. Too much at stake. Cameron didn't even return to Douglas. Broward County had an online course program for homeschooling, and Cameron enrolled in that to finish his high school education. He would spend most of the fall in Los Angeles. Alfonso also enrolled in most of his courses online, heading over to school just for drama class. He skipped the play but kept the class.

Several of the Chicago kids went on to college. Alex King headed to Grand Valley State University. He was majoring in theater, a happy coincidence after six months with the Parkland drama kids. "My mind was set on it long before I met any of them," he said. Alex was the first in his family to make it out of the neighborhood and into university. Realizing the dream.

When the movement was just beginning, and its future uncharted, Jackie foresaw a generation of struggle, to make the world safe for the kids she would raise someday. Five months later, with thousands of miles in the rearview, she confirmed that assessment. "Though election cycles can change things, it'll take a generation of people to understand that they don't need these weapons," she said. She met a lot of people in gun country, and heard a lot of them say, "I'm a responsible gun owner; I didn't do anything wrong." She understands that. But her generation, trained to expect a gunman to burst into their classroom any day, tends to see it differently.

Her goal was not a decisive win in November and sweeping gun reform the following spring. It was passing one reasonable law after another, to reduce gun violence without cramping the style of responsible young gun owners. "When they have kids, when they grow up with this all the time, and they've seen the positives that these laws will create from a young age, they will understand," she said. "It'll take a generation. And it's unfortunate, but I just hope that when we have children, they will probably, hopefully, end up in a society where these laws are implemented."

3

The tour wound down toward a finale at Sandy Hook, with a reunion of all the kids from both buses. The penultimate stop was New York City, and many of the kids from the Southern Tour had already rejoined them there. Spirits were high. It was exciting to be in the big city, but Lauren Hogg was downright bubbly. She bound around the auditorium on the Upper West Side, chatting, giggling, and hugging old friends and new. The pop band AJR made a surprise appearance, and closed a short set with "Burn the House Down," which the MFOL kids had adopted as their theme song. Lauren said they played it all summer long on the bus. The bouncing beat, and the lyrics about casting aside doubt to take a stand against injustice had saved her on all those long, dreary rides.

Lauren sang along to the first verse and danced in her seat. As the first chorus approached, she could barely contain herself, until the stage door flew open, and Emma, Matt, Cameron, and a dozen more friends rushed out to join the band, while she dashed up the short steps, with more friends at her heels. They sang along, and danced about with silly moves, but no one matched Lauren's glee. Still not out of the woods, but on her way.

4

Cameron Kasky, who had gathered the team in his living room, was the first leader to depart. September 15, he tweeted: "Taking a break from Twitter for a bit so I don't lose my mind. I encourage you all to try the same if you think it's becoming too much." Four days later, he announced his departure from MFOL on Fox News Radio. "If I thought that my friends and the people I worked with couldn't do it without me, I would not have done that," he said. "But alas, all of our efforts looking forward looked like they didn't really need my involvement." He could have helped, but he wasn't crucial, he said. "These kids are the real experts. Look, I have some very intelligent friends. Some friends who can intellectually run circles around me, but I'm not the expert in pretty much anything. I'm a Spider-Man fan, and I can tell you with great platform comes great responsibility."

Cameron looked back on the bus tour plaintively, describing a person he met in Texas who had bought a semiautomatic to protect his family. "I learned that a lot of our issues politically come from a lack of under-standing of other perspectives." Just as disheartening were all the young firebrands locking horns in debate with the sole intention of beating each other. "I'm working on some efforts to encourage bipartisanship," he said.

And he lamented his own role in that. "I'm very re-gretful of a lot of the mistakes that I've made along the way," he said. "One of the things I never really did was watch myself. If I was on a screen I kind of tried to run away from it. I'm not entirely sure why." His deepest re-gret was setting out to embarrass Marco Rubio. He said there were seventeen people in the ground, and he was looking for someone complicit in the killer getting the weapon. He saw Rubio. "I'm not going to kick myself for it, because I'm seventeen," he said. But then he did. "I went into that wanting less conversation and more to embarrass Rubio and that was my biggest flaw. I even name-dropped the murderer." He didn't even think about that at the time, but it had weighed on him since. "Looking back, it ticks me off so much when people do that, because then you're getting that person's name out there and making them a celebrity. That's one of the worst things you see come out of these horrific mass murders, is name recognition."

Cameron didn't stop tweeting entirely, but he scaled back from his earlier frenetic pace. Three weeks later, on October 9, he revealed why—in a series of tweets: "Lately, I've been a lot less active not only online, but in general. I understand the timing is pretty inconvenient with midterms around the corner, and I apologize. I've been struggling with depression and anxiety in a stronger form than I've ever seen it." He asked people to be kind to each other, simply because they are people. "And sometimes, people hurt. And it's OK to hurt. Waking up is hard for me lately, and for the first time ever, it's not because I was staying up late. And that's just something I have to deal with. I started medication today and I'm hoping that'll put me on a better path, but please . . . Remember that the sun will rise in the morning and the world will spin on. It's so hard, I know. It really is. But we can do it."

And then Cameron really took a Twitter break—for a while. He was back to tweeting heavily leading up to the midterm elections. And he never lost his sense of silliness. In November, he landed in the hospital for an intestinal virus, and tweeted, "I actually like being in the hospital. I get to wear a dress all day withOUT being judged."

5

Most of the group remains committed. They expect MFOL to endure, and plan to lead it for a long time, but no one really knows for sure. Five or ten or twenty years from now, MFOL may be a powerhouse organization, or it may have faltered, or evolved into something new. But somehow, in some way, the fight will go on. And when Jackie, Emma, David, Matt, or whoever is still fighting hands the reins to the next generation, their vision for this movement will prove a force more powerful than the NRA.

They will need some big wins for that to happen. They expect some punishing losses as well. But they had to score some blows the first round. That was coming November 6.

As their mobile home for the summer pulled into its final stop in Newtown, Connecticut, August 12,

MFOL had another frantic agenda. They had to get those waves of new voters to the polls. They had thousands of new affiliates in the field, and the big task for the fall would be building a stronger infrastructure, "so a random kid from Texas could talk to someone in Idaho and connect and organize together," Jackie said. They had twelve weeks to tighten up their organization for Election Day, and two years to prepare for 2020.

Three days later, Jackie was back in Parkland for the first day of her senior year. A week later, I asked about school, and she groaned. "Oh God. It feels like a side project for me now. Every year of my life it would've been my main priority, and now it kind of feels like an extracurricular. Every day I go to school, and then I go work on March for Our Lives for the rest of my night. I don't really know what my main thing is, but I'm pretty sure it's March for Our Lives."

As she looked forward into a gloriously uncharted future, and wistfully back at the past—at the crazy summer on a tour bus, and the thousands of aspiring activists pouring into her life—a single face stood out. Jackie had met Natalie Barden at the *Teen Vogue* summit in June. Natalie was in fifth grade when she lost her little brother, Daniel, at Sandy Hook. For five years, Natalie avoided the gun conversation; it was just too painful to talk about. Parkland changed that. Parkland changed everything. Natalie went to the march on Washington, "and was moved beyond belief," she wrote.

"When she saw us do it, she felt empowered," Jackie said. "Because when her little brother died, she was ten." Natalie was Jackie's lead organizer in Newtown, helping her plan the four-hour rally with food trucks, entertainment, speakers, and a meeting of MFOL kids and Sandy Hook survivors. "She did an amazing job," Jackie said. "When you have a connection to the issue, it doesn't even feel like a job."

Jackie felt like she was passing the torch, but she was really lighting activist flames. "March for Our Lives does not belong to us anymore," Jackie said. It belongs to every kid in America who is ready to heed the call.

21

The Third Rail

1

The midterms. The first big test finally approached. MFOL upped the pace. August 30, David Hogg appeared with New York City mayor Bill de Blasio on MSNBC's *Morning Joe* to announce the group's next big initiative, Mayors for Our Lives. They had enlisted more than fifty mayors from both parties around the country in a program to register new voters under thirty, particularly at high schools and colleges.

They would need them. All indications still pointed to enthusiasm in their swath of the electorate, but the gun issue was getting less and less attention. The Supreme Court nominee Brett Kavanaugh was accused of sexual misconduct, and the country was riveted by the battle over his confirmation in late September and early October. Pollsters reported the fight energizing the Right. And the Supreme Court suddenly leapt to voters' number one issue in a Pew poll, pushing gun policy down to fourth. CNN had it down to fifth in August, right behind "corruption," presumably due to Robert Mueller's investigation of President Trump. Endless political upheavals would follow.

And journalists were sometimes speaking about the Parkland kids in the past tense. In October, Katy Tur's MSNBC show did a "Battleground College Tour," speaking to students on different campuses each day. She mentioned Parkland as a huge factor in the spring that had seemed to disappear. Keeping guns a priority would be a challenge. On bad days, it felt like this time might be like all the other times: The nation would gasp at another slaughter, vow to really do something, and then forget. Guns never seemed to stick.

Also in October, Ariana Grande posted an Instagram story urging her fans to register, posting imminent deadlines in each state, with a swipe-up link to the MFOL website. So many people followed the link to register that it temporarily crashed the site. And MFOL announced twelve more cities on its Vote for Our Lives tour, a final sprint for the last three weeks to Election Day. "I was so exhausted," Jackie said. "The last two weeks, I was starting to burn out. And I was like, 'Well, I've got to stick it out. It's like when you're really tired, you stay up for two more hours, it's like, 'Stay up! You have to do this.'"

Her grades were taking a hit. The same was true for all the kids who were back in school. Teachers had been very forgiving in the spring semester, but that was over. Even after she scaled back to one AP class, an academic breeze for Jackie, her grades were ugly. Choices had to be made.

Emma was coping with college—a big adjustment for everyone, but strange to enter as an icon. "A lot of people here feel like it's weird that they know about me without me having gotten to know about them," she said. Shortly before Election Day she reported classes going well, but she was struggling still with the social transition. "You can't bond at the base soul level when you first meet somebody at school like I did with these [MFOL] people," Emma said. "I'm working on it. Nobody else is ready to share traumatic experiences with each other."

It helped to bring someone with her who understood. She had made it through the terror holding hands with two friends, and one of them, Lenore, was her roommate at New College of Florida. That helped. "She and I are the only two people who know what each other

was going through," Emma said. "We already have little movies set up, communicating with pictures instead
of words, because sometimes it's hard to always figure
out what words we're feeling."

2

As election day beckoned, hopes ran sky high. Election *day*—the concept was anachronistic in much of
the country, where more people voted in the lead-up
weeks than on the day. And early voting was through
the roof. All the demographics MFOL was counting on
seemed to be coming out.

Dreams were taking shape. When MFOL marched
on Washington, pundits were batting about a "blue
wave" scenario, and a big enough wave might actually turn over the House. That seemed like a best-case
scenario all spring. Because of gerrymandering, and
Democrats being concentrated in cities, it seemed
highly unlikely that they could win much more than
the twenty-three seats needed to retake the House. And
because of a fluke of history, most of the thirty-five
Senate seats up for election were Democratic incum-
bents, several in deep-red territory. They had to defend
seats in Montana, West Virginia, North Dakota, and
Missouri, states Trump had won by 18 to 41 points.

And they had few pickup opportunities, mostly in the Deep South. Tennessee? Arizona? Texas? All seemed like fantasies. The conventional wisdom through the spring and into the summer was that the best the Dems could hope for in the Senate was to give up a few seats. They would have to wait until 2020, when the Senate map reversed, and they could make a potential killing.

But late polls showed some of the long-shot races coming into reach. And with all that early voting, all bets were off. Beto O'Rourke was the breakout star of the year, an unabashed progressive, winning over huge swaths of Texas. A week out, polls showed him within three points of the Republican incumbent, Ted Cruz. A Democratic senator from Texas? Two blue houses of Congress? The fantasy might actually materialize.

3

Election night brought reality crashing down. Much of the MFOL crew and their allies, along with parents of the victims, gathered at Hurricane Grill & Wings to celebrate the returns. David was there, and Emma, Jackie, Daniel, and the Deitsch brothers. As polls closed from east to west across the country, the mood turned sour. Twitter felt like a Democratic wake. The House was going blue, but the Dems picked up *only* two dozen seats. The Senate was going the other way: probably five seats lost. No Texas miracle. The Dems were picking up a lot of governorships, that was nice, but no historic black woman to lead Georgia. And there was a painful personal blow: they were losing both big races in Florida. They were about to have gun safety foes in their governor's mansion and for both of their senators.

But none of that was the worst of it. Their generation might have let them down. There were only preliminary numbers available, but early exit poll numbers were indicating that young voters made up about the same share of the electorate as in previous elections.

"I'm shaking with anger right now," Jackie said. "It's like the same feeling I was getting the night of February fourteenth. I'm so angry and I don't know what to do with that anger." But maybe she did know. "We're not going to stop fighting," she said. "I can tell you, I'm doing this for the rest of my life."

There was anger, then guilt. "I felt like I disappointed some of the families that lost their kids," Jackie said. She looked around the room. Guac's family: Tío Manny and Patricia Oliver. She looked at the Guttenbergs and saw their daughter, her lost young ballerina friend, Jaime. "I was just like, 'Damn, we couldn't do this for them.' But they comforted me. Patricia, she was like hugging me and telling me to relax, and I was like, 'Oh my God.'"

4

The gloom was premature. By Wednesday morning, they regained sight of the best-case scenario they had envisioned in the spring: a big surge in youth voting, candidates unabashedly running on gun safety, candidates winning on gun safety, and maybe, if all that happened, the Democrats taking control of the House to begin implementing their agenda. They had accomplished all four.

The early returns proved misleading. The late-counted vote trended heavily Democratic. They took back two of the Senate seats that appeared lost the night before, both in deep-red states, Montana and Arizona—in the latter, the first Democratic senator elected there in thirty years. But the House was truly startling. When all the races were over, the Democrats had picked up forty seats—their biggest night since the post-Watergate landslide of 1974. And Democrats won the popular vote in House races by 8.8 million, beating even the number in 1974. They had also flipped 349 state legislative seats, six state legislative chambers, and seven governorships, mostly from large battleground states. Those would be crucial to the big redistricting fights ahead, following the 2020 census.

Voter turnout among the under-thirty voters was 31 percent, dwarfing the 21 percent from the previous midterms. It was the highest-recorded turnout since the premier organization studying them, at Tufts University, began collecting data in 1994. And those new young voters swung overwhelmingly liberal. They supported Democratic House candidates by a 35-point margin, exceeding even the margin for Barack Obama's election. Their vote had been apparently decisive in the Democrats' winning the Senate seats in Montana and Nevada, and the governorship in Wisconsin.

And people were finally voting on guns. Exit polls showed gun control as voters' fourth-most-important issue, surpassing any previous result. And they were finally voting on both sides. Professor Robert Spitzer, a gun politics expert at SUNY Cortland, said that about 16 or 17 percent of people voted on guns as a primary issue in the past, mostly against gun safety. NBC News' exit poll indicated that 60 percent of voters favored stronger gun laws—even 42 percent of gun owners. Gun country hadn't quite boarded the MFOL bandwagon, but 42 percent was a hell of a start.

Candidates had been watching those polls all year,

and many decided it was finally safe to come out of the gun closet. "Candidates embraced the gun safety agenda this cycle to a degree not seen since at least the 2000 elections," Professor Spitzer said. It could be hard to take the pulse of 435 different House races, but the Democratic Party's "red to blue" list was telling. That's their list of districts they hope to flip each cycle. In 2016, only four of thirty-six candidates in those races included gun safety in their platforms. This time, it was thirty-eight of fifty-nine candidates.

And MFOL had achieved one dream, of drawing some Republicans to their cause. In some key swing districts, like the Philadelphia suburbs of Bucks County, the House candidates ran on gun safety on both sides.

Both the NRA and gun safety groups claimed victories in several House races—itself a game changer. For the first time in a long time, the gun issue was at play, Spitzer said. "It worked mostly to the benefit of gun safety in a way we have not seen for almost twenty years. I think it has also given the gun safety people real momentum to continue their activities for the next election cycle, which of course will be a presidential year."

The NRA was also losing the money battle, another first. Earlier in the year, it admitted to big fund-raising problems, and in this cycle, it spent only $11 million, half what it spent in the previous midterms. For the first time ever, it was outspent by gun safety groups, which spent $12 million.

The NRA's aura of invincibility had been ruptured, Spitzer said. "It had this reputation, if they target you for defeat, that (a) they'll make your life miserable, and (b) they'll probably succeed." That was never true, he said—there was a mountain of data disproving it. But it was believed and feared, and acted on. But this election really blew a hole in that marked-for-extinction narrative, he said. "They have no visible effect on the outcome at all."

The fight would really get hot in the presidential year, but Spitzer was actually looking past that. "The question is, what does the Republican Party look like in a post-Trump world?" he said. "Either it's very small and even more hard-core, which means they won't be winning many elections, or they're going to have to broaden their base somehow. And an issue like gun safety could be one amenable to bipartisan support."

Spitzer said the gun safety movement had a long way to go, but they had broken a huge barrier. Their cause had been seen as untouchable, the third rail of American politics. "It's no longer a third rail," he said. "It's been deactivated, de-electrified."

5

The best evidence that the gun third rail has been deactivated came two days later, from the presumptive House Speaker, Nancy Pelosi. She announced that House Democrats would prioritize "bipartisan legislation to have commonsense background checks" on gun sales. That obviously wouldn't pass the Senate, and President Trump would veto it anyway, said Professor Spitzer. "But it has a very forward-looking objective, first because it's low-hanging fruit. Pelosi knows that well. It's a good campaign issue. And once the House passes it, she'll have bragging rights to say that every Democrat in Congress supported this bill, and the Republicans killed it. It gives them kind of bragging rights to say, 'Look, we're doing what the majority of American people want us to do, but the obstructionist Republicans turn a deaf ear to that.' It's a useful club in the next round of elections."

Epilogue

1

"I'm sure you saw a video of me crying," Jackie said after Thanksgiving. "I was very emotional. It was months and months of work compounding into one single decision. Obviously it was very much more dramatic in the moment. The next day I woke up, I was breathing, I was fine, the world didn't end. It continued to motivate me. I'm very much fired up again."

The election brought another reckoning. The MFOL had cleared the highest hurdle yet. Time to re-evaluate. "People are going to college—Brendan and Delaney and Sofie—so we just need to figure out what the internals are going to look like in 2019," Jackie said. They had a big group meeting set for the first Sunday in December, to see how involved everyone wanted to be, and restructure a bit accordingly. They were also looking into creating some full-time paid staff positions. If they were going to last as an organization, it was going to require more than volunteers.

For Alfonso, the reckoning came about a month before the election. "Before, my life used to be one hundred percent march, one hundred percent gun control," he said Thanksgiving weekend. "And now I'm trying to do a fifty-fifty. Because I'm realizing that in order to get the message that we want—change laws, policy, get people registered to vote—we need to do some growing of our own as well. I have to apply for college; I have to get a job."

He said he had watched a few of his MFOL peers land in the hospital from exhaustion, and he was on the same path. "I had gained weight, I didn't shave for a while or cut my hair, I was wearing the same clothes," Alfonso said. "I was slipping in my grades, I had less energy, I slept in way more, working at the office more than doing homework, I looked like a shell of my former self." And it wasn't just him suffering. His room was a disaster, he wasn't helping at home—but little Putin was taking it hardest. Alfonso had a lizard the size of his forearm, and Putin's cage was messier than Alfonso's room. Some days, he was out of water. That was bad.

His parents had cut Alfonso a lot of slack in the spring, but by fall they were concerned, and telling him so. "I ignored my dad, I ignored my mom, I didn't want to hear any of it," Alfonso said. "And one day I kind of realized, 'OK, you're seventeen, he's fifty.'" Alfonso was barely seventeen, just had his birthday in October. He admired his dad, always looked up to him—when had he stopped listening to him? "I realized I gotta grow up," Alfonso said. "So about a week goes by, and then I just start changing little things. Like, finally shaved, finally cleaned my room, right? And in about a week and a half, one night I was just restless, I couldn't sleep, it was about three in the morning, I basically said, 'OK, I gotta do something.' So I cleaned my room spotless. I did some chores, which was three in the a.m., which was ridiculous, but I was having a little breakdown. I was like, 'OK, let's start.' And in the last month or so after, it really sank in. I've been losing weight, I've been more responsible, I've been more respectable, I've just been a better overall human being."

He was thinking about seeing a therapist now. "Even though I'm doing so much better, I can't just fix myself physically. I also have to fix why I was like that for some time." He still wrestled with survivor guilt. He was unnerved by the anxiety that still pervaded Parkland. "Out of nowhere every time there's a fire alarm, kids start crying in school. Or people still have mental breakdowns or panic attacks. Like I've had."

Alfonso needed to pace himself for the movement too, he realized. And his future in it. School had become an afterthought, as though he had learned all he needed already. "I'm not even an adult yet," he said. He planned to take on better debaters than Marco Rubio one day. He needed to get educated about history, and politics and rhetorical devices, and logical fallacies . . . He had to go to college. And make it a priority. He got serious about his applications, and his study habits. This was a marathon. He was seventeen.

2

MFOL had a long-term plan. "We created March for Our Lives and we want to see it demolished," Jackie said. "We want it to demolish itself so it doesn't have to exist. It shouldn't have had to exist ever." But that might take a while. "I just really hope by the time I am thirty years old, March for Our Lives is a thing of the past," she said.

Meanwhile, they had big plans. As of December 2018, they had mapped it out only through the following summer, because they liked to stay nimble and keep revamping on the fly. And more kids would be going off to college then, including Jackie. She would have to pull back somewhat, but would still be involved. She, Matt, and David were the student members of the 501(c)(4) board.

Jackie's goal for the next nine months was to set MFOL on a course whereby it could function with a lot less of her. She laid out three big focuses for the organization in 2019: policy, creativity, and infrastructure.

They were eager to help Congress take on the gun issue, as well as all those state legislatures in which gun safety advocates had seized control. They planned to be a big part of that conversation—and were looking for creative ways to keep the public engaged. Especially their generation, with videos and collaborations with entertainers—having fun had always been a big part of their appeal.

But as always, Jackie would take the lead on the more mundane stuff. Infrastructure, and building out the network behind the scenes. They had recruited over seven hundred sibling marches, and most of those organizers had remained active, but about a hundred had matured into full-fledged chapters, doing powerful work on their own. "I'm going to spearhead moving forward, like making sure the network of chapters is completely clear and very well organized," Jackie said. That had been difficult to do while also working on the election, but now they could do it right. Her next big push was college campuses, where she expected to soon establish many more outposts.

In January 2019, MFOL planned to announce a big event to help organize around. They planned to commemorate the one-year anniversary of the march with a major youth summit. "We're bringing thousands of young people together to advance leadership skills and show the world that the younger generation plays a pivotal role in our political process," she said.

And their plans for the anniversary of the shooting? "We're not doing anything," Jackie said. "It should be a day of complete and total solidarity with the community. I'm just going to be with my friends that day. I don't want to be organizing or facilitating anything." Why commemorate the day that jerk took something from them? They're going to celebrate the weekend they answered.

3

Fall brought a big round of awards and accolades, but the biggest thrill was winning the International Children's Peace Prize, and traveling to Cape Town, South Africa, to accept it from Archbishop Desmond Tutu. Two ChicagoStrong leaders came with them to accept it: Alex King from the Peace Warriors and Trevon Bosley from BRAVE. They had earned it. Alex had to apply for a passport first. Alex had never seen a house like Emma's before March, had been afraid of how to act there—to walk on the grass or wear his shoes inside. He had never left the country, never expected to. "I never thought I would ever have a passport, ever need a passport," he said. "My first time out the country going to Africa, that was just incredible."

At the ceremony, Archbishop Tutu described March for Our Lives as one of the most significant youth movements in living memory. "The peaceful campaign to demand safe schools and communities and the eradication of gun violence is reminiscent of other great peace movements in history," he said. "I am in awe of these children, whose powerful message is amplified by their youthful energy and an unshakable belief that children can—no, must—improve their own futures. They are true change makers who have demonstrated most powerfully that children can move the world."

Tío Manny introduced the kids, standing beside a 3D-printed statue of Guac holding a sunflower. "Joaquin Oliver is officially a member of March for Our Lives," he said.

It was the fifteenth anniversary of the KidsRights Foundation, the organization that bestowed the award, so they brought most of the prior winners to Cape Town for the celebration. Jackie said the highlight for her was meeting the 2017 winner: "A Syrian refugee that made his own school in Lebanon. It was just insane to compare the two types of activism, because you can't really compare them. It was definitely really cool and kind of overwhelming, because there's always a sense of, 'Oh, I don't deserve this.'"

But she was sure enjoying the adventure. They got to explore outside the city, out to Boulders Beach, still a long way from Antarctica, but close enough to spot penguins in the wild. "I was on a beach, a literal beach, and there were penguins and it was incredible," Jackie said.

Alex spoke gleefully about the penguins too, but reverently about another excursion. He rose hours before dawn one morning, to climb Lion's Head in the darkness. As the sun rose over the mountain, a breathtaking vista took shape below him: the South Atlantic and the cape reaching into it, the distant outcropping of the continent he had dreamed of, that he'd come from, but unseen by his family for generations. A whole new life seemed to be coming into view. "That was my highlight of Africa," Alex said.

They took a long trip home, doing more press and conferences across Europe, missed Thanksgiving in America, and then Jackie was starting to recharge. She said she had begun to catch up since the election, and her grades were rising again. The last week of November, she took the whole night off to hang out with her family to put up the Christmas tree. (But then I texted her about some follow-ups, and she hopped on the phone for an interview lasting nearly an hour.)

They had a few more awards to accept, and were ranked number four in *Time*'s Person of the Year issue. But Jackie was actually looking forward to finishing all that. "Then we're done for the holidays, so I'm just excited to stop traveling so much, because I just need to be a normal freaking kid."

She was also thinking about college. In March, Jackie had laughed at the idea of her at an Ivy—and then blown her class rank with a second B plus. But she had reconsidered. December 13, announcements were sent online: "Congratulations! . . . the Committee on Admissions has admitted you to the Harvard College Class of 2023 under the Early Action program."

David, who had been mocked by Laura Ingraham for some college rejections in March, got the same acceptance message.

They also got the chance to give some awards. Alfonso got to present a Courage Award to ChicagoStrong, which included the Peace Warriors and BRAVE and most of their comrades there. "I think those kids in Chicago are bigger heroes than we are," Alfonso said. "And it meant more to me than almost anything I've done to justify to them that what they're doing is important. What they're doing is really big."

4

As they took a breath for the holidays, the kids gazed back on that crazy year. With just a whiff of hindsight, it was the road they harkened back to most. The Road to Change. And all that summer, as they rumbled across America, right about the time that night's town hall was beginning, Bruce Springsteen was taking a Broadway stage. He regaled his audience with guitar and harmonica, but mostly with spoken stories of his lifetime traveling those same dreamy highways, in beat-up cars, borrowed pickups, and endless rowdy tour buses—out of Freehold, New Jersey, and all the way back again—realizing his dream to "collide with the times." Bruce spun his story chronologically, and each night it climaxed as he reached the present, about four minutes to ten. The stories were deeply personal, but he made an exception there, squeezing in one topical incident, a late addition to the tightly scripted show. He lamented the bleakness of the Trump years, and how it shook his faith in our future, until a sunny day in March, when a group of kids from Parkland, victims refusing victimhood, drew hundreds of thousands of soul mates to our capital, to remind America what we stand for. What we are capable of. The March for Our Lives Day, he called it. A day that changed America. A day that changed him. He described it so vividly, experiencing it from a distance, the sights and sounds invigorating him through his TV, the faith flowing back into him, the wonder restored. *The dream of life. The rising.* "It was a good day," he said. "A necessary day." And just like Jackie Corin, a young woman he has yet to meet, Bruce reached back fifty years, and drew a straight line to Martin Luther King Jr., assuring us that "the arc of the moral universe is long, but it bends toward justice"—but adding a stern corollary: "That arc doesn't bend on its own." Bending it takes a whole lot of us, bending in with every ounce of strength we've got.

And right about then, in a church or gym in Bismarck or El Paso, another town hall was wrapping up, and Jackie and Cameron, Delaney, Dylan, Daniel and Brendan, Bradley, Jammal, John, Pippy, Adam, Amaya, Annabel, Sarah, Sofie, Alex, Alfonso, Samantha, Matt and Ryan, Morgan, Sheryl, Lex, Chris, Carly, Charlie, Michelle, Kyrah, Kevin, Naomi, Robert, Gabriel, Diego, David, Lauren, and Emma, and whatever freedom riders hitched a ride that week, were bending in. They would stagger to some strange bed, wake weary, bleary, a bit confused about where their pillows lie, but certain, absolutely certain, of one thing: that to their cause—to save every kid of every color from the ravages of gun violence—history will bend.

Time to stuff their suitcases, board the Bus to Somewhere, recharge each other with road giggles, and exhale that hope and wonder into another American town.

Acknowledgments

First and foremost I want to thank all the survivors who shared their stories and their lives, taking me into their confidence, their offices, and many of their homes. I won't rename everyone in the story, but this is your story, and thanks for trusting me with it. Equal thanks to all the MFOL team mentioned only in passing or not at all. I'm sorry our paths didn't cross, or came too late. (Charlie Mirsky, can't wait to meet you!) Also their parents, especially Tío Manny and Patricia Oliver, Rebecca Boldrick and Kevin Hogg, Natalie Weiss, and Paul and Mary Corin. Equal thanks to all the MSD students, family, and Parkland residents who helped me understand their community, especially Carol Chenkin, Wendy Hunter, and Christine Barclay, all your staff, and the casts of *Spring Awakening* and

Legally Blonde. Steven Sater and Duncan Sheik, that talk-back and your story of adapting *Spring Awakening* was a master class for me. Your musical helped me step out of this madness I've been immersed in for two decades and see it with new eyes. I listened to the songs on Spotify at the gym several nights a week for inspiration, and a bar to aspire to. If I could capture just a whiff of what I feel each time I hear "Those You've Known" I'd be a happy man. (Though I admit the one on heaviest rotation was "Totally Fucked.")

I owe a huge debt to my brilliant, tireless editor, Gail Winston, who raced through so many rewrites with me to get this book tightened up and so much better with the clock ticking loudly the whole time. Her advice and encouragement really got me through. When the stress was high, it was calming to know I was in good hands. Emily Taylor played traffic cop with the army of people it takes to create a book, and pull all the pieces together. I'm grateful to Jonathan Burnham and the whole Harper team, including Leslie Cohen, and Nicholas Davies, Theresa Dooley, and Emily VanDerwerken on her publicity team; the production team, including John Jusino, Diana Meunier, and Nate Knaebel; copy editor Douglas Johnson; the sales and marketing teams under Leah Wasielewski and Jennifer Murphy; senior designer Bonni Leon-Berman, who designed the lovely interior; lawyer Trina Hunn, who did the legal read; and a hundred others on the Harper team whom I may never meet but who played a role in bringing this story to the page. (And still more to bring it to your e-reader or audiobook, including Robert Fass, whom I was lucky enough to have read it.) I was already working with Harper on my book on two gay soldiers, and I chose them for that project because I was so impressed by their entire team and the way they wanted to approach it. So when the possibility of a Parkland book came up, I knew exactly whom I wanted to work with, and I was thrilled to see how enthusiastically they embraced the project and allowed me to interrupt the gay soldiers book to plunge right into this one. (And I want to thank the two gay soldiers I've now been working with for nineteen years, and their families, for being so understanding to wait even longer to bring their story to the page. I don't want to reveal your names yet, T. and S., but you know who you are.)

This book grew out of my work at *Vanity Fair.* Big thanks to everyone who got the project rolling and helped there, especially Mike Hogan, my editor on most of the stories, and the one who first called and suggested I go. To Radhika Jones, for having the faith to green-light the project, to send me down with little sense of what might be possible, and then to extend and expand the project several times. To so many people there who helped, but especially the copy editors and fact-checkers Katherine Commisso and Mary Flynn, who saved my butt countless times, by questioning, digging, and checking. And Sarah Shoen, who got me on planes and booked me rooms and sorted out any little problem I had. And to the photographers and videographers who worked with me, Paul D'Amato, Ron Beinner, Tim Braun, Abie Troen, and especially Justin Bishop. And of course Matt Alston.

Thank you to the experts who advised me on various matters, especially John Della Volpe, Professor Robert Spitzer, Dr. Alyse Ley, Dr. Frank Ochberg (so many roles), and all the journalists I cited in the notes on sources. Special thanks to retired FBI profiler Mary Ellen O'Toole and the anonymous friend at the University of Virginia, who has been so generous in helping me understand these killers all these years.

Eternal thanks to my great writer (and a few reader) friends who responded to my absurd request to read the first draft of the manuscript and offer feedback in eight days—and right over Thanksgiving. I sent the Hail Mary request to several people, hoping for one or two responses, and I was stunned that so many took it on, to read all or part of it: Miles Harvey, Kevin

Davis, Patty Wiater, William Lychack, Staci Amend, Dr. Frank Ochberg, Bethany (aka BethAnnie) Belle, and Matt Alston. Special thanks to Staci, who made so many amazing and thorough edits.

To my incredible research sleuth, Marc Greenawalt, and my additional researchers Colson Lin and Manola Gonzalez. To the ACIA team and Dr. Frank Ochberg and everyone at the Dart Center, including Bruce Shapiro and Kari Pricher, who helped cure me the first time, so I was capable of going down there again. Dr. Ochberg, retired FBI SSA Dwayne Fuselier, and my shrink Pat Patton all helped pull me out of my second Columbine breakdown in 2006, which I'll never forget. You've all become great friends too, along with Mimi Fuselier.

So many survivors from so many tragedies have shared their insights and their friendship. I can only name a handful, but thank you Coni Sanders, Paula Reed, Kiki Leyba (plus Kallie and Samson), Frank DeAngelis, Heather Martin, and Chris and Jenny Babij.

Friends have kept me sane, and let me start with a few: Mike and Elise Jordan, who created the "Sag Harbor writer's retreat" for me to stay for weeks at a time, so I could get away from the city. And Patrick Brown and Chris Nyce, who did the same for shorter stretches in Boulder. And for so many more: Samuel Morett, Alejandro Morelos, Ira Gilbert, Tito Negron, Gregg Trostel, Octavio R. Lavoignet, Dave Yoo, Elizabeth Geoghegan, Brian Cookstra, Miles Harvey, Kevin Davis, Bill Lychack, Bill Kelly, Dennis Grech, Jeronimo Sochaczewski, Paul Campbell, Juan Carlos Alvarez, Joseph Leskody, the Cosbys (Doug, Monica, and Cecilia), Kyle Bradstreet, and of course Bobby Sneakers.

For my family, who have been so encouraging, my dad, and my siblings Linda Reinert, Kathy Pick, Marie McGrath, Patty Wiater, and Joe, Danny, Peggy, and Kelly Cullen and their spouses. My nieces and nephews, who bring such joy to my life, and who remind me what it was like to be young: Chris Pick, Cari Pick, Steven Pick, Matthew Wiater, Michael McGrath, Caitlin McGrath, Kaylee Wiater, Seamus Cullen, Kennedy Cullen, Liam Cullen, and Siobhan Cullen. And my mom, who died a few months before this began, but whom I still carry with me, and who oddly in the final stages of dementia reminded me how much I loved her and why. To my extended family, the Eustises, Kachuriks, and Lerches, and the Phillipses. Special thanks to Aunt Mary Ellen and the other Phillipses who found the poetry and writing of my grandfather Joe Cullen from 1914, and fresh bits about his grandfather Matthew Cullen, the revolutionary Irish newspaper publisher, to open up a whole new understanding of how long writing has been in my blood.

For all the readers of *Columbine* still emailing or tagging me on social media nearly every day, especially the high school students—and the teachers and librarians bringing the book into their lives. Writing can be a lonely life, with so many frustrating and sometimes fruitless days, wrestling with the page. The encouragement coming in, and the personal stories of its impact on you, saved me from countless shame spirals, that I'm just some goofball, typing up drivel in my little writing cave.

I apologize to everyone I left out, because I left this chapter till last, and kept writing and editing up till the last minute. Finally, I will never repay the debt to my writing mentors along the way; chronologically, Mrs. Barrows, Linda Tufano, Joan Walsh, Jonathan Karp. My trusted agent, adviser, and friend Betsy Lerner was the first person to believe in this project as a book, and helped me shape it throughout. The singular being Lucia Berlin is in a class all her own. She taught me so much, about writing and living, in the guidance she gave and the example she set, in person and on the page. But she gave me something so much bigger.

Lucia was the first person not dating or related to me to tell me she loved me. That gave me permission to finally say it back—to her, and to everyone else I loved. I never would have told my mom I loved her without you, Lucia. Thanks. I miss you.

Notes on Sources

The bulk of the material in this book comes from my own reporting, following the MFOL kids around the country and meeting and interviewing hundreds of people who interacted with them. I first made contact by phone on Sunday, February 18, when David put me on speakerphone with the entire group. I arrived in Parkland the following day. I stayed in regular contact until we finished fact-checking this book in mid-December. I spoke to nearly everyone in the group at some point, but I focused on a manageable number, and spent the most time with Jackie Corin, David and Lauren Hogg, Cameron Kasky, Matt Deitsch, Alfonso Calderon, Daniel Duff, and Dylan Baierlein.

I did several formal interviews with all those students and with many others, but more often my interactions were brief, informal exchanges in the field, or checking in by text. I visited several kids in their homes, and got to know some of their parents. I also followed them on social media, and in the traditional media, observing how they interacted with people there. Cameron and Alfonso liked doing late-night Instagram Live chats, which are always fun—and I'm happy to report they're exactly the same there as in person. Wherever the MFOL kids traveled, I tried to talk to as many people who were interacting with them as possible, including fellow Douglas students, youth activists, teachers, coaches, clergy members, mental health workers, survivors of other tragedies, academics, and political professionals. It's all about hearing multiple perspectives, and I tried to cast as wide a net as possible.

Most quotes from the kids are from my interactions with them—or occasionally from statements they made at events I attended. Exceptions are noted here, with brief citations for readability, and the full details are given in the bibliography. The main exception is Emma. She grew concerned very early that she was becoming the face of the movement, and she was determined to share the spotlight. She rarely did substantial interviews after that and never agreed to an in-depth interview with me. I observed her in person on well over a dozen occasions, and I got an occasional question, as well as recordings of her speaking to individuals and groups. The longest interview I got with her was about five minutes with a few other reporters in the media tent the morning of the DC march. Of course, I got stories and impressions from everyone in her orbit constantly. So I developed a good feel for her, but I had to rely on published sources for a lot of her quotes.

I could not be everywhere, and I wouldn't want to rely on my own impressions alone. So I am indebted to a great number of wonderful journalists whose work I relied on to fill in many pieces. They added so much more than details and quotes. I learned a great deal in the field just by comparing notes and impressions with smart reporters also immersed in this story, and by discovering fresh insights from reading their work. I want to call out two journalists in particular: Lisa Miller at *New York* magazine and Emily Witt at the *New Yorker* did deep dives into this story, and their work was invaluable.

A few words on quotes and thoughts. I adhere to standard journalistic practices: everything in quotation marks was either (a) heard by me, (b) published by a reputable source, or (c) recorded on TV or other media. (I watched all the TV passages cited, but I often relied on published transcripts. However, the punctuation of spoken speech is subjective, and I frequently changed some odd transcript choices. I tried to preserve language the way the speaker delivered it. I also corrected mistakes in the wording, which is why online transcripts may vary slightly from what you see here.)

I recorded most of my conversations on my iPhone, an e-recorder, and a notepad, typically all three. (I get nothing from Sony, but if you're looking, I've been very happy with the Sony ICDUX560BLK.) Everywhere I went, I took photos and videos on my phone (a few thousand total), which allowed me to re-create the visuals with precision later. I edited quotes for length without inserting ellipses, and made minor edits for grammar and readability—obviously taking care to preserve (and clarify) the intended meaning. (For example, when someone used a pronoun to refer back to a name used earlier, I've substituted the name without adding brackets. I've also generally eliminated stumbles, midsentence backtracks, and so forth.) Whenever I say a person thought something, it's because that person told me so.

PROLOGUE

1

Nearly all Jackie Corin's quotes in this book come from my interviews with her. Exceptions are noted. We did around ten formal interviews—some in person, but usually by phone—plus several dozen follow-up calls and texts. We met in person over a dozen times. Up until October, we checked in every few weeks at a minimum. Then I let her focus on the election and me on the final rewriting and editing of this book, and I remained in contact sporadically until early December. In general, I tried to get her impressions of any event two different ways: (1) within a few days (or while it was happening), and (2) much later, to see if her impressions had changed. Many of the events in the book involving her I witnessed firsthand, others she told me about. She described the North Carolina rally in the opening scene.

2

Until the final draft of this book, the first portion of this section read, "discovered that post-traumatic stress can strike without experiencing a trauma directly." Dr. Frank Ochberg was kind enough to vet sections of the manuscript medically and advised me to change "experiencing" to "witnessing." He served on the committee that first created the concept and diagnosis of PTSD, and said it actually had been a major point of debate whether secondary observers like me experienced an event. The committee concluded that we do, and experience has borne this out. It's telling that I still don't fully believe I experienced it without having been in the building. It's a lesser experience—secondary—but still very real, and enough to take me down.

This story harkens back to Columbine and to my two decades on the wider story. I am frequently asked why I chose it, so I'll use up my cliché quota early: I didn't, really; it chose me. I was a freelancer living in Denver, just returning to part-time journalism after two decades. I happened to sit down for lunch just as the Columbine reports were hitting local news. Shots had been fired, but no injuries confirmed. I figured it would be nothing, but I hopped in my car just in case. First I left a voice mail for Joan Walsh, an editor in San Francisco I'd done one story for, apologizing for bothering her. I had never heard of Columbine, but my then-boyfriend had a vague sense of where it was. He sent me down Highway 6, with several possible exits to choose from, and I figured I'd fumble my way there. (It would be years before I owned a cell phone.) Driving toward the mountains, I spotted a ring of helicopters in a tight circle to the south. That was alarming. I tried to line them up with the best exit, and I drove toward them until I hit a police barricade. I pulled into a strip mall and asked the cops which way the school was. They pointed and said, "That way," and I ran toward it. I had no idea what I was hurtling into.

The iconic photograph was published in the *Rocky Mountain News*, which deservedly won the 2000 Pulitzer for Breaking News Photography for its collection of twenty Columbine photographs. The *Rocky* went bankrupt and its site disappeared, but the photos are all collected at the Pulitzer site mentioned in the bibliography.

The CNN ratings I document are from 1999, and which I included in *Columbine*. We rechecked the number of consecutive *New York Times* front pages from its archives.

All information on the Columbine shooting in this book comes from *Columbine*, which we carefully vetted at the time. Many basic logistical details about the attack in it come from the Jefferson County sheriff's report, but see the endnotes for details.

I have consulted with many trauma experts about norepinephrine, and vetted this passage with Dr. Frank Ochberg. The quote is from my interview with him in November. I relied on several sources to summarize the attack. Three were particularly helpful: "What Happened in the Parkland School Shooting" (*New York*

Times), "What Happened in the 82 Minutes" (*Chicago Tribune*), and the Broward County Sheriff's Office's official report.

I read a wealth of news material on the suspect, but relied heavily on a series of articles in the *Miami Herald*, which did a stellar job. They included: "'You're All Going to Die' . . ." and "Uber Driver Says . . ." The *New York Times* also published several informative articles: "Parkland Shooting Suspect Lost Special-Needs Help" "[His name], Florida Shooting Suspect, Showed 'Every Red Flag,'" and "'Kill Me,' Parkland Shooting Suspect Said." I also incorporated details from "Teacher Told Students to Run" (CBS News).

The figures for mass shootings in America come from *Mother Jones*'s open-source database of mass shootings since 1982.

4

We published an expanded edition of *Columbine* in 2016 with a new epilogue. In it, I document how frequently mass shooters cite Columbine and its killers as their inspiration, and copy their costumes, technique, timing, imagery, and so forth. I discuss the false Columbine narrative of those killers as heroes for the downtrodden, which so many perpetrators have bought into. Others have written about this as well.

The figures for numbers of mass shootings and Americans killed in mass shootings are pulled from *Mother Jones*'s database on American mass shootings. We included data from Columbine (April 20, 1999) through the Chicago Mercy Hospital shooting (November 19, 2018).

1. VALENTINE'S DAY

1

I have been talking to Laura Farber about her Columbine documentary for several years, since its inception phase. It eventually debuted at the Minneapolis Saint Paul International Film Festival in April, and has since won a string of film festival awards.

David and Lauren Hogg, and their parents, discussed their Valentine's Day experiences with me many times, individually and together. They had a chance to crystallize their thoughts over time and home in on them in their excellent joint memoir, *#NeverAgain*, so I used many of the quotes about that day from their book.

I followed up with Lauren while fact-checking in November, to see which friends she learned about each day. She said she first learned about Alyssa, and then it's all a blur.

2

Authoritative sources on David Byrne seem split on whether his hair is black or dark brown. We examined photos closely and fall in the dark brown camp, though if it's black to you, we won't argue. David Hogg's hair also appears black to many people, but he assures me it's dark brown.

We rounded the school's student body to 3,200 students. The exact figure was 3,158 students enrolled at MSD during the 2017–18 school year, according to the National Center for Education Statistics.

MSD has fourteen permanent buildings, confirmed in an email exchange with Nadine Drew of the Broward County Public Schools Public Information Office in November. As of that date, there were about forty temporary buildings, most of which serve to accommodate the closing of building 12.

3

I did not expect this to be a book. I actually began writing about Parkland the morning after the shooting, when a *Politico* magazine editor saw one of my tweets and asked me to write a piece about my becoming the media murder guy. I was so stunned by David—and his peers, whom I watched the rest of the morning—that

I proposed writing the piece about whether this time might actually be different. I was wrapping that up Saturday when Michael Hogan called. He is a good friend and the digital director of *Vanity Fair*, who knows my restrictions and edits my occasional pieces for that publication. He said he knew I wasn't allowed to go to these places, but . . . would I consider it anyway? I did consider it. But I had another problem: I was eighteen years into my book on two gay soldiers whom I'd first written about in 2000. (Half of that time was overlapping with *Columbine*, which was my primary occupation until 2009.) I was three years late on the gay soldiers book, the end in sight, and vowing to stay laser focused. But Parkland seemed too important to ignore.

I thought about it overnight, and hashed it out with Mike on Sunday. I agreed to cover Parkland for five weeks, publishing three to five pieces for *Vanity Fair*, and helping produce a documentary video short. Under no circumstances could I stay more than five weeks.

I had become so engrossed in working that out that I missed the Sunday-morning shows announcing the march. When I heard that, I knew I had made the right call. I started packing while hitting up my media and survivor networks to find a way to make contact with the kids.

I was down there Monday, and once I met those kids, I was hooked. I have spent much of the past two decades working with children. Countless high schools and colleges have brought me in as a speaker, and I had been Skyping with classes regularly until I put that on hold to finish the soldiers book. So I am used to being amazed by kids, and I never really bought into the idea that they're incapable of huge undertakings. Still, the march was a lot. Once I saw Jackie and her team pull off Tallahassee, I had no doubts.

I got so enthused the first month that I toyed with the idea of a book a few times. I kept deciding it was a terrible idea. One book at a time. But my second trip to Parkland, mid-March, turned my head around. I was meeting several of the kids in person for the second round, with many phone calls in between. They were feeling more comfortable with me, and I was getting a real sense of them, and I could not bear the idea of not telling their stories. I had already written about several of them in *Vanity Fair* dispatches, but that canvas was way too small. I was staggered by the scope of this, and I wanted room to convey their personalities as well.

Vanity Fair signed on for a long piece in the October issue of the print magazine, which committed me for much longer. I told my agent, Betsy Lerner, that I was serious about a book, and she helped me work out an approach—leaving the content open-ended, to see how the story played out. (God, I hate it when journalists arrive at a story with it already written in their heads.) We worried about Harper's possible reaction. I was already under contract and three years late on the gay soldiers book—would they be horrified at my suggesting another delay? (Or what if they suggested replacing the overdue book with *Parkland*? That would be far worse.) Luckily, they were eager to tackle both. (The new plan is for me to finish writing the gay soldiers book in 2019.)

Survivors showed me the Hokie Stones when I visited Virginia Tech at the Academy of Critical Incident Analysis (ACIA) conference. I recalled some very particular memorials at Newtown, but couldn't remember what they were, so I dug through old news reports. I found the painted bedsheets and small cardboard angels in "Asking What to Do With Symbols of Grief as Memorials Pile Up" (*New York Times*) and "Christmas Day in Sandy Hook" (*New Yorker*).

All the details from Pine Trails Park are my observations and impressions.

I didn't realize it at the time, but the young women were singing "What a Beautiful Name" by Hillsong Worship. They actually sang the fourth line out of order. The group leader would call out a line, and the rest would sing it back, and I recorded and transcribed it the way they performed it.

2. LIGHTNING STRIKE

1

Jackie described her lockdown experiences to me in interviews, and we went over them several times. Cameron laid his down in a series of Facebook posts the first night, and pieces he later published, including his CNN op-ed the next day. I later discussed them with him and his mother, Natalie Weiss. Cameron has made his Facebook posts private, but those posts were captured before he did so. I ran them by his mom. (The kids have enormous demands on their time and get overwhelmed by media requests. I tried to offload routine matters to people around them whenever possible. His mom had all the posts and could vouch for them 100 percent.)

If you have never watched a "Run. Hide. Fight." video, I highly recommend them for preparing yourself if you ever find yourself in this situation. They stress three simple concepts, and they offer lots of ideas that you can visualize when there is no time to think. Just google the phrase, or check out the great one I feature in the resources section of my website.

MSD's alternating silver and burgundy days are named after the school's colors.

The profile by Emma I cite was published in *Harper's Bazaar* in February.

All the major investigations into the issue of school shooters and mental illness have issued the same caution: that most perpetrators never received a formal psychological evaluation, and they've then died during their attacks. Our inability to interrogate such perpetrators afterward has led to woefully incomplete data. Given that these statistics are pulled only from the cases in which a history of mental illness could be documented, the incidence of such issues among perpetrators may actually be considerably higher.

Though I only briefly touch on the mental health issue here, I have explored it in greater depth in several publications over the past few years. If you're interested in this topic, my piece "What Does a Killer Think?" (*Newsweek*) summarizes the three major motivations of mass murderers other than terrorism: depression, psychosis, and, rarely, psychopathy. (The last two sound similar and are often confused by laypeople, but are in fact completely different.) I have written related pieces for the *New Republic, Slate,* and the *New York Times.* They are linked at my site.

3

I relied on several sources to document the perpetrator's actions, including the Broward County Sheriff's Office's official report. The *New York Times* had several excellent pieces: "What Happened in the Parkland School Shooting," "Parkland Shooting Suspect Lost Special-Needs Help," "[Suspect name], Florida Shooting Suspect," and "'Kill Me,' Parkland Shooting Suspect Said." I also consulted "'You're All Going to Die' . . ." (*Miami Herald*), "Uber Driver Says . . ." (*Miami Herald*), "What Happened in the 82 Minutes" (*Chicago Tribune*), and "Teacher Told Students to Run" (CBS News).

4

All quotes in the book from Cameron's mom, Natalie Weiss, come from my interviews with her. I met her at the first two *Spring Awakening* shows, and asked if I could interview her. She said she would be happy to, but only if Cameron approved it. He did. I interviewed her for a few hours at their home on May 7, and followed up periodically by text afterward. The descriptions come from my time there. She let me tour their home and take lots of pictures for reference.

It was widely reported that Jackie's post was made to Instagram, with "MAKE IT STOP" formatted as a picture, and the rest in the text. That is understandable, because her Instagram feed is public, and her Facebook timeline is not. However, Jackie assured me as far back as February that she posted it to Facebook first, and then created the Instagram post, using the last Facebook line for the Instagram picture. (She sent me the Facebook post.) It was also the Facebook post that made its way to the family of Debbie Wasserman Schultz, setting in motion the events described next in this chapter.

5

All the details and quotes about the development of the Tallahassee trip come from numerous interviews and follow-ups with Jackie, Claire VanSusteren, and State Senator Lauren Book in February and early March, primarily the first two. (We also did a lot of fact-checking calls and texts in the late summer, prior to a *Vanity Fair* piece.)

The primary interviews with all of them took place by phone, about a week after the trip. I spoke to Senator Book several times on that trip, and spoke and texted with Claire constantly—she was invaluable at getting us into sessions, sending urgent texts to hightail it over—but most of the reflection, and re-creating all the details, came later.

I shadowed Jackie through much of the trip, but she did not grant any media interviews during or prior (other than her brief chat on my Sunday call with David on speakerphone with the team).

State Representative Kristin Jacobs made her comments to me in an interview late Tuesday night, immediately after the training inside Leon High School covered in the "Tallahassee" chapter.

3. #NEVERAGAIN

1

The re-creation of the first few days at Cameron's house come from interviews with many of the kids over the course of several months, as well as trusted media accounts. Emily Witt's excellent *New Yorker* piece "How the Survivors of Parkland Began the Never Again Movement" was incredibly useful. I borrowed liberally, checked it all out with the kids, and I'm indebted to Emily for capturing it so well.

Emma's quotes come from her *New York Times*

op-ed "A Young Activist's Advice," and her feature on the Instagram account Humans of MSD.

2

Estimates of attendance at the first Women's March were determined by crowd scientists who conducted a digital image study, the results of which were reported in "Crowd Scientists Say Women's March . . ." (*New York Times*).

Statistics on crowd size for the Women's Marches and the March for Our Lives come from the professors Kanisha Bond, Erica Chenoweth, and Jeremy Pressman, who reported their articles "Did You Attend the March for Our Lives?" and "This Is What We Learned . . ." (both in the *Washington Post*). The authors belong to the Crowd Counting Consortium (CCC), which collects "publicly available data on political crowds reported in the United States, including marches, protests, strikes, demonstrations, riots, and other actions," according to its website. The CCC was formed to collect data for the first Women's March and its sibling marches, and it has continued to publish data on its website and in monthly articles for the *Washington Post*. It offers by far the most definitive numbers, so I relied on them throughout.

Eleven days before the Women's March, the *New*

York Times reported donations at $849,000 ("Women's March on Washington . . ."). As of November 2018, the March has received $2,069,783 in donations.

3

The five recent grads were Matt Deitsch, Dylan Baierlein, Brendan Duff, Kaylyn Pipitone (Pippy), and Bradley Thornton. (All come up in the book except Bradley. Sorry Bradley—I wish our paths had crossed. I think they did briefly in Chicago.)

Statistics on Parkland's demographics, median income and home value, and poverty rate are from City Data, DataUSA, and the US Census.

The Parkland Historical Society was invaluable in providing history on the area. The society's president, Jeff Schwartz, and vice president, Jim Weiss, described the area as it was and is to my researcher Marc Greenawalt. (These were among the few interviews I did not conduct personally.) Jim Weiss also wrote articles on the Parkland Historical Society's website that contribute to the background. Additional information comes from the city of Parkland's website.

I relied on several sources to situate Parkland's role in the Everglades, especially the US Geological Survey's articles on the Everglades and the South Florida environment, and Michael Grunwald's book *The*

Swamp: The Everglades, Florida, and the Politics of Paradise.

For biographical information on Marjory Stoneman Douglas, I relied primarily on "At the March for Our Lives . . ." (*Washington Post*) and Tim Collie's "Marjory Stoneman Douglas, 'Voice of the River'" (*Sun-Sentinel*). That *Washington Post* piece also provides the number of stoplights in Parkland.

The statistics on Marjory Stoneman Douglas High School come from the National Center for Education Statistics and pertain to the 2017–18 school year. Additional statistics come from *U.S. News & World Report*.

Basic facts on the rally, including sponsors, come from the event's Facebook page.

4

Emma's experience in AP US government class that day and her thoughts about gun legislation at that time come from "Emma González Hated Guns . . ." (*Washington Post*).

The information about David Hogg recommending Emma for *Anderson Cooper 360°* initially came from the same article. I also spoke to the producers about David at the time, and appeared on the show that night.

Quotes from Emma in this section come from her appearances on *Ellen* and *60 Minutes*, her interview with Milk.xyz, and the articles "Emma González Hated Guns . . ." (*Washington Post*) and "What We Know about Emma Gonzalez" (CNN).

Like most of America, I had never heard of Emma until Saturday, and I was unaware of the rally until Saturday afternoon, when I started seeing clips of her speech online. I watched it online many times. All quotes and descriptions are from that recording.

4. TALLAHASSEE

1

All descriptions and quotes from the Tallahassee trip— including the organizational meeting and the parking lot—are from my interviews and observations. I rented a car and followed the first two buses in a long media caravan up to the capital. We made three rest stops along the way. At first, I left the kids alone to have quiet time, but at each break, more of them wandered over to chat with me. I pulled into Leon High School right behind the first bus, convinced a cop to let me into the parking lot, and then watched the kids get off the first two buses, receive a hero's welcome, and make their speeches. Then the Leon kids went inside with them, and Claire let me inside the school. I spent the next few hours interviewing kids and observing the training. I was covering it with a two-man documentary film crew hired by *Vanity Fair*, so we often split up and compared notes, and I watched the video footage as well. The third bus arrived while I was inside, so I didn't witness that. Jackie was on it, and she described their unceremonious entry to me later.

2

I watched Jackie and Cameron hop onto the SUV in the parking lot from a few feet away, but did not hear what they whispered to each other. I got the brief snatch of dialogue used in the book first by interviewing Jackie about it, and then I pasted it into a text message to run it by Cameron. He remembered a few bits slightly differently. I adjusted accordingly to match his memory, then ran that by Jackie, until they were both satisfied it was accurate. (This scene was included in a March *Vanity Fair* online story, and its fact-checker then checked most quotes like that, but I can't recall for certain if she did that one.)

Jackie's comment to the school board member is an exception to her providing the commentary later. I heard and recorded that at the time.

I filmed more than an hour of video on my phone in the Publix parking lot alone, and filmed much that evening and the next day in the capitol, as well as teaming up with the *Vanity Fair* video crew once we got to Tallahassee. I found it somewhat amusing that in all that time, the only person who asked me not to use what I had shot was a journalist. While the CNN producer was having the slightly heated disagreement with Jackie, she noticed me filming it. She then found me later and begged me not to use it. It was understandable. I could have made her look awful, by appearing to give a seventeen-year-old survivor a hard time. I assured her it was clearly a legit problem, which Jackie agreed with as well once she understood. I chuckled that the kids were fine, but a professional had gotten worried. But she had reason to—and it was a painful reminder that it's very easy to make an innocent person look horrible if you come with an agenda, or if you're just sloppy and don't bother to sort out what actually happened.

I interviewed Jackie's dad, Paul, in the parking lot. Her mom did not want to do interviews, but I spoke to her informally near the end of the trip, and a bit by phone and text days and weeks later.

I did not witness the dispute with the bus driver. We were already lined up in our cars with motors running, waiting for the buses to leave at any moment. (The bus engines had been running the entire time, and everyone had boarded the buses.) We were wondering what the holdup was. Jackie filled me in on those events later.

3

David, Cameron, and Alfonso all told me about their roles and the logistics getting there.

Information on the march's projections comes from the group's permit application. I discussed various aspects of it with the kids over the next month.

I did not interview Emma Collum. Her descriptions come from "Parkland Students Have a Cause and $3.5 Million . . ." (*Miami Herald*).

The information on the celebrity donations and their statements was widely reported, but I got them all from *Deadline*. I pulled Oprah's statement from her Twitter feed.

I was flipping around the dial as we drove, and I heard the promotion on Sean Hannity's radio show and the opening report on *All Things Considered*.

The comments from Jeff Kasky and the MFOL spokesman are from "Parkland Students Have a Cause and $3.5 Million . . ." (*Miami Herald*).

4

My approach to sizing up expectations was to pose the question to dozens of students twice: before they arrived at the capitol, and then late in the day to see how they matched up. Daniel Duff's reaction was the most common, so I used him to stand in for the whole. In his case, I followed up with him with two phone interviews over the next few weeks to elaborate and reflect more in depth.

This seems like a good time to talk about how I chose the kids I would focus on in the book. There were about two dozen kids in the original MFOL group, and I knew I could not feature all of them, or the reader would get a strong sense of none. I knew I wanted to focus on a small number, with a mixture of perspectives: all the obvious things like male, female, and different ethnicities, but also the roles they played. I wanted leaders in a central role and foot soldiers a bit further out. The first time I interviewed Daniel in Tallahassee, I knew he was a strong possibility. I asked him to spell his name and give his age and year in school, and I was astounded he was a freshman.

I also frequently get asked how I made contact with all the kids. Woody Allen famously said that "showing up is eighty percent of life." I quote that often, because I find it surprisingly true, particularly in journalism. Getting David's number took some doing, but the rest was mostly showing up. Nearly a hundred kids went to

Tallahassee (a few dropped out at the last minute), and I must have spoken to at least two-thirds along the way, plus lots of parents. I used to be reticent about asking minors for their phone numbers, and I'd ask for emails instead. That has all changed. Now they give their cell numbers out with barely a thought, so I didn't feel bad about it. Over the course of the year, only a few kids said they would feel more comfortable giving me their emails, which I respected. Many kids rarely check email, so it's frequently useless. (Of course I never share cell numbers. When someone wants to contact a particular individual, I send a message to the source conveying the request.) I came home from Tallahassee with forty to fifty numbers—more than I could ever follow up with. From there, one person recommended me to the next, and I kept bumping into more of them along the way. They generally gave me their cell number at that point, and we'd stay in touch. (In Jackie's case, it was actually her dad who gave me his number in the Publix parking lot, and he conveyed the message to Jackie afterward, and she called me back.) Sadly, I never connected with a handful, which was mostly just odd luck. It was very hard to get to the kids through official media channels, because they were besieged. It was much more effective just to go to their events and connect with the kids in person. Even once we connected, it was sometimes hard to get a response, because they had so many more media requests than they could handle. But I found that when I actually flew down there—or wherever they were headed—they tended to respond. Showing up.

I obviously didn't spend the night with them. Claire, Senator Book, and lots of the kids described the scene to me later. Everything else in this chapter I witnessed directly. (As in all cases, some of the quotes came in real time, and some were later follow-ups. It was a frenzied schedule, and impossible to get everyone's impressions as they occurred.)

I rejoined them at the capitol as soon as they arrived, and I spent the day running around with different groups. Claire set up the same large chamber for both the kids and the press to stash our stuff and to use as a break room (and they ate their box lunches there), so we were really thrown together. In that room, I respected their need for downtime, and generally kept to the informal press side of the room. A few times—like right after they met with Governor Scott—I wandered over and asked, "Anyone want to talk?" (No one did then, because they were hungry, but several said they would come find me after they ate, and they did. That's generally how it worked. They made it pretty clear when they wanted to talk, and they knew where to find us.)

5

"Seventeen bills that could have saved seventeen lives," a mom told me, a senator told me, aides told me, and the incoming president of the Florida PTA told me.

6

Jackie was taking a brief respite from the press—and from everything—in Senator Book's office. She was with just a few people, but Claire was one of them, who texted me to come confer with her about something I've now forgotten. So I happened to see Jackie playing with the babies, but I kept my notepad and recorder in my pocket, and gave her some space. Then I ended up playing with the babies myself. They were adorable, and we all needed a break. (Senator Book was there and handed one of them to me—sorry, I forgot which.)

Alfonso's quote beginning "I'm extremely, extremely angry and sad" comes from "'Look Me in the Eyes.' . . ." (*Miami Herald*). He (and many others) characterized it the same way to me directly, but I thought he said it best there, so I used that version.

5. SPRING AWAKENING

1

All the descriptions of Cameron's childhood come from his mom, Natalie, mostly in our May interview. We stayed in touch by text through the end of November, and I followed up on small items that way periodically.

Natalie gave only a brief description of Cam's stand-up set on the cruise ship. She let me know videos of the act were on YouTube, and I watched quite a few. I used the footage to re-create the specifics of that scene. As of November 2018, a video was still there, titled "Cameron Kasky-Norweigan Sky-040509-'Jokers Wild' open mike night." (Note the typo of "Norweigan" to find it.)

French Woods was the name of the performing arts camp Cameron attended where he discovered his passion for drama. Campers attended and put on shows: ventriloquism, magic, circus. YouTube video of Cam there also helped me flesh out the scene.

2

Most of the backstory details on the *Spring Awakening* production before and after Valentine's Day come from Christine Barclay, whom I interviewed and visited numerous times. (All her quotes in the book are from those interviews or from direct observations.) I also conferred with the kids about it, and attended the first two performances, a rehearsal and warm-ups before one of the shows, and the talk-back with Duncan Sheik and Steven Sater and the cast and crew after the opening-night performance. I also talked to Cam's mom about her impressions of Christine Barclay, and how Cameron described their connection. All those impressions aligned.

Most of Steven Sater's quotes in this chapter actually come from the talk-back in May, but I felt they made more sense in this chapter, especially for readers not familiar with *Spring Awakening*. There are additional quotes from the talk-back in chapter 18. In all cases, I went over the quotes with Steven in November, and he elaborated on several and rephrased a few. I also asked Steven to look over my summary of his play, and he helped me get it right—especially where I was summarizing his intentions, based on his talk-back. (I tried to collapse a great deal into a short space, and I'm grateful for his help.)

4

Concerning the pervasive feeling after these tragedies: I have observed it and discussed it with trauma experts countless times over the past two decades. The Columbine example is portrayed in that book.

6. BACK TO "NORMAL"

1

Daniel's father, Brian, his two brothers, Brendan and Connor, and Connor's girlfriend, Haley Richardson, came to the march in DC with him. My photographer and helper friend and I arranged to spend most of the day with them. Then the family had me over to their house for a sit-down interview in early May. Daniel, his dad, and his mom, Debbie Duff, attended that, along with Pippy, who was staying with them. Of course I interviewed Daniel throughout the year and chatted with him at events. All the quotes in the book from the family come from those various meetings.

I know Robin Fudge Finegan from Columbine, and have used her as a source many times. She posted her remark as a comment on one of my Instagram posts about the kids.

A large number of students talked to me about their anxiety returning to school. I chose a few incidents from Daniel and Jackie that were representative of what I heard. As always, I've tried to give you a sense of how this affected all the kids through the eyes of a handful.

There was *a lot* of eye-rolling from Douglas kids about the Play-Doh. But everyone seemed thrilled with the comfort dogs.

The basic facts behind the Washington Mall being previously booked were widely reported, and I consulted various news accounts. The application filed by Deena Katz provided the most significant details. Of course, Jackie's reaction, summarizing the group's response, comes from her directly. Others in the group described it similarly.

7. PEACE WARRIORS

1

We calculated the gun fatality numbers using data from the Gun Violence Archive online. I defined a "kid" as someone between the ages of zero and seventeen and included perpetrators of gun violence who were killed or injured in the act in my total.

Delaney Tarr's quote comes from Lisa Miller's excellent *New York* magazine piece "On the Ground with Parkland Teens as They Plot a Revolution." The kids were very open with journalists, including me, about their privilege. But I thought Delaney's quote to Lisa was the most articulate I saw or heard, so I went with that one.

2

Everything about the meetings between the Chicago and Parkland kids comes from the kids from both groups, and from Father Pfleger. I first heard about it from Matt Deitsch on March 15. He and other MFOL kids talked to me about it several times, but I wanted to convey it from the perspective of the Chicago kids, so my account primarily relies on Alex King and D'Angelo McDade. (And on Father Pfleger for much of the origin.) Alex and D'Angelo also texted me pictures from the meeting, and Emma posted a few pictures online, which also helped with a few details, like the furniture in her house. (I've not been there.)

Matt put me in touch with all three of them, but I was juggling a lot of stories and didn't interview them until June, about a week before I was set to meet them all at the Peace March (all three by phone, and separately, D'Angelo in two installments). I stayed in touch with all of them, particularly Alex, who spent the next two months on the bus tour, so I ran into him throughout the summer. We chatted many times.

During the meeting at Emma's house, Alex and D'Angelo each told a powerful story of how gun violence affected them, which I recount here. No journalist was at the meeting, and I'm not aware of anyone recording it. So Alex and D'Angelo each re-created those moments for me, by retelling their story as they typically do. That is what appears here.

The snatch of dialogue between D'Angelo and Emma at the end of the chapter comes from him. I ran it by Emma via her publicist through email, and she confirmed it was accurate.

All quotes from Alex King and D'Angelo McDade in this book are from our interviews. (The exception would be snippets of their public speeches and statements at MFOL town halls. All of those quoted I witnessed in person.)

Martin Luther King Jr.'s six principles of nonviolence are:

1. Nonviolence is a way of life for courageous people.

2. Nonviolence seeks to win friendship and understanding.

3. Nonviolence seeks to defeat injustice, not people.

4. Nonviolence holds that suffering can educate and transform.

5. Nonviolence chooses love instead of hate.

6. Nonviolence believes that the universe is on the side of justice.

8. STRATEGY

1

I talked to many of the MFOL kids about the strategy formulation covered throughout this chapter, but Matt was the chief strategist, and I relied heavily on his account. David also had a lot of input.

It was Martin Luther King Jr.'s second principle that came up most commonly with the kids.

2

All quotes from Professor Robert J. Spitzer come from my interview with him.

3

Jackie made the rough calculation of thirty thousand miles for me in early June, so it includes only travel to that point.

4

Counts of NRA Twitter activity include only original tweets, not retweets.

We searched the NRA's official Twitter account from Valentine's Day through mid-fall and found only one tweet that tagged David's handle (from August), and none that tagged Emma.

Wayne LaPierre's comments come from "N.R.A. Chief, Wayne LaPierre . . ." (*New York Times*).

The *Times* story I cite describing the debate on NRATV is "Where the N.R.A. Speaks First and Loudest."

5

David Hogg's comments come from our May 13 interview.

The summary of the origins of the two National School Walkouts come from "Meet the Students Who . . ." (NPR) and the Women's March Youth EMPOWER's publicity materials.

The Ashcroft in America Research Project is conducted by Lord Ashcroft Polls. Elise Jordan is a colleague and also a friend. I have discussed the results of her focus groups regularly with her for the past two years; they have been very helpful in reading the political climate, particularly with Trump voters. We had a lengthy conversation about the Mississippi and Memphis focus groups in March. Her quotes are from those conversations and a follow-up interview in November. The quotes from participants are from the Lord Ashcroft Polls site and her *Time* magazine article titled "I've Supported the Second Amendment My Whole Life. It's Time for Reasonable Gun Control," in March.

9. CHANGE THE REF

1

I interviewed Tío Manny (Manuel Oliver) in his office in Boca Raton in May. I later met him and his wife, Patricia, at other events during the bus tour, and spoke to them then. Most of the information and quotes in this chapter, and the later episodes with the family, come from these conversations.

Exceptions are noted here, with two big ones:

1. Maria Alesia Sosa and Luis Velarde wrote an incredible piece for Univision, "Where Is My Son?" It is the basis for most of section 1, interspersed with my reporting in Columbine. I later confirmed the veracity of their account with Tío Manny. The Univision piece provided the last names of Sergeants Rossman and Brown, but I was unfortunately unable to track down their first names for inclusion in this book.

2. My descriptions of the murals come from photos and videos of Manny creating them, as well as what he described to me. I was present in Chicago for the mural he created there, noted in chapter 18.

2

Tío Manny provided vivid descriptions of Joaquin, and he told me about the poem mentioned here. He directed me to the *Eagle Eye*'s special memorial issue for the Parkland victims for the precise wording and additional background. Some details and the quotes from Joaquin's sister, Andrea Ghersi, and his teacher, Stacy Lippel, come from that issue.

3

Tío Manny's account of dropping Guac off at school the morning of the shooting is from Manny and Patricia's August interview with *Democracy Now!*

4

Tío Manny's quote about giving a voice to Joaquin comes from his video message on the Posts Into Letters website.

A 2005 study by the Congressional Management Foundation titled *Communicating with Congress* reports, "Nearly all staff surveyed (96%) reported that if their Member of Congress had not arrived at a firm decision, individualized postal letters would have 'some' or 'a lot' of influence on the Member's decision."

The Posts Into Letters website keeps a running tally of all of the letters that have been sent to congress-people through its app. As of November 2018, the tally stands at over 19,700 letters.

Posts Into Letters won Silver Lions in the PR and Print categories and a Bronze Lion in the Direct category at the 2018 Cannes Lions International Festival of Creativity.

10. EXHAUSTED

1

In this chapter, I tried to illustrate how various MFOL kids were dealing with the situation at a single point in time, about a month after the tragedy, and just over a week before the march on Washington. Therefore, nearly all the quotes in this chapter come from in-person interviews I did with them on successive days: Alfonso, Daniel, and Ryan together on March 12; David and then his parents, March 13; David and Lauren at the school walkout rally, March 14; Jackie, March 15; and Matt Deitsch, also March 15 (but separately). There were a few exceptions. The first is a few great quotes by David from published sources, noted in the main text. I also spoke to Daniel by phone several times that week in addition to the group interview.

My first sit-down interview with David was in his kitchen, May 13, for just under an hour. I spent the next few hours with his parents, Rebecca and Kevin. They gave me their perspective, filled me in on David's childhood, gave me a tour of the house, and showed me some of his favorite gadgets, like his first drone, and the newer model he had recently wanted badly and then gotten. Lauren was also there some of the afternoon, and we chatted just briefly. All the quotes from them in this chapter come from those interviews, except as noted. (And a few are from the rally the next day, where I ran into David and Lauren again.)

The *Outline* piece on David was written by Gaby Del Valle.

2

Beth González's comments are quoted from her interview with *60 Minutes* that aired March 18.

4

David's comments on meeting Michael Bloomberg come from Lisa Miller's excellent profile on David for

New York magazine. (It's easily the best profile of him I've read.)

Though many of David's quotes in this chapter come from my conversations with him, a few come from Miller's piece.

11. WALKOUT

1

All of section 1 is from my direct observations and real-time interviews. I watched the Douglas kids march out to the football field and back for their walkout from just outside the fence, along with the press and locals. I met Christopher Krok and the other Westglades students on the street as the Douglas kids were filing back in. I first interviewed Christopher and many of the others there (including big groups of the other junior ROTC kids), and then the big wave of students from Westglades arrived, and everyone started running. Where I wrote that reporters kept asking where they were going, I heard a few other reporters asking, but that was mainly me, asking over and over. I sprinted to the front of the pack and then let them start passing, and kept asking, and no one seemed to know, until that person finally yelled out "Pine Trails!"

The police had told the media to park our cars along the side of that road, and we happened to be running right toward my rental car. So I stayed with the pack for a bit, interviewing kids on the move, then back-tracked to my car and drove to the park so I could beat them there and watch it unfold from start to finish. It was nearly two miles away, so it took them a while, and I also had a chance to walk the field to gather impressions of the state of the memorials, and to take a lot of pictures. That's when I noticed Peter Wang's sign had come free and was lying on the ground.

During and after the rally, I interviewed lots of other students, including all the ones quoted here. That's when Susana Matta Valdivieso filled me in on all her planning for the prior month. Rabbi Melinda Bernstein and Angel Lopez gave me the background on what they had been doing. I spoke to dozens of Douglas students, and most said they'd gotten wind of the plan early that morning, but none of them thought it was actually going to happen. Lauren Hogg and others showed me the Instagram and Snapchat messages from that morning, which were still on their phones.

We consulted local news reports just to fact-check the spelling of names (although most of the kids spelled them for me, sometimes I couldn't read their writing later).

2

Jackie's exchange with her math teacher was conveyed entirely by her, which she recited to me from memory the following day. (This was the same interview used in the prior chapter. We met after school, at a Starbucks nearby.)

I cringed when Jackie told me about the friendships. It made me sad that it was happening, and it scared me that Jackie was sharing it with journalists (for the reason stated in the text). I decided to put it off the record for several months, to see how it played out, and I struggled for days about whether to advise Jackie to consider keeping that from people like me. Eventually, I decided that would be too intrusive, but I still wondered whether I made the right choice. These kids have never been in this position, and sometimes those of us with more life experience are in a better position to see the potential ramifications of certain decisions. In the end, Jackie was right, and as I made near-final edits over Thanksgiving, I decided it was safe to divulge.

3

This is the same group interview as that described in the prior chapter. We met on the patio of the restaurant at the Heron Bay Marriott (the same hotel that was used as a rendezvous point on Valentine's Day). Daniel arrived first and I chatted with him for a while, then the others came. The entire session lasted about two hours.

12. THE MEMES MEN

2

I followed Jackie's car to the MFOL office immediately after our Starbucks interview on March 15.

That was the first time I met Matt and Dylan. I interviewed Matt that afternoon and Dylan the next day. All the quotes from them in this chapter are from those interviews.

As soon as I met Matt and Dylan, I knew I wanted to feature them, at least in a magazine piece. In fact, I was in the final stages of a very different story for the online edition of *Vanity Fair*, to run less than a week later, as a preview to the march. I walked out so excited that I called my editor from the parking lot to say I wanted to drop that story and replace it with a much better story about these guys. He agreed. I would continue to interview them and chat with them at events over the ensuing months.

Pippy was also in the office that day, and I recognized her, because she had assisted Jackie on the Tallahassee trip and had helped me out before and during. (For what it's worth, I wanted to feature Pippy as well. She said she doesn't like to be the center of attention, and I could use little bits from her, but she didn't want to be featured. She was very helpful over the course of the spring coordinating things. And she finally agreed to be part of my sit-down interview with the Duff family in May.)

I spent a bit under two hours in the office that day, and less than two the following day. The kids gave me permission to take photos to use to describe the space later, and I took dozens, including close-ups of the Post-it notes and anything written on the wall, which is how I was able to reproduce it here. I also kept the tape running as we toured and narrated some of it as we walked—and asked Jackie about things.

The photos were intended for documentation purposes, but Jackie later gave me permission to publish several on *Vanity Fair*'s website with my March 22 story.

3

Several of the kids told me about the Fight for Our Lives rebranding, under strict confidentiality. Not all of them were sure exactly when the change was going to happen, but I got the impression it was going to be at the DC march. As we were leaving the march, I asked Daniel about it, and he was a bit surprised too. He noted that many of them had tossed out "little Easter eggs," and thought it would be coming soon. I asked some of the kids a week or two later (I can't recall exactly who), and although they were unsure about timing, they were sure I should keep it quiet. I didn't ask about it again for a few weeks, and by then they had let it go.

The best count of actual sibling marches that took place in the United States comes from the *Washington Post* data, published in "Did You Attend the March for Our Lives?" The number given in the article is smaller than the figure stated in this chapter, because 84 of the marches were abroad.

5

Matt told me most of the *Cold Beak* stories, and Dylan filled in more.

13. HARVARD

I did not attend the Harvard conference. Most of the information in this chapter comes from my interviews with John Della Volpe, as do all quotes from him in the book. He also sent me the slideshow cited, and I pulled the passages directly from it. I interviewed him by phone in June, with several follow-ups. I talked to the kids about it as well.

His key polling question—"Does political involvement have any tangible results?"—has changed wording over the years, so I paraphrased him. His most recent statement, to which he asks potential voters to respond on a five-point scale, is "Political involvement rarely has any tangible results."

Like Della Volpe, I wondered for a while whether Alfonso and David had choreographed that one-two punch. I was going to ask them about it when I saw them both at a community barbeque on the Road to Change tour in Aurora, Colorado, in July, but I could never get them together. (They move around!) I was talking to Alfonso as he was about to board the bus after the event, and David was off riding a bike to decompress. Just then, David rode up, so I asked them the moment I had them together. They both laughed out loud. It had been a last-minute situation.

14. MARCH FOR THEIR LIVES

1

In the weeks leading up to the march, I thought about how I wanted to cover it. I figured there would be all sorts of reporting on Emma's day, and David's (a documentary crew was scheduled to follow him around). I was most curious what it would be like for someone not quite at the center of the organizing, outside the media storm. I knew immediately who I wanted. I pitched Daniel Duff the idea of spending the day with him and whoever he was going with: from first thing in the morning, through the day. He was game and checked with his family, and they agreed too. *Vanity Fair* also liked the idea, and sent a great photographer, Justin Bishop, to capture it visually. (My assignment was just to write extended captions, but it turned into a piece.) We knew it would be a crazy day, so my writer friend Matt Alston agreed to come down with us and help. He was working on a profile on me, and by sticking by my side, he could help me out and get a firsthand look at my process. 42 West gave us all access to the media interview tent.

Joan Walsh was *Salon*'s news editor when Columbine was attacked, and she edited nearly all the four dozen stories I published for it. (About two-thirds of those concerned Columbine.) That was my first time back into journalism since college, and she was really helpful in guiding me and honing my stories, and has been one of the major influences on my work. Joan was at *Salon*'s main office in San Francisco, so we did it all by email and phone, and didn't meet in person for more than a year. We are now friends, and she is now national affairs correspondent for *The Nation* and a CNN political analyst. We coaxed the 42 West people to position us together in the interview tent, and we spent a good chunk of the day together, sharing findings, impressions, and ideas. Joan is one of the wisest people I know, and a great mentor, and we have been on this larger story together for nearly twenty years. She was incredibly helpful as a sounding board. She has also been covering civil rights issues within the African American community for decades, and that insight was invaluable.

We agreed to meet Daniel and his family at their hotel lobby a bit before eight a.m. and head to breakfast. It (stupidly) had not occurred to me that all the MFOL kids would be staying there, so I was surprised to see most of them in the lobby. I decided to give them their space. Some of them were clearly just waking up, and we were in their home for the day, and they didn't need to deal with media yet. I just nodded and said hi when they came over to see Daniel, and tried to observe as inconspicuously as possible.

Brendan Duff played a major role in MFOL, but he kept such a low profile that I was not even aware he was part of it until I met him with Daniel at breakfast. Brendan was the key adviser on media and image early on, which was critical. The entire family has an interesting story. Brendan and Connor Duff were both in North Carolina when the shooting happened, but they were determined to come home immediately. The Duffs had moved to Parkland from New Jersey only a few years earlier, after Connor graduated from high school, so he had less of a connection to Douglas. But he wanted to be there for Daniel, and for Brendan, whose good friends had been traumatized. I had every intention of telling much more of Brendan's story, and the family's, but I just had too much material, and was never able to backtrack. (I also stayed in contact with the other kids by running into them at events, and Brendan was away at college.)

2

Most of the technical specs for the stage and equipment come from the National Park Service's event permit, with a bit from the group's application. The rest was from my observations.

David Hogg explained the orange $1.05 tags in his speech. They were used at later events as well.

3

I hated that the press area sealed us off from the crowd, but it gave us a good view of the stage, plus the Jumbotron for close-up detail. There was a metal barricade that separated us from the crowd, so we spent most of the rally leaned up against it, so we could watch them react and chat with the people inches from us on the other side. I wanted to get an immersive sense of the event, though, and to see what it was like for people several blocks back. So midway through, Matt and I took one long, slow walk all the way to the back (around Twelfth Street). We stopped along the way to gauge responses and chat with revelers here and there. I was slightly surprised to see the excitement level nearly as high all through. (Anyone who's been to a concert knows how different being in the back can feel. I'm glad we did it, but we couldn't always see or hear what was happening onstage during the trip to the rear. We missed Sam Fuentes throwing up. I heard about it back in the media area, and watched it later online to write that scene. The walk took twenty to thirty minutes, so we did that only once.)

Background on Naomi Wadler and her school walkout come from "A Parkland Father and . . ." (*Alexandria News*).

Media wasn't permitted in the VIP area where Daniel was, so we had to part ways with him until after the rally. But our photographer, Justin, managed to score a wristband, so he spent most of it beside Daniel taking pictures and jotting notes. Justin provided most of the details of Daniel's and Ryan's experiences during the rally (which I confirmed with them later).

4

I tell a fuller version of Linda Mauser's story in the afterword of *Columbine.*

5

I texted Daniel right after Emma finished, and we realized they were about to pass us on their way out. So we reconnected moments later, and they were elated, so I hit the record button on my iPhone to get their immediate impressions. Then we found both their dads and family members. We all walked over to the Capitol, but Daniel and Ryan were so amped up that they kept running ahead and then circling back to us. I stayed back with the dads and got their impressions for much of that time. We caught up with the boys at several stoplights, while they searched for their documentary team. I was beside them with the tape rolling when they stopped in traffic, and when they chatted up the cops.

6

The Crowd Counting Consortium published its results on the march, along with historical comparisons, in "Did You Attend the March for Our Lives?" (*Wash-*

ington Post). I drew additional historical references—including on the Vietnam War and Iraq protests—from "This Is What We Learned . . ." by the same authors in this piece on the Women's March.

The University of Maryland sociology professor Dana R. Fisher led a research team to gather very specific data on the composition of the Women's March in 2017. They surveyed every fifth person in the crowd to compile a wealth of detail about who the attendees were, why they came, and what their backgrounds were. It was very successful. Major demonstrations continued in the months that followed, so Fisher redeployed her team for every large protest in Washington from that date forward, and she was continuing her crowd analysis at least through October 2018. Her results on the MFOL march were published in "Here's Who Actually Attended the March for Our Lives" (*Washington Post*). This is incredible data, and my source for crowd analysis.

The Trace's data comes from the article "Parkland Generated Dramatically More News Coverage Than Most Mass Shootings."

15. PTSD

All quotes and reflections from Dr. Frank Ochberg and Dr. Alyse Ley come from interviews with them. I have been consulting with Dr. Ochberg about trauma issues since 1999, when he played a big role at Columbine. I became an Ochberg Fellow at the nonprofit organization he founded, the Dart Center for Journalism and Trauma, at Columbia University's Graduate School of Journalism. I first discussed the Parkland kids' situation at length with both doctors during the ACIA conference in Las Vegas mentioned in the prologue in May—both individually and in panel discussions. It was enlightening to also involve two recent survivors of the Las Vegas tragedy, Chris and Jenny Babij, in that discussion, and for their real-time coping experience to inform it. I followed up with Dr. Ochberg periodically, and he helped vet portions of the manuscript medically and filled in and fleshed out many ideas in an interview in mid-November (though I of course take responsibility for the material in this book). I then followed up with Drs. Ochberg and Ley in separate lengthy interviews in late November. Dr. Ley followed with citations from the DSM-V.

16. DENVER NOTICED

1

I again used the Crowd Counting Consortium's (CCC) data for the sibling marches. However, a major distinction is necessary between estimates of the DC and the sibling marches. A wealth of different organizations weighed in with estimates of the DC march, and the consortium evaluated all of them to create both a range and a best guess. With the sibling marches, there were far fewer sources. The CCC relies on estimates published in local news outlets, and on Twitter posts in the cases of small demonstrations. Typically news reports are intentionally vague, with terms like "thousands" or "hundreds." Local authorities used to estimate crowd sizes, but the numbers grew so politically charged that they stopped doing that years ago. So the CCC conservatively converts "hundreds," "thousands," and "tens of thousands" to "200," "2,000," and "20,000." That can result in a gross undercount. Because much of this chapter is set in Denver, I dug a little deeper. Most local news reports used the "thousands" catch-all, but everyone I spoke to felt the actual number was toward the upper end of that range. Denver's alternative weekly *Westword* was the only news outlet to offer a harder number, reporting "almost 100,000."

I wanted to experience how the walkouts played out in many different places, but I could be in only one place at a time. For the first walkout, I decided it was most important to attend the Douglas event, and I used news accounts to gauge the impact nationwide. (That was just for background, and I didn't describe any other walk-outs in the book, but the *New York Times* had a thorough roundup of them, and the TV networks offered great video footage.) For the second walkout, I decided to risk something big happening in Parkland to check out what was happening further afield. Columbine's choice to hold a walkout-related event a day early allowed me to experience it in two cities. I flew to Denver on April 17 and spent three days meeting with organizers and others related to their big event, watching them handle last-minute logistical details (like walking the site and choosing where to put the Porta-Potties, and so forth), interviewing the Parkland kids who had flown in, and then attending all the events on the nineteenth.

Then I caught a six a.m. direct flight to Austin, to take part in its walkout rally. Nine local high schools organized a joint rally on the steps of the Texas State Capitol, busing in students from some of the further schools. Full disclosure: Cecilia Cosby, the daughter of old friends, is now in high school and was one of the organizers. She asked me to speak at the rally, and I accepted. (I was not paid, but the organizers offered to cover my travel expenses, and ended up purchasing a flight one way. *Vanity Fair* covered most of my travel, since I tacked it on to the Columbine trip I was covering for them.) The gist of my speech was:

The Parkland kids have demonstrated so much more power than parents of survivors, because when adults see their teen faces, we see our own kids. Similarly, you [Austin kids] have a different kind of power: when adults see you, we see future targets, kids in power. You all are the face of this movement. Use that power as you see fit.

The Austin event drew several thousand and was very powerful. I had hoped to include it in this book overtly, but it was also crowded out. (*Most* of my reporting was crowded out. There was room for only a small fraction of it.) The Austin trip was great for perspective, though. It gave me a chance to witness how MFOL was affecting kids in cities where they hadn't been (i.e., most cities). I spoke to the Austin organizers and to dozens of kids who came out to the event. Many came up to talk to me immediately afterward.

Austin also gave me an added behind-the-scenes peek for several reasons. I know how long the various groups had been organizing, because Cecilia first emailed me on February 27: just thirteen days after the Parkland attack, and nearly two months before her event. It's kind of extraordinary that by then, the Austin high schools had already formed their alliance and were deep enough into planning that Cecilia had taken on the role of fund-raising and acquiring speakers, had a budget to do so, and was lining up speakers. Of course I also had backstage access during the event, but the biggest insight came via Cecilia's parents, Doug and Monica Cosby. I often interview parents, but of course they tend to be highly protective of their kids and wary of what they disclose to reporters. I have known Doug and Monica since we worked together as consultants at Arthur Andersen in the early 1990s. Monica actually worked for me on several jobs, and she is driven, and a perfectionist, and badly wanted to help the kids. It was amusing to hear her frustration at how adamantly they rebuffed all her attempts. The kids insisted they were doing this themselves. It was helpful to get the perspective of someone who would give me the unvarnished truth. (Cecilia even insisted on making the initial reach-out to me. She was born after I moved from Texas, and I had never met her or spoken to her before receiving her email in February.) I spoke to faculty members at some of the Austin schools, and while they told me they were offering advice and some logistical support, they assured me that the kids were just as firm with them on directing the project. This stance of kids organizing themselves, on their own terms, was central to the MFOL narrative, and it was interesting to see how profoundly that template had permeated distant communities, with whom the Parkland kids had no direct contact.

All the quotes from Colorado sources in this chapter and the next are from my interviews. Depictions of all Colorado events were from my direct observations, with one exception: because I was in Austin on April 20, I did not attend the service events. I spoke to Frank DeAngelis and the kids about what they had scheduled, and then confirmed those details with local news coverage.

The Denver sibling march and the April event outside Columbine were huge undertakings, and I talked to dozens of people involved in organizing them. I could name only a few in the text without confusing the narrative, so I focused on Emmy, Kaylee, and Madison, but I don't want to give the impression they did it alone. Emmy's copresident was Sam Craig, who deserves recognition.

Emmy's group was originally organized under the name Jeffco Students United for Action—and that was still its name at the time of the events depicted here. However, the group soon rebranded itself as Jeffco Students Demand Action—which I use in the narrative to avoid confusion. (My researchers had trouble even verifying the original name ever existed. If you google to learn more, it's the current name you'll want to use.) The reason for the change is actually interesting, and it was duplicated around the country, as kids learned the power of branding. Groups were sprouting around the country with their own creative names, but Students Demand Action quickly developed into a brand, with T-shirts, hashtags, a logo, principles, and so forth. When kids networked around their region and tweeted around the world, SDA was a known quantity, so large numbers of them quickly began to coalesce around the name.

2

Full disclosure: the leaders of MFOL and the Columbine survivor community both knew I was connected with the other, and both sides reached out to me for contact names and numbers. In a strange coincidence, Frank DeAngelis and Jackie Corin texted me at almost the same time for help in reaching each other. (Frank didn't specify Jackie in particular, but wanted to invite the MFOL leaders to the April 19 event. Jackie wanted to invite Frank to Douglas High to advise them on the grieving process.) That was the full extent of my role: helping connect them—and advising Frank that Jackie was a reliable person to use as a primary contact there. However, it gave me an early window into what the groups were planning long before they revealed it to media, and I kept in touch with both sides about the developments.

3

My interview with the four *Legally Blonde* kids actually took place a few weeks later, on May 8. As a rule, I tried to use quotes in the narrative when they occurred, or very close to that time, to give the reader a sense of how individuals' impressions evolved. Two weeks is longer than I usually like to stretch it, but this was the place in the story where this material was relevant for readers, and it was clear that the kids had settled on these feelings for quite a while. I had also heard bits and pieces of this sentiment from many Douglas students for weeks before and after this point in the narrative (April 20). Of all those conversations, I felt this foursome really captured many shadings and perspectives of those feelings. I hope this scene provides a sense of so many more like it.

4

The meeting with survivors was by far the most intimate exchange between survivors I've ever witnessed in two decades covering such events. It was closed to the press and public. However, since I've known several of the Columbine survivors so long, they trusted me to observe quietly in the back of the auditorium. I took notes but did not record it. To augment my notes, I taped several minutes of impressions immediately after walking out. Because no one taped the session, I used only the few brief quotes—which I jotted down and then confirmed with the source later. Because it was private, I used only names and quotes from people who gave me permission afterward.

More disclosures: I have gotten close to many of the Columbine survivors over the years. After *Columbine* was published, I foolishly believed I had moved on from this horrible story, and became good friends with some of my "former" sources, including Kiki and Paula. The reality is that after two decades, we have all been pulled into the strange gravitational orbit of these awful events, and are part of it together. Normal journalistic boundaries have blurred.

In the years after *Columbine* was published, I also faced an ethical dilemma. I had always sought to remain neutral and objective on issues like the gun debate. However, I am now frequently sought out for advice on mass shootings by students, parents, school administrators, academics, and law enforcement officers. (For example, I was the keynote speaker one year for the annual threat management conference organized by the FBI and LAPD.) I realized at some point that

I had blended into being part of this, and with people dying—so many children dying—and such an obvious national problem with guns, I could no longer stay completely neutral. I avoid public positions on specific gun legislation, but I take the overt position that we have badly failed to do anything, and some reasonable action is clearly called for.

Paula and Kiki are both articulate and empathetic, and I often recommend them as speakers when reporters, TV producers, or others ask me for suggestions. In 2014, John Ridley, the executive producer of ABC's *American Crime*, contacted me for help selecting survivors for the second season of the series, which involved a school shooting. He wanted to weave clips of actual survivors into the show. I suggested Kiki and Paula, and ABC eventually hired me (for the day) to interview them and three survivors of other brutal situations on camera. It aired in February 2016. Kiki has taught *Columbine* as a text in one of his English courses for the past several years. The first year, I Skyped in with the class. He knows writers struggle to make ends meet, and on several of my trips to Colorado, he and his wife, Kallie, invited me to stay at their house for a few days, and I accepted. That included both trips covered in this book: the April trip in this chapter, and the August trip in chapter 19.

I see people like Kiki and Paula now less as sources and more as friends, as well as valuable conduits into the closely guarded world of trauma survivors. When tragedy strikes or controversy arises, and insiders seal themselves off from the press or recite talking points, I have abundant sources who will share the blunt truth. So now I rarely use Paula or Kiki as direct sources, but because the Parkland kids sought out the Columbine community, Paula and Kiki ended up at the center of a few powerful scenes that I thought readers would appreciate. So I've included them, with this disclosure of our friendship.

This boundary crossing comes with risks, but I think they are heavily outweighed by the insights and access they afford. These people have been living with this for twenty years, and they trust me to share feelings they otherwise never would with a reporter. On the April trip, staying at Kiki's home provided extraordinary access, including long conversations with him immediately before and after events, in his kitchen or living room. He also arranged for me to interview Kaylee there, and then to visit at her home, where about twenty of the Douglas kids were hanging out and preparing to go on the Lookout Mountain trip. (I made sure all those kids knew I was a reporter, and a few chose to do interviews with me there. I got another window into them behind the scenes.) It's also highly unlikely I would have known about Kiki's car crash without staying there. I learned about it when I landed in Denver and switched on my phone from airplane mode. Kiki had texted that he might be late meeting me at his house, because he had just crashed his car. (He was not injured.) I saw the car crumpled in the driveway for the next three days. I talked to Kallie about him being too upset to call the insurance company.

5

Two years after Paula Reed taught Dylan Klebold, he and Eric Harris attacked Columbine. Most of Dylan's friends shared Reed's perception that Dylan was a sweet kid, and were shocked that he participated.

17. SETBACKS

1

Because of my existing relationships with Frank DeAngelis and others in the community, I was monitoring the evolving controversy for weeks while it remained private. I had agreed to keep it off the record at that time, because everyone involved supported the movement and didn't want to sow public discord. They eventually hit an impasse and DeAngelis went public—taking issue only with the timing. (He was an enthusiastic supporter of MFOL both publicly and privately.)

2

My quotes from Diego Garcia come from my interview with him. That was June, when I met him the weekend of the Peace March, but his comments about the walk-out were pertinent here.

3

Most of the information about Alfonso and Charlie's trip comes from my interviews with Alfonso and an Arizona representative who spoke on the condition of anonymity. I also spoke to several other MFOL kids about it and its implications, including the passage quoted from Dylan. Alfonso didn't cover all the nitty-gritty details—and he was not present to the end of the die-in—so I augmented his account with news reports: "Hamilton High and Other . . ." (*Arizona Republic*), "We're Not Going to Give Up" (*Arizona Republic*), "Parkland Student to Campaign for Hiral Tipirneni" (*Arizona Republic*), and "Arizona Students Stage 'Die-In'" (*Arizona Daily Independent*).

Background on Arizona's and Pennsylvania's special elections come from the *New York Times*. In the Senate race, the bisexual woman leading in contention for the Democratic nomination was Kyrsten Sinema. She won the nomination and the seat.

Officials eventually chose not to arrest five students who remained in the Arizona capitol building, but they shut off the lights and left the students in the dark. When that failed, officials carried them out around ten thirty p.m.

Gadsden flags are the yellow ones embellished with a coiled snake, which read DONT TREAD ON ME.

5

In addition to David's *Axios* interview, he made similar comments at a Twitter Live Q&A with Alex, Cameron, Emma, Jackie, and Ryan earlier in the week.

Yahoo News picked up the *Newsweek* story on David's *Axios* quote, and Tyah-Amoy Roberts actually linked to Yahoo's version in her tweet.

18. GRADUATION

1

The company put on four performances of *Spring Awakening*, and I attended the first two. I bought my ticket to the first show early, a front-row seat, on the far aisle, stage right. That put me beside the front VIP table, which Cameron's family happened to purchase, so I got to see their reactions during the show. (I learned who they were only later, though it was clear they were connected to him in some way.) Cameron also performed some of his major scenes at that edge of the stage. For the second performance, I got a seat toward the center, several rows back, which allowed me a much wider view of the show. I didn't design it that way, but the two seats were highly complementary in giving me different perspectives on the show.

I attended the talk-back with Sater and Sheik. I hope my account doesn't give the impression that Duncan was silent. They both had great insights, but Sater wrote the lyrics, which are most pertinent to this story, so I ended up quoting just him. The talk-back was intended to be held in the theater and open to the public, to begin after the cast had a chance to meet with friends and family outside on the boardwalk. But while that was happening, the theater owner locked up the venue, so Barclay was forced to come up with a quick plan B, and she moved the talk-back to her studio, just steps away. It was a small space, so the event had to be restricted to the cast, crew, Sater, Sheik, and a few journalists. It made for an intimate setting, with the two dozen of us barely squeezing in. They brought in chairs for Sheik and Sater, and the kids sat or lay on the floor, many curled up together. The adults mostly stood. All the questions came from the cast and crew. I got it all on tape. As stated earlier, I went over Sater's quotes with him in November, and he clarified and expanded on them. (For the most part, he added back bits that were either included in the question or a previous answer.) It was also in November that Sater shared his poem and gave me his permission to include it.

Sheik and Sater had also met with the students earlier, visited their school, and met with their drama instructor, Melody Herzfeld. I should also note that Melody played a big part in these kids' lives, and they really liked her. I contacted her in March (with Daniel Duff's help), and we texted several times, all off the record. She was extremely gracious but decided that she wanted to be there for her kids and keep the focus on them. That was very understandable. I always intended to follow up, but as with some other sources, the story got so big and great story lines got crowded out. The *Spring Awakening* material was so powerful, and so aligned with what they were going through, that I decided to focus on that. If I had another few months and could write a few more chapters—and were she willing—I would definitely include Melody. Sadly, I also intended to interview Ed Stolz on that trip, but our paths kept missing. He was assistant musical director at Douglas High, and was with most of the kids in lockdown in the drama room. He was also the musical director for Barclay's company. I regret not finding the time or space to include him. Eric Garner is also on that list, the broadcasting teacher at Douglas.

I did not attend the master class with the original Broadway cast. I spoke to Barclay about it, and some of the kids mentioned it from time to time, but I relied heavily on Alexis Soloski's excellent *New York Times* feature "Parkland Survivors Get a Broadway Master Class in Healing." Most of the quotes I used from the event come from her.

2

When I write "Everyone saw a change in David," that was an understatement. The kids were often bringing it up, and just walking into a room with David, you could feel it. He was also quite aware of it.

I had already spent a lot of time with Cameron and David over the previous months, but it was really concentrated that week. I spent a good chunk of the late part of the week shadowing Cameron and the rest of the *Spring Awakening* company, and then about five hours on Saturday at the Hoggs' house (with David there for a bit more than half of that). The contrast was so extraordinary that I bounced my impressions off David.

3

I was in town for prom weekend because of *Spring Awakening,* and I also took the opportunity to talk to some of the kids about their plans. But I felt strongly they needed a break from the media that night, so I stayed away and made no contact that evening. I used the kids' social media posts and media reports for most of the details about it, including "Marjory Stoneman Douglas High Plans 'Over the Top' Prom" (*Los Angeles Times*), "Marjory Stoneman Douglas High Prom" (*Sun-Sentinel*), and "Parkland's Seniors Celebrate Prom, but Four Are Missing" (NBC News).

By coincidence, I happened to spend much of prom day at the Hoggs' house. I was actually supposed to do an interview with Rebecca and Kevin on Thursday, but Kevin was rushed to the ER with a kidney stone. He was back on his feet quickly, and they suggested I come by Saturday morning. They were held up a bit, and only Lauren was home when I arrived, but she was open to an interview, so I caught up with her. (This is when she told me about the incident with the special issue of the *Eagle Eye,* among other things.) Then I did a long interview with Kevin and Rebecca while the kids went to lunch. Rebecca showed me the unique wrist corsage she had gotten Emma and let me photograph it. She could barely contain her giddiness about her only son going to prom. (I agreed to keep everything about Emma and David going together off the record.) We were still talking when the kids returned, and David sat down on the couch and just listened for about twenty minutes. Eventually he chimed in, and it gradually morphed into a long interview with him. Prom came up several times, and that's when David broke the news about no pictures, and he and Rebecca had it out. Eventually, Rebecca left, and Kevin spoke to David again about it, trying to find some compromise. They both felt terrible about it for Rebecca, but David said the price for letting the information out would be terrible. Eventually David went up to get dressed, while I chatted more with Kevin. (Kevin is the introvert in a very extroverted family, so it's best to get him alone. And David said he was fine with my staying.) When David came down in his tux, I got out of there to give him some space, wished him well, and promised not to text.

I regret not finding more space for Rebecca in this book. She is hysterical in person and also extremely caring. (All the parents I met were incredibly gracious and kind to me.) Rebecca always put me in a good mood. I also appreciated her candor. I hope all that comes across. I wrote and deleted much more material about Rebecca, but decided the focus needed to stay on the kids.

4

I was concerned about Lauren the first time I met her. Of all the Parkland kids I spent time with, she reminded me most of the shell-shocked Columbine kids I'd come to know. All three of the assessments of Lauren in this section (by Lauren, David, and Rebecca) came over the course of prom day. (Kevin did not weigh in.)

5

I interviewed Tío Manny on May 8, five days before Mother's Day, and he was really worried about the upcoming holiday. It seemed unthinkable for Patricia. But then when he considered it, he realized graduation would likely be the worst day of all. All the quotes in this section are from that interview.

6

My reflections at the start of this section come from nineteen years watching survivors go through the process. It tends to be a much bigger milestone than most of them foresee at the beginning.

I next saw Tío Manny in Chicago on June 15, and

met Patricia then. They had just been through graduation, and they were bracing for Father's Day two days later. We talked about all three occasions. Mother's Day had been as bad as expected, and graduation was terrible, but they'd felt much better after they devised Patricia's silent protest of a T-shirt.

I did not attend the graduation. I discussed it later with many of the MFOL kids, and particularly with the Olivers, who were still reeling from it. I composed this section primarily based on those interviews. For details, I watched much of the graduation online. I drew additional details and quotes from the *NowThisNews* article "Joaquin Oliver's Parents Appear on Their Son's Behalf at Parkland Graduation."

19. ROAD TO CHANGE

1

The kids talked to me about the tour throughout April, May, and early June—with all conversations embargoed until it was announced. During much of that period, they were still figuring out what it would really look like. (I didn't hear about the Florida bus until rather late in the game, but perhaps it just didn't come up.) I went most in depth about it with Matt and Jackie, and to a lesser extent with David and several others. All quotes and descriptions in this section are from those conversations.

Earlier in the book, I refer to Father Pfleger organizing the Peace Marches (plural), a series of marches held every Friday night throughout the summer. But with MFOL coming to the kickoff march this year, it became a big event, and the church itself dubbed it the Peace March (singular), which is how everyone I encountered before, during, and after spoke of it. So for clarity, I used the singular in this chapter.

2

I attended the Peace March on Friday, and also all the related events that evening and Saturday. Friday's activities included the MFOL students touring the area around the church, Tío Manny creating his mural, the rally, the march, and street interviews after. (The march lasted a long time, and the MFOL kids were dispersed throughout the crowd. I ran up and down the length of it watching the MFOL kids, and speaking briefly to get a quick impression, but mostly giving them space to enjoy it. Daniel was feeling chatty, so I marched with him for a while and talked with him and his new friends.) Saturday included the press availability with kids at Saint Sabina, a public barbeque in a park nearby, and then the first town hall Saturday evening in Naperville, and more press availability afterward (and a bit informally squeezed in before). We also did a *Vanity Fair* group portrait session with twelve of the MFOL kids early Saturday afternoon. In all, there were opportunities to catch the kids in a multitude of different settings and moods. I checked in with many of them repeatedly throughout the weekend. All depictions and quotes come from that reporting, as well as my preinterviews. I spoke to the MFOL kids about the Peace March many times leading up to the event, and interviewed Alex, D'Angelo, and Father Pfleger by phone several days before. I spoke to all of them throughout the weekend.

Terrell Bosley was shot outside the Lights of Zion Church on Halsted and 116th on Chicago's Far South Side.

The "freedom riders" added at the last minute were literally last-minute, or close. When the barbeque ended, I stayed to write down my impressions, so I was one of the last to leave. I pitched in with the cleanup and found a manila folder, which looked like something someone would need. So I looked inside, and it was the release forms for one of the Chicago kids to join the bus tour. I had just interviewed him at the barbeque, and we were all headed to the town hall in suburban

Naperville, so I texted him that I would bring it to him there. He had signed up to join the tour in the final hour. And he was not the only one.

3

All quotes and depictions from Naperville come from my reporting there. Several of the organizers from Downers Grove North High were also at the Peace March, and I chatted with them briefly on Friday, but we were interrupted and didn't talk long. (There was a lot going on.) I had done some basic research on their car wash the week before, and followed it on Facebook, because I was planning to attend. (There were some protests planned, and they also got so many RSVPs that they moved to a bigger location.) I ended up not going, because the barbeque was too interesting to leave. I talked to a whole lot of local activists there, and also people from the neighborhood who had come to check them out. (And the food was delicious!)

The quotes from Jackie reflecting on Naperville are from a phone interview I did with her Monday morning (two days later). When we settled on a time for the interview by text, she gave it to me in EDT. (By the way, Jackie is very precise, and includes time zones to avoid confusion.) I asked if she really meant EDT, because she was going to be in Missouri, and that was central time. No, she meant eastern. Jackie, Emma, and one of the other team members (sorry, I lost track of the third) were flying to Atlanta for a big event, and then right back to rejoin the tour. They were three days into a marathon bus tour and already tacking on extra travel? But I wasn't *too* surprised, because they had been behaving that way all spring. Still.

4

The July TargetSmart report is titled "Analysis: After Parkland Shooting, Youth Voter Registration Surges." The *Miami Herald* article cited is "Youth Voter Registration Went Up 41 Percent . . ."

5

I attended Road to Change tour dates in and around Chicago, Denver, and New York City, checked in with the kids regularly by phone and text, and monitored the tour by social media postings daily. (When something interesting happened, I would follow up by phone or text.)

All the quotes and depictions in this section come from my reporting.

6

All the quotes and depictions in this section come from my reporting, with one exception: I consulted local news accounts in Salt Lake City for background on the theater owner canceling the venue there. I did not quote any of those.

I had one of my researchers track down one of the Second Amendment protesters in Texas to pre-interview him to get his perspective. I normally conduct all my own interviews, but I was on a tight deadline for a *Vanity Fair* piece for which I was considering using it. I didn't, so I never interviewed him personally, but he was forthcoming with my researcher, and it was informative to get his perspective.

I have followed Tom Mauser's efforts since 1999 but had not checked in for a while. It was stirring to see how he had really come into his own, and how the MFOL kids looked up to him as a sort of elder statesman in their cause. Because he was. He was a pioneer.

20. HOMEWARD BOUND

1

When I saw the kids at the two Colorado stops midtour, I had the sense that some of the kids were nearing the ends of their ropes. Then and in New York City, some of them made offhand comments, but no one wanted to name names, as they were all still working it out. But it was clearly coming, and it seemed natural.

The Joni Mitchell song is "Coyote." I recommend the live recording on The Band's farewell concert album, *The Last Waltz*—and Martin Scorsese's film of the same name.

2

Everything in this section is from my reporting, except the paragraph on David, where I got most of the details and the quoted phrase from Lisa Miller's *New York* magazine profile on him, "Parkland Activist David Hogg . . ."

3

This section is from my reporting.

4

Cameron announced his departure on the Fox News Radio show *Benson and Harf* on September 19. A transcript of the key passages is online on the Fox News Radio website.

5

This section is from my reporting.

21. THE THIRD RAIL

1

The kids briefed me about the Mayors for Our Lives initiative in advance, and I watched the *Morning Joe* interview. I happened to see Katy Tur's comment while watching her show.

All quotes from the kids in this chapter are from my interviews, except as noted.

Ariana Grande's push for voter registration was reported in *Billboard*: "March for Our Lives Website Crashes . . ."

Quotes from Emma in this chapter come from her interviews with *Diverse* magazine, *The Alligator*, and *Variety*.

3

I was not at the Hurricane Grill & Wings gathering. I relied on accounts from the kids, augmented by news accounts. Jackie's quote about shaking with anger and vowing to keep fighting comes from "Pain for Parkland Students . . ." (*The Guardian*). Her other quotes come from my interviews.

4

All quotes from Professor Robert J. Spitzer in this chapter come from my interview with him. His cogent op-ed about the results of the midterms in the November 12 *New York Times* also provided context.

EPILOGUE

1

All quotes and updates from the kids in this chapter come from interviews and texts with them, up through early December.

4

I was a huge Springsteen fan in my youth. In high school, I bought the first four albums of my life at one time, and *Darkness on the Edge of Town* was one of them. I had never seen Bruce in concert, though. His Broadway show played for over a year just a few blocks from my apartment in Manhattan's Hell's Kitchen, but I couldn't afford tickets, so I didn't enter the lottery. But June 21, less than a week after the Peace March, I was invited to attend a performance less than an hour before the show. I always carry a pen and paper. I try to keep one letter-size sheet folded into quarters in my back pocket, but art often inspires me, so I packed two. I'm so glad I did. When Bruce mentioned the March for Our Lives kids, I was stunned. I immediately pulled the paper out and jotted down everything I could. I'm pretty sure I got the quotes right, but the way they appear in this book is from my notes, in the dark, as I heard them. I wrote a first stab at this section in the dark, during the final minutes of the show. I filled both sides of both papers, though I was writing very large, praying that I was not overwriting and that it would be comprehensible. It was. I walked straight home and fashioned the first draft of this section over the next hour, and refined it over the next several days.

I figured word must have gotten to the kids, but I texted Matt and Jackie (separately) that night just in case, and they were shocked and awed. And honored.

I said Bruce "has yet to meet" Jackie, because it's true; they haven't met, as of the final edits in December 2018. But I have a feeling that will prove temporary.

Works Cited

Alfonsi, Sharyn. "Students Calling for Change after the Parkland Shooting." CBS News. March 18, 2018.

"Animals." National Park Service. October 13, 2017. https://www.nps.gov/ever/learn/nature/animals.htm.

Ashcroft, Lord. "'We Didn't Elect Him to Be a Saint, We Elected Him to Be a Leader': My Latest American Focus Groups." Lord Ashcroft Polls. March 23, 2018.

Basler, Cassandra. "Meet The Students Who Dreamed Up Friday's National School Walkout." NPR. April 19, 2018.

Beatty, Hannah, and Christopher King. "March for Our Lives Team Encourages UF Students to Vote." *The Independent Florida Alligator*. November 6, 2018.

Beckett, Lois. "Pain for Parkland Students after Pro-gun Candidates Win: 'I'm Shaking with Anger.'" *The Guardian.* November 7, 2018.

Blair, J. Pete, and Katherine W. Schweit. (2014). "A Study of Active Shooter Incidents, 2000–2013." Texas State University and Federal Bureau of Investigation, US Department of Justice, Washington, DC. 2014.

Bond, Kanisha, Erica Chenoweth, and Jeremy Pressman. "Did You Attend the March for Our Lives? Here's What It Looked like Nationwide." *Washington Post.* April 13, 2018.

Bonier, Tom. "Analysis: After Parkland Shooting, Youth Voter Registration Surges." TargetSmart. July 19, 2018.

Brainwrap. "UPDATE X2: *MUST-READ* Facebook Post from One of the Students Who Survived the #Parkland Shooting." *Daily Kos.* February 15, 2018.

Britzky, Haley. "Hogg: Stoneman Douglas 'Is a Prison Now.'" *Axios.* March 23, 2018.

Chavez, Nicole, and Saeed Ahmed. "What We Know about Emma Gonzalez, the Fiercely Outspoken Teen Who Stunned America with Her Silence." CNN. March 26, 2018.

Chenoweth, Erica, and Jeremy Pressman. "This Is What We Learned by Counting the Women's Marches." *Washington Post.* February 7, 2017.

CNN. Report. August 15, 2018. http://cdn.cnn.com/cnn/2018/images/08/14/rel7b.-.2018.pdf.

"Co-Founder of March for Our Lives Cameron Kasky Explains the Mistakes He's Made & Why He Left March for Our Lives." Fox News. September 19, 2018.

Collie, Tim. "Marjory Stoneman Douglas, 'Voice of the River.'" *Sun-Sentinel.* July 12, 2008.

Contrera, Jessica. "At the March for Our Lives, You'll See Her Name Again. But Who Was Marjory Stoneman Douglas?" *Washington Post.* March 22, 2018.

Damasceno, Pedro, and David Morales. "A Student Take: Emma Gonzalez." *Milk.* March 20, 2018.

Daugherty, Alex. "Parkland Students Have a Cause and $3.5 Million. Here's How They're Going to Spend It." *Miami Herald.* February 21, 2018.

Daugherty, Alex. "Youth Voter Registration Went up 41 Percent in Florida after Parkland." *Miami Herald.* July 19, 2018.

"Digest of Education Statistics, 2016." National Center for Education Statistics (NCES), US Department of Education.

The Ellen Show. "Stoneman Douglas Activists Discuss the School Shooting with Ellen." YouTube. February 23, 2018.

Eller, Claudia. "Emma Gonzalez Opens Up about How Her Life Has Changed Since Parkland Tragedy." *Variety.* October 12, 2018.

Falkowski, Melissa, and Eric Garner, eds. *We Say #NeverAgain: Reporting by the Parkland Student Journalists.* New York: Crown, 2018.

Fausset, Richard, and Serge F. Kovaleski. "[Killer's name], Florida Shooting Suspect, Showed 'Every Red Flag.'" *New York Times.* February 16, 2018.

Federal Bureau of Investigation. "School-Associated Student Homicides—United States, 1992–2006." Centers for Disease Control and Prevention. January 16, 2008.

Feller, Madison. "Emma Gonzalez Shares the Story Behind Her Moving 'We Call B.S.' Gun Reform Speech." *Elle.* February 23, 2018.

Fisher, Dana R. "Here's Who Actually Attended the March for Our Lives. (No, It Wasn't Mostly Young People.)" *Washington Post.* March 28, 2018.

"Florida Everglades." SOFIA-Mangroves, Hurricanes, and Lightning Strikes-Nutrient Cycles. https://archive.usgs.gov/archive/sites/sofia.usgs.gov/publications/circular/1182/.

"Florida Student Emma Gonzalez to Lawmakers and Gun Advocates: 'We Call BS.'" CNN. February 18, 2018.

Follman, Mark. "New FBI Study Shows Mass Shooters Aren't Loners Who Suddenly Just Snap." *Mother Jones.* June 20, 2018.

Follman, Mark, Gavin Aronsen, and Deanna Pan. "US Mass Shootings, 1982–2018: Data from Mother Jones' Investigation." *Mother Jones.* November 19, 2018.

The Founders of the March for Our Lives. *Glimmer of Hope.* New York, NY: Razorbill and Dutton, 2018.

Fox News. "Student Says Heroic Janitor Saved Many Lives During Shooting." YouTube. February 14, 2018.

Gallagher, Dianne, and Jason Hanna. "The Price Tags around These Marchers Are Meant to Reflect What They Say Their Lives Are Worth: $1.05." CNN. March 24, 2018.

Gardiner, Dustin, Alexis Egeland, Derek Hall, and Angel Mendoza. "'We're Not Going to Give Up': Arizona Students' 'Die-In' Puts Focus on Gun-Safety Reform." *Arizona Republic.* April 21, 2018.

Geggis, Anne. "Marjory Stoneman Douglas High Prom: Dancing Away from Tragedy, Mindful of the Missing." *Sun-Sentinel.* May 17, 2018.

González, Emma. "A Young Activist's Advice: Vote, Shave Your Head and Cry Whenever You Need To." *New York Times.* October 5, 2018.

González, Emma. "Parkland Student Emma González Opens Up about Her Fight for Gun Control." *Harper's Bazaar.* March 7, 2018.

Grunwald, Michael. *The Swamp: The Everglades, Flor-*

ida, and the Politics of Paradise. New York: Simon & Schuster, 2007.

"Gun Violence Archive." Gun Violence Archive. Accessed November 10, 2018. https://www.gunviolence archive.org/.

Hogg, David, and Lauren Hogg. *#NeverAgain: A New Generation Draws the Line.* New York: Random House, 2018.

Humans of MSD. Profile of Emma González. Instagram. January 22, 2018.

Huriash, Lisa J. "Students Recount Horror of School Shooting." *Sun-Sentinel.* February 23, 2018.

"In Memoriam." *The Eagle Eye.* April 2018.

"Joaquin Oliver's Parents Appear on Their Son's Behalf at Parkland Graduation." *NowThisNews.* June 5, 2018.

Jones, LaMont, and Monica Levitan. "Guns on College Campuses Debate Ushers in New School Year." *Diverse: Issues In Higher Education.* September 5, 2018.

Klas, Mary Ellen, and Elizabeth Koh. "'Look Me in the Eyes.' Douglas High Students Press Florida Politicians for Answers." *Miami Herald.* February 21, 2018.

Kochaniec, George, Jr. "The Pulitzer Prizes." *Rocky Mountain News.* April 20, 1999. https://www.pulitzer .org/winners/photo-staff-2.

Latifi, Fortesa. "Arizona Students Stage 'Die-In' Outside Governor's Office to Demand Action on Gun Violence." *Arizona Daily Independent.* April 20, 2018.

Longhi, Lorraine, and Lauren Castle. "Hamilton High and Other Phoenix-Area Students Walk Out over School Gun Violence." *Arizona Republic.* April 20, 2018.

Loudenback, Tanza. "Middle-Class Americans Made More Money Last Year Than Ever Before." *Business Insider.* September 12, 2017.

Lowery, Wesley. "Emma González Hated Guns Before. Now, She's Speaking Out on Behalf of Her Dead Classmates." *Washington Post.* February 21, 2018.

Magness, Josh. "Who Is Naomi Wadler, the 11-Year-Old Speaker Who Electrified the March for Our Lives?" *Miami Herald.* March 24, 2018.

Mazzei, Patricia. "'Kill Me,' Parkland Shooting Suspect Said after Rampage." *New York Times.* August 6, 2018.

Mazzei, Patricia. "Parkland Shooting Suspect Lost Special-Needs Help at School When He Needed It Most." *New York Times.* August 4, 2018.

Miller, Lisa. "On the Ground with the Parkland Teens As They Plot Their Revolution." *New York.* March 2, 2018.

Miller, Lisa. "Parkland Activist David Hogg Is Taking

His Gap Year at the Barricades." *New York.* August 19, 2018.

Moyer, Justin Wm. "'March for Our Lives' Gun-Control Rally Bumped from Mall by 'Talent Show.'" *Washington Post.* March 1, 2018.

Nass, Daniel. "Parkland Generated Dramatically More News Coverage Than Most Mass Shootings." *The Trace.* May 17, 2018.

National Park Service. Permit for the March for Our Lives. US Department of the Interior. March 19, 2018.

Neal, David J. "Uber Driver Says [killer's name] Told Her: 'I Am Going to My Music Class.'" *Miami Herald.* February 28, 2018.

"New Day Transcript." CNN. February 15, 2018.

Ovalle, David, and Nicholas Nehamas. "'You're All Going to Die.' [Killer's name] Made Cellphone Videos Plotting Parkland Attack." *Miami Herald.* May 30, 2018.

"Parents of Murdered Parkland Student Joaquin Oliver on Using Art to Demand End to Gun Violence." *Democracy Now!* August 15, 2018.

"Park Profiles." City of Parkland. Accessed November 10, 2018.

"Parkland, Florida." City-Data. http://www.city-data.com/city/Parkland-Florida.html.

"Parkland, FL." Data USA. Accessed November 10, 2018.

Peters, Jeremy W. "N.R.A. Chief, Wayne LaPierre, Offers Fierce Defense of 2nd Amendment." *New York Times*. February 22, 2018.

Peters, Jeremy W., and Katie Benner. "Where the N.R.A. Speaks First and Loudest." *New York Times*. February 22, 2018.

Rogers, Katie. "Women's March on Washington: What You Need to Know." *New York Times*. January 10, 2017.

Rosenblatt, Kalhan. "Parkland's Seniors Celebrate Prom, but Four Are Missing." NBC News. May 6, 2018.

Smidt, Remy. "Here's What It's Like at the Headquarters of the Teens Working to Stop Mass Shootings." BuzzFeed News. February 20, 2018.

Smythe, Katie. "Never Again: A Parkland Father and Two Congressmen Advocate for Sensible Gun Laws, School Safety." *Alexandria News*. March 8, 2018.

Solomon, Lois K. "Marjory Stoneman Douglas High Plans 'Over the Top' Prom for Survivors of Mass Shooting." *Los Angeles Times*. April 14, 2018.

Soloski, Alexis. "Parkland Survivors Get a Broadway Master Class in Healing." *New York Times*. April 18, 2018.

Sosa, Maria Alesia, and Luis Velarde. "'Where Is My Son?' The Agonizing Wait of Parents Searching for Their Children after Florida School Shooting." Univision. February 15, 2018.

"The South Florida Environment: A Region Under Stress." United States Geographical Survey. September 4, 2013.

Spitzer, Robert J. "The Gun-Safety Issue Is Actually Helping Democrats." *New York Times.* November 12, 2018.

"Stoneman Douglas Student Tells *60 Minutes* Why Arming Teachers Is 'Stupid.'" CBS News. March 16, 2018.

"The Student Body at Marjory Stoneman Douglas High School in Parkland, FL." *U.S. News & World Report.* https://www.usnews.com/education/best-high-schools/florida/districts/broward-county-public-schools/marjory-stoneman-douglas-high-school-4749.

Sullivan, Kevin. "What Happened in the 82 Minutes between [the killer's] Arrival and Arrest during Florida Shooting." *Chicago Tribune.* February 16, 2018.

Sullivan, Kevin, Tim Craig, and William Wan. "'People Are Angry': Pain Turns Political in Parkland after School Shooting." *Washington Post.* February 17, 2018.

"Teacher Told Students to Run after Encountering Florida School Shooting Suspect." CBS News. February 16, 2018.

"US Existing Single-Family Home Median Sales Price." YCharts. https://ycharts.com/indicators/us_existing _singlefamily_home_median_sales_price.

US Secret Service and US Department of Education. *The Final Report and Findings of the Safe School Initiative: Implications for the Prevention of School Attacks in the United States.* July 2004.

Valle, Gaby Del. "David Hogg Is Mad as Hell." *The Outline.* March 5, 2018.

"Voters More Focused on Control of Congress—and the President—Than in Past Midterms." Pew Research Center for the People and the Press. June 20, 2018.

Wallace, Tim, and Alicia Parlapiano. "Crowd Scientists Say Women's March in Washington Had 3 Times as Many People as Trump's Inauguration." *New York Times.* January 22, 2017.

Walsh, Joan. "6 Minutes and 20 Seconds That Could Change the World." *The Nation.* March 28, 2018.

Weiss, James. "5—The Ranches—The Heart of Parkland." Parkland Historical Society. http://www .parklandhistoricalsociety.com/portals/the-ranches ---the-heart-of-parkland.

Witt, Emily. "Calling B.S. in Parkland, Florida." *New Yorker*. February 21, 2018.

Witt, Emily. "How the Survivors of Parkland Began the Never Again Movement." *New Yorker*. April 17, 2018.

Witt, Emily. "Launching a National Gun-Control Coalition, the Parkland Teens Meet Chicago's Young Activists." *New Yorker*. June 26, 2018.

"Wolf Transcript." CNN. February 21, 2018. http://transcripts.cnn.com/TRANSCRIPTS/1802/21/wolf.02.html.

"Women's March On Washington." Crowdrise. https://www.crowdrise.com/womens-march-on-washington/fundraiser/womens-marchon-washington.

About the Author

DAVE CULLEN is the author of the *New York Times* bestseller *Columbine*. Cullen has also written for the *New York Times, BuzzFeed, Vanity Fair, Politico Magazine,* the London *Times,* the *New Republic, Newsweek,* the *Guardian,* the *Washington Post,* the *Daily Beast, Slate, Salon, The Millions, Lapham's Quarterly,* and NPR's *On the Media.*